MOVIE MUTATIONS

The Changing Face of World Cinephilia

Edited by
Jonathan Rosenbaum and Adrian Martin

To the memory of

Serge Daney
(1944–1992)

and

Raymond Durgnat
(1932–2002)

The British Film Institute promotes greater understanding and appreciation of, and access to, film and
moving image culture in the UK.

Cover design: Squid Inc./Jethro Clunies-Ross

Set by Fakenham Photosetting, Fakenham, Norfolk
Printed by Cromwell Press, Trowbridge, Wiltshire

British Library Cataloguing-in-Publication Data

A catalogue record for this book is available from the British Library
ISBN 0 85170 984 2 (pbk)
ISBN 0 85170 983 4 (hbk)

Contents

Acknowledgments

In Chapter 1, Nicole Brenez's letter is translated by Kent Jones and Jonathan Rosenbaum; Alex Horwath's letter is translated by the author and Petra Metelko; and Raymond Bellour's letter is translated by Lynne Kirby. In Chapter 13, Brenez's letter is translated by Martin and Rosenbaum.

Chapter 1 was first published, in French translation, in *Trafic* no. 24, Winter 1997; a list of subsequent translations appears within the text. It appeared in English in shorter form in *Film Quarterly* vol. 52 no. 1, Fall 1998. An earlier version of Chapter 3 first appeared in French translation in *Trafic* no. 25, Spring 1998. Chapter 4 appeared in French translation in *Trafic* no. 26, Summer 1998, and draws some material from 'Remaking History', *Chicago Reader*, 10 November 1998. Part of Chapter 5 appeared in French translation in *Cinéma 03*, 2002. An earlier version of Chapter 8 appeared in *Senses of Cinema* no. 12, February–March 2001. An earlier version of Chapter 10 appeared in Philip Brophy (ed.), *Cinesonic: Experiencing the Soundtrack* (Sydney: Australian Film, Television and Radio School, 2001). A different version of Chapter 11 appeared in *Chicago Reader*, 8 June 2000. Chapter 13 first appeared in Spanish translation in the booklet *Movie Mutations. Cartas de cine* (Buenos Aires: Ediciones Nuevos Tiempos, 2002).

Our thanks to: for their unstinting help with the manuscript, Grant McDonald and Helen Bandis; for assistance with the Masumura research, Chika Kinoshita, Mikiro Kato, The Japan Foundation, Tokyo's National Film Centre, Pacific Film Archives, Bernard Eisenschitz and Adriano Apra; for their work on *Movie Mutations. Cartas de cine*, Flavia de la Fuente, Marta Alvarez, Lisandro A. de la Fuente, Gabriela Ventureira and Javier Porta Fouz; and Quintín, Lynne Kirby, Muhammed Pakshir and Bérénice Reynaud.

Preface

Jonathan Rosenbaum and Adrian Martin

ADRIAN MARTIN: The *Movie Mutations* project made its first public appearance in a 1997 issue of the French magazine *Trafic* – in a series of letters that appears here as Chapter 1. Why did you initiate that exchange, Jonathan?

JONATHAN ROSENBAUM: The project literally began with a taped dialogue between you and me in a Melbourne suburb in 1996. I was trying to solve a riddle that had grown out of some of my previous travels and international contacts – such as that first letter and that package containing your first two books that you'd sent me out of the blue in 1995. What piqued my curiosity was having met four extremely knowledgeable and highly energetic professional cinephiles based in different parts of the world who were all born around 1960 and had very similar film tastes, tastes which weren't my own. The fact that none of you knew one another – except for Kent Jones in New York and Alex Horwath in Vienna – was what especially intrigued me, because all four of you, including also Nicole Brenez in Paris, gravitated towards the same set of film-makers. What were the generational conditions of this unconscious bond between strangers that traversed so many national and linguistic borders? That's what I wanted to explore in our dialogue, and, for practical reasons, this ultimately grew into a series of letters that I asked the editors of the French magazine *Trafic* to consider publishing. The fact that *Trafic* – founded by the late Serge Daney, who invited me to become an early contributor – was already highly international, grounded in cinephilia, and favourable towards highly personal expressions such as journals and letters made it an obvious choice.

Then the fact that these letters sparked off discussions in still other countries, such as Holland and Italy, involving cinephiles who were younger than the four of you, suggested a somewhat different development growing out of the initial project: an exploration of what cinephiles (and, in some cases, film-makers) around the planet have in common and what they can generate, activate and explore by linking up together in various ways. Though I started out wanting to explore the phenomenon of a certain unconscious 'global' simultaneity – which I found not only in the tastes of certain far-flung cinephiles, but also in the styles and themes of certain far-flung directors (which became my starting point in Chapter 5, comparing Yasuzo Masumura with several American directors) – the international exchanges and collaborations that ensued are cases of willed and deliberate simultaneity. In other words, a recognition of common interests, which include making certain films and critical positions more accessible and better known. A way of broadening the options.

The remainder of this book more or less traces that development, step by step. Some of the early chapters, such as the dialogues with Abbas Kiarostami in Chicago in 1998 and with Shigehiko Hasumi in Tokyo in 1999, followed by various email exchanges between others over the next three years, were generated specifically for the book, while some others – such as Kent's essay on Tsai Ming-liang, pieces of mine about the Rotterdam Film Festival and *The Circle*, and your own reflections about international musicals – were initiated independently of the book, but then became integral parts of it by suggesting new yet related avenues to follow.

AM: Of course, some of these chapters developed concurrently, but their order, which is mainly chronological, reflects the overall process through which this book was defining itself – a kind of ongoing narrative leading us at times into unforeseeable directions, and inflected by contemporary events ranging from the attack on the World Trade Center to the death of Raymond Durgnat. All of which culminated in a second round of letters, five years after the first, sparked by the invitation of Quintín, a film critic and festival director based in Buenos Aires. So there's a certain widening geographical spread as well as a chronological development reflected in the book's structure.

So, what began as your inquiry into an intriguing generational phenomenon became something else – a larger, collective meditation on many sorts of 'mutation' affecting film, and film culture, today. Let's start with the technological mutation that comes up in Chapter 1: this mysterious thing popularly called 'digital cinema', which brings with it a new definition of the filmic image.

JR: Daney was the first to raise this issue in the early 90s. For him, the cinema we once knew was based on the photographic registration of the world – a notion dear to his mentor at one remove, André Bazin. But with the digital image we can fake the world, paint the image. So what does this mean for our almost religious belief and faith in the cinema?

On the other hand, you have something resembling a reinvention of Italian neo-realism in the Iranian New Wave and in some of the notions of Dogme, so it's not as if Bazin's notions of reality are completely outmoded. There's still some carry-over of Bazin's idea as a kind of humanism. I mean, what was the cinema for, according to Bazin? It was a way for the world to keep in touch with itself – and that's clearly an issue today, even an urgent one when faced with the consequences of, say, American isolationism.

AM: Isolationism is the opposite of another kind of mutation which this book pursues: the changing map of world cinema, and how our perceptions of it and accounting for it must keep pace with that mutation. The cinemas of Asia and the Middle East have, over the past decade, assumed a prominence in world film culture unimaginable twenty years ago. Many of us are still a long way from knowing either the breadth or depth of production and film thought in most countries of the world. But the old prejudices and assumptions are giving way. This book looks into a number of the 'masters' of this new map of world cinema, like Kiarostami, Hou and Tsai – which is maybe an old-fashioned, auteurist way to proceed, but absolutely necessary when you flip open the latest edition of David Thomson's *The New Biographical Dictionary of Film* and still read the ill-informed lament that 'there are so few masters left now'.[1]

JR: Yes – it's alarming how certain critics are valued precisely because of their capacity to keep certain doors closed, making it so much easier for their lazier colleagues to function – which leads inevitably to mutations in film criticism itself, in modes of writing, of publishing, and in that state of mind or way of being we're calling cinephilia. During the period in which we've worked on this book, various magazines have appeared that have a specific relevance to our undertaking – the online, Melbourne-based *Senses of Cinema*, with which you were closely involved during its first two and half years; Mark Peranson's Toronto-based *Cinema Scope*, which started shortly afterwards; and now *Rouge*, another international online journal, which you're helping to found and edit, launching in 2003. And there are at least half a dozen new journals in France now, such as *Balthazar* and *Exploding*, which explore new methods of analysis (such as 'figural' criticism) and draw interesting connections between, say, 'trashy' horror films and the most radical experiments of the avant-garde. All these new publications have created a context that is unabashedly intellectual – rather than pandering to the anti-intellectual defences of so much 'fan' culture today – and we've tried to bear witness to this commitment in the book.

AM: I'm very struck with how these magazines – we can also cite *El Amante* and *Otrocampo* from Argentina, *Schnitt* from Germany and *De Filmkrant* from Holland – all have some sort of website, even if they're not all primarily web magazines. And they're all created by people who have a real curiosity about things happening in other countries. So, for the first time in my experience, we're getting a true sense of internationalism in such humble acts of film culture as little magazines, which are no longer bound by the film cultures they're in, involved in an effort to share knowledge across countries. *Otrocampo* and *Senses of Cinema*, for instance, adopt a policy of publishing articles in their original languages whenever possible alongside the English translations.

JR: What's interesting is that each magazine seems to have one foot in its own national culture and the other foot in a new kind of shared, international space – the kind of new space where, for instance, thanks to multiregional DVDs and players, you can easily order films from the other side of the world rather than wait for them to turn up in local cinemas. It's that growing community that really interests me, in part because it reminds me of the film community I saw being formed between, say, New York, LA, London, Paris and Rome during the early 60s; and I'm enough of an old fogey now to feel nostalgic for those links. The friendships between certain *nouvelle vague* directors provided a model for that sense of mutual empowerment. And in New York, where I was living at the time, the community was new enough to be truly pluralistic, so that you could find Stan Brakhage, Manny Farber, Pauline Kael, Jonas Mekas, Andrew Sarris, Jack Smith and Parker Tyler all writing in the same issues of *Film Culture*. And a little later there was a short-lived effort to bring out an edition of *Cahiers du cinéma* in English – something that's been done more recently in Japan.

AM: And with community comes dialogue, conversation. That's why so much of this book takes the form of dialogues, letters or email exchanges. All these types of collaborative writing can create a different way of speaking and thinking about cinematic objects. Modes and tones get mixed, digression has a place, the personal voice is valued. But our goal is not merely personal, is it?

JR: I've often said that one of the key functions of film criticism is or should be information, and one handicap the West has in accessing certain kinds of information regarding film is the radical splintering of film culture that has come about through the growth of academic film study. For me, what caused an enormous detour in this study was the way the so-called social sciences took over – making art itself a suspect notion, as Gilberto Perez has pointed out, at least in the Anglo-American branches of academia.[2] And because of its institutional basis, this orientation began to avoid certain kinds of politics as well, despite some appearances to the contrary. Yet it's equally reprehensible when the critical mainstream simply ignores academia, an attitude which is no less parochial.

Traversing both academia and the mainstream is something of great concern to me, the question of availability: when films become available, or whether they remain unavailable, wherever you happen to be. This is an issue that always exists and is particularly acute in America. I think that, generally, where there is a group of cinephiles that know one another across the different sectors of a film community, the problem exists to a lesser extent. But I would say for example in a place like New York or even Los Angeles, where you have totally autonomous groups composed of academic film study people and industry people and journalists, it's a big problem. There's a lot of waste involved because people are duplicating the same work, the same research, discussing the same issues, when there could be a coming together of all of this. In effect there's absolutely nothing that could be called a single film community.

AM: *Movie Mutations*, then, is our way of showing how such a community might be conjured, through the book's own actions of information-sharing and mutual reflection. There's a trap here, however, which is the classic imperialist takeover: taking an Asian film (say), extracting it from its specific, national and cultural context, having a fantasia about it, bringing it back to the West and writing it up. Our hope is that, through the collaborations we set in motion, we can get past that sort of myopia, into a cross-cultural understanding. But we are also trying to stay open to the exciting possibilities that can emerge from not always remaining bound to the 'culture-specific': we're looking to find certain insights into our own situations whenever we can, in the process that Bérénice Reynaud has called using the defamiliarising mirror of another culture.

JR: My initial understanding of Taiwanese cinema was as the articulation of a certain existential crisis of Taiwan in relation to history – which was instructive for its similarities to and differences from certain questions about American identity. But that should be only the first step. As I pointed out in my exchange with Hasumi, there's a very disagreeable American trait that finds other cultures interesting only if they echo or duplicate American culture, and I suspect that alternate versions of that trait can be found in (say) France, England and China. On the other hand, a big stage in my education about Iran was learning from Mehrnaz Saeed-Vafa how Bresson could speak directly to the experience of post-revolutionary Iran – not only in *A Man Escaped* (1956), which deals directly with the French Occupation and Resistance, but more generally through the notion of souls in hiding.

My point is that national identities are generally helpful and relevant at the outset of such discussions; eventually they become hindrances because they're becoming outdated. I mean, we're obviously where we're from when we're on the Internet because of the cultural baggage we're carrying, but in other respects we're getting a taste of potential statelessness, the sense in which we're all citizens of the world (which George W. seems so intent on denying). There's a new international culture growing out of this shared perception and some of the kinds of empowerment it can bring. That's part of what makes Naomi Klein's *No Logo*,[3] which has been translated into quite a few languages by now, so exciting, and I think it's significant that it was written by a Canadian; the biggest countries are usually the last ones to know what's going on – and to realise that the more the big multi-corporations go on doing the same things across the planet, the more that people across the planet have something in common, and a reason for joining forces with one another. I like to think that the chain reaction of Tiananmen Square in 1989 among Chinese-speaking people around the world was a burst of energy made possible as well as evident by the fax machine, and that the World Trade Organization uprising in Seattle a decade later was largely organised via the Internet. The possibilities are in fact limitless, and at this point they've barely been scratched.

AM: As Ray Durgnat might have written, the 'usual disclaimers' apply: this book offers its own map to a changing film culture, but it does not pretend to be definitive or comprehensive. It's more an extended example, a 'rhizome', of the kinds of explorations and connections that can be made today.

JR: Some of the sections of this book that were planned at one point or another but which never materialised include discussions with the film-maker Richard Linklater about his long-term involvement with the Austin Film Society; Edward Yang about how recent films from the West are read by Asian spectators and conversely how recent Asian films are read by Western spectators; and a dialogue between French film historian Bernard Eisenschitz and Russian film historian Naum Kleiman about suppressed Soviet films. It's important to emphasise that much of the material in this book is conceived of as work in progress. It can and should be extended beyond the parameters of a single project or publication.

Between Melbourne and Chicago, December 2002

Notes

1. David Thomson, *The New Biographical Dictionary of Film* (New York: Knopf, 2002), p. 22.
2. Gilberto Perez, *The Material Ghost: Films and Their Medium* (Baltimore: Johns Hopkins University Press, 1998).
3. Naomi Klein, *No Logo* (London: Flamingo, 2001).

Notes on Contributors

Raymond Bellour is director of Centre Nationale de la Recherche Scientifique de Paris, a founding editor of the magazine *Trafic*, and the editor of the Gallimard edition of the complete works of Henri Michaux. His many books include *Alexandre Astruc* (1963), *Le Livre des autres* (1971), *L'Analyse de film* (1980) [translated as *The Analysis of Film* (2000)], *L'Entre-Images: photo, cinéma, vidéo* (1990), and *L'Entre-Images 2: mots, images* (1999).

Catherine Benamou teaches at the University of Michigan. In New York she curated and occasionally subtitled films for public exhibition and discussion by Latin American women film-makers and indigenous video-makers from the Andes and the Amazon regions. Her publications include articles and reviews in *The Independent*, *Afterimage*, *Cineaste*, *Nuevo Texto Critico*, *Cahiers du cinéma* and the forthcoming *It's All True: Orson Welles at Work in Latin America*.

Nicole Brenez teaches cinema studies at the University of Paris-1. Her many publications include *Shadows de John Cassavetes* (1995) and *De la figure en général et du corps en particulier. L'invention figurative au cinéma* (1998). She has initiated and organised many film events and retrospectives, notably 'Jeune, dure et pure, une histoire du cinéma d'avant-garde en France', and has been the curator of the Cinémathèque Française's experimental and avant-garde film programmes since 1996. She is preparing a book about Abel Ferrara.

Fergus Daly, resident of Galway, is the co-author of a book on Leos Carax (University of Manchester, 2003). His essays have appeared in *Film West*, *Senses of Cinema*, *Realtime* and *Metro*, and he is the director of a documentary on Abbas Kiarostami.

Nataša Durovičová is an editor for the International Writing Program at the University of Iowa, with a long-standing research interest in various forms of polylinguality in cinema and, more recently, in film historiography beyond the paradigm of the national.

Shigehiko Hasumi, President of the University of Tokyo between 1997 and 2000, has also taught film as well as French literature there, and published widely on both subjects. His texts in English include essays in *Suzuki Seijun: The Desert under the Cherry Blossoms* (Rotterdam Film Festival, 1991), which he edited; *Mikio Naruse* (San Sebastian Film Festival, 1998), which he co-edited with Sadao Yamane; and *Ozu's Tokyo Story* (Cambridge, 1997), edited by David Desser.

Alexander Horwath, director of the Austrian Film Museum and former director of the Viennale (1992–7), has published widely on film and art. An English translation of *The Last Great American Picture Show: New Hollywood 1967–1976*, a 1995 collection he edited and contributed to, is forthcoming from the University of Amsterdam Press.

Kent Jones, program director of the Walter Reade Theater in New York and a member of the New York Film Festival selection committee, is a frequent contributor to *Cahiers du cinéma*, *Film Comment* and *Trafic*, and the author of *L'Argent* (BFI, 1999).

Abbas Kiarostami has been making films since 1970. Some of his best known features are *The Traveler* (1974), *Where Is the Friend's House?* (1987), *Homework* (1990), *Close-up* (1990), *Life and Nothing More...* (1992), *Through the Olive Trees* (1994), *Taste of Cherry* (1997), *The Wind Will Carry Us* (1999) and *10* (2002).

Adrian Martin is the film critic for *The Age* (Melbourne, Australia). He is the author of *Phantasms* (Penguin, 1994), *Once Upon a Time in America* (BFI, 1998), *The Mad Max Movies* (Currency, 2003) and a forthcoming BFI book on Terrence Malick. He is co-editor of the Internet journal *Rouge*, and a Doctoral Candidate in Art and Design, Monash University.

James Naremore is Chancellors' Professor of Communication and Culture at Indiana University. He is the author of several books on film, including *Acting in the Cinema* (1988), *The Magic World of Orson Welles* (1989), *The Films of Vincente Minnelli* (1993) and *More Than Night: Film Noir in its Contexts* (1998).

Mark Peranson is editor and publisher of the Canadian magazine *Cinema Scope* and a programmer for the Vancouver International Film Festival. His writing on film appears frequently in the *Village Voice* and the Toronto *Globe and Mail*.

Quintín [the pen-name of Eduardo Antin] is a former maths teacher and soccer coach, an editor and writer for the monthly Argentinian film magazine *El Amante/Cine* and, since 2001, director of the Buenos Aires International Festival of Independent Film.

Jonathan Rosenbaum is film critic for the *Chicago Reader*. His books include *Midnight Movies* (with J. Hoberman, 1987), *Greed* (BFI, 1991), *Moving Places* (1995), *Placing Movies* (1995), *Movies as Politics* (1997), *Dead Man* (BFI, 2000), *Movie Wars* (2000), *Abbas Kiarostami* (with Mehrnaz Saeed-Vafa, 2003) and *Pantheon Movie Picks: Recanonizing Cinema* (2003).

Mehrnaz Saeed-Vafa is an independent film-maker and a full-time film teacher at Chicago's Columbia College. Her publications in English include *Abbas Kiarostami* (with Jonathan Rosenbaum, University of Illinois, 2003) and essays about location and cultural identity (in *The New Iranian Cinema: Politics, Representation and Identity* , I. B. Taurus, 2002) and Sohrab Shahid Saless (in *The New Iranian Cinema*, BFI, 1999).

Lucia Saks teaches transnational cinema and film theory at the University of Michigan. From 1997 to 2002, she was Senior Lecturer and Program Director of Media and Communication at the University of Natal in Durban, South Africa. She has written for *Spectator*, *Communicare* and *Change Reels: Film and Culture in South Africa* (forthcoming from Wayne State University Press).

I

Movie Mutations: Letters from (and to) Some Children of 1960

Jonathan Rosenbaum, Adrian Martin, Kent Jones, Alexander Horwath, Nicole Brenez and Raymond Bellour (1997)

Chicago, 7 April 1997

Dear Adrian,

Almost a year has passed since I wrote in *Trafic* about 'the taste of a particular generation of cinephiles: an international and mainly unconscious cabal (or, more precisely, confluence) of critics, teachers and programmers, all of whom were born around 1960, have a particular passion for research (bibliographic as well as cinematic), and (here is what may be most distinctive about them) a fascination with the physicality of actors tied to a special interest in the films of John Cassavetes and Philippe Garrel (as well as Jacques Rivette and Maurice Pialat)'.[1] I named four members of this generation: Nicole Brenez (France), Alexander Horwath (Austria), Kent Jones (US) and you, Adrian Martin (Australia). Each of you, I should add, I met independently of the other three, originally through correspondence (apart from Kent), although Kent and Alex already knew each other. By now, I'm happy to say, all four of you have become acquainted, either by letters or in person, which has opened up many possibilities of both testing my hypothesis and, even more, of extending, refining, qualifying and better understanding it. I've noted, for example, other common enthusiasms among most or all of you, starting with Jean Eustache, Monte Hellman and Abel Ferrara. And differences that usually relate to your (and my) separate nationalities: Kent and I are much cooler towards Brian De Palma than the rest of you, and Nicole is the only one among the five of us not excited by the recent work of Olivier Assayas.

What fascinates me most of all about the 'confluence' I was discussing earlier (Nicole objects to 'cabal' for what she perceives as its right-wing connotations) is how it came into being. After all, the main message someone of my generation (born in 1943) hears almost daily is that cinephilia as we once knew it is dying; the cinephilia, that is, that took root in the *nouvelle vague* around the same time that you four were born. In the mainstream American press especially, articles by (among others) Susan

Sontag, David Thomson and David Denby about the 'death of cinema' and/or cinephilia have become common currency – a position which of course becomes easier to take in a country where not a single film by Hou Hsiao-hsien, Edward Yang, Abbas Kiarostami or Mohsen Makhmalbaf has yet been properly distributed, and where the most important European and (in some cases) American features (such as *Dead Man* [1995] and *Thieves* [1996]) are usually acknowledged only in the alternative or underground press.

Though clearly my own tastes are not the same as yours, I still feel that your generation may be the first to have emerged since the 70s that is in rebellion against the amnesia regarding both film and criticism that affects nearly everyone else – which is why it seems relatively easy for me to communicate with all of you. I'm reminded of a beautiful novel of 1936 by my favourite science-fiction writer, Olaf Stapledon, *Odd John*, about a group of superhuman mutants scattered across the world who gradually come to know one another – in secret, of course, because an open acknowledgment of their special talents would frighten most people and threaten existing institutions.

What seems dangerous to me about your collective sensibility (if I can describe it as such) is a familiarity with the paradigms and master theories of the past combined with a willingness to update and alter them according to current needs. For much too long, spectators of my and Sontag's generations have been arguing that if you weren't around in the 60s when Jean-Luc Godard, Michelangelo Antonioni and others were changing the face of cinema, then you can't be expected to understand what's lost or missing today. But I would counter that if you don't understand what morphing is and does – what the alteration of a pixel does to an on-screen event – then you can't be expected to understand the contemporary relevance (or irrelevance) of André Bazin's theories about the plan-séquence and deep focus. Moreover, if you fail to understand the changing face of film commerce since the era of Bazin – a subject involving such disparate matters as state funding, corporate ownership, video and publicity – you don't stand much chance of perceiving contemporary film aesthetics and the formation of canons.

So much for the need for new paradigms and theoretical models. But what were the specific needs of your generation that gave rise to your particular brand of cinephilia? As you indicated when we discussed this in Melbourne last year, the specific lure of minimalism as evidenced in films by Garrel and Chantal Akerman and by Eustache's *The Mother and the Whore* (1973) was a historical response to a certain surfeit of intertextual reference that grew out of the *nouvelle vague* – the sense that every text was to some extent an anthology of cross-references to previous texts, a palimpsest of film history that beyond a certain point became so encoded in its own textual processes that a certain simplification of concerns and affects became desirable. And, as you pointed out, this simplification appeared in different forms: Cassavetes, by stepping outside the usual process of contextuality, was injecting a new version of raw life and lived experience into the cinema, and so in a different way was Garrel. Akerman, whose minimalism derived in part from painting, was clearing away the cobwebs in a different if related fashion, and Hellman, who may have taken some of his cues from the theatre of Samuel Beckett, had his own ways of draining away outdated significations. The process can perhaps be seen most clearly in *The Mother and the Whore*, where Eustache was deliberately taking some of the most cherished emblems of the *nouvelle vague* – Jean-Pierre Léaud, extended dialogues in Left Bank cafés, literary aphorisms, black and white cinematography – and showing in his disillusionment how some of that era's utopian notions of love and freedom could no longer be supported or sustained; how, in fact, they had become a certain camouflage and holding action for blocking despair. (The fact that this also implied a certain defeatism and conservatism, where Catholic bourgeois 'necessity' implicitly becomes a kind of biological truth – above all in Françoise Lebrun's tearful extended monologue – was for me the limiting factor in this enterprise.)

An even clearer illustration of what was happening to cinema during this period can be traced though the career of Jacques Rivette in the early 70s. Two separate versions of the same threshold are crossed – the first roughly halfway through *Out 1* (in both its 1971 and 1972 versions), the second between *Celine and Julie Go Boating* (1974) and *Duelle* (1976). I realise that you haven't been able to see these pictures apart from *Celine and Julie* – such are the vagaries of Australian distribution, not to mention distribution of Rivette's work in general – so I hope you can bear with my somewhat abstract interpretation of what took place, which in each case involved an emptying-out of meaning. It's a process that Roland Barthes spoke about with Rivette and Michel Delahaye many years before: 'The best films [to me] are those which best withhold meaning. To suspend meaning is an extremely difficult task requiring at the same time a very great technique and total intellectual loyalty.'[2]

Barthes' model for this delicate operation was Luis Buñuel's *The Exterminating Angel* (1962). But it seems to me that an even clearer illustration can be found almost a decade later in the master narrative of *Out 1*, which begins by accumulating all sorts of meanings – meanings related to conspiracy, to theatre, to all sorts of human interactions and exchanges (including implicitly the accumulation of meanings that clustered around such dreams as those of the *nouvelle vague*, those of the counterculture and those of May 68 – in short, utopian 60s' dreams of collective effort) – and then remorselessly records the draining away of those meanings and connections, the gradual splintering of the very idea of collectivity into solitude, unsolvable puzzles, paranoia, madness. Perhaps it's just another version of the dialectic Rivette (like many other film-makers) experiences between the collective adventure of shooting followed by the more solitary activity of editing, but in this case it provides a mythical and formal model for the artistic and political Zeitgeist of the 60s and 70s themselves, at least in that particular corner of the world.

A related threshold is crossed between *Celine and Julie Go Boating* and *Duelle*. The first of these features represents to my mind a final flowering (or is it last gasp?) of the referential aspect of the *nouvelle vague*, the aspect where Rivette's previous career as a film critic is most apparent – an explosion of references to Hollywood musicals, Louis Feuillade serials, Alfred Hitchcock thrillers, other films of the *nouvelle vague*, and so on. All these references are allowed to interact with and enhance particular locations, actresses and actors, everyday moods and details. But in *Duelle*, which may have just as many references to other films (especially Hollywood noirs like *The Seventh Victim* [1943], *The Big Sleep* [1946], *The Lady from Shanghai* [1948] and *Kiss Me Deadly* [1955], but also fantasies by Jean Cocteau and Georges Franju), the references no longer connect with material reality in the same manner. The world of the characters seems congealed, under glass, disconnected from the natural locations and to some extent from the actresses and actors as well – a private and more obsessive world populated by the bodies of actors more than their faces or souls.

This, at any rate, is one version of what happened between the *nouvelle vague* and its aftermath – the version of someone seventeen years older than you who tends to see the *nouvelle vague* as a kind of nostalgic family homestead that has been levelled for the erection of a high rise. But there are other and I'm sure more fruitful ways of viewing this evolution, and I would be eager to hear yours.

Your pal,
Jonathan

Melbourne, 30 June 1997

Dear Jonathan and Kent,
Although I am technically – it is true – a child of the 60s (born 16 September 1959, the day after Godard completed shooting *A bout de souffle*), I don't have the same magical relation to the cinema of that epoch that Jonathan and others of his generation have. As a child who grew up in the 60s – which is a rather more mundane way of putting the situation – my most intense memory of 60s' cinema as it unfolded was dreaming in perfect clarity and detail, when I was seven years old, several scenes from *Planet of the Apes* (1968) several months before I knew the film even existed.

Actually, these days, my relation to the 60s finds its precise image in the dream or myth of that decade which I believe animates Assayas' *Irma Vep* (1996): a whirlpool of cultural traces, Franju and Serge Gainsbourg and Chris Marker and the *nouvelle vague*, pulled through some foggy filter of longing and fascination into our confused and desperate present day. As for the tastes that align me with my brothers and sister in this cabal we have going here, I can more truthfully trace that moment of rupture and self-identification to a specific stage of the 70s. It is the time of high theory in full flight and force: Louis Althusser, Jacques Lacan, Christian Metz's film semiotics, Stephen Heath and the British mob at *Screen* magazine, the feminist analyses in the first issues of *Camera Obscura* in America, Wollen and Mulvey's 'new talkies' or essay films dutifully read (and taught) through the template of theory. Plus the various Australian outposts of this loose, broad but powerfully influential movement. I remember this as the era of hard words, of viciously exclusionary intellectual sects, of the 'necessary destruction of pleasure' and neo-puritanism, of political correctness before its time and anti-humanism, of signs and meanings, interpretative grids and avant-garde holy grails.

If I caricature this movement now for the purposes of shorthand, I lampooned it even more wildly back then through the sheer force of my angry, peeved passion. The 70s, at least within this circuit that I had to endure in the universities, was not the time or place for a starstruck, buffish cinephile like myself. Nor was it a time for any kind of poetry or lyricism or even simple fun in cinema or its critical writing; there was programmatic work to be done. When I was young and impressionable, I too wrote briefly under the sway of the march of theory, until the day that a wise, kindly friend said to me, 'Adrian, why don't you write your articles the way you write your letters?' And that is, in a sense, what I have tried to write ever since: love letters to the cinema, if we remember to include in our working definition of love every kind of passion and need and exasperation and exacting, critical demand.

I like the way that Nicole Brenez's survey 'The Ultimate Journey: Remarks on Contemporary Theory' politely sidesteps this whole nasty legacy of the 70s and starts its story with the freer, more creative intellectual moves of the 80s: for her, that means Gilles Deleuze, Serge Daney, Jean Louis Schefer ... and also certain golden oldies skilfully excavated, reread, translated and inserted into the present tense, such as Vachel Lindsay.[3] In my part of the world, I felt the need to trace a similar kind of loop: to join Manny Farber, Raymond Durgnat and others from the past to exemplary voyagers of the present like Bill Routt and Stanley Cavell.

But it was cinema itself that really led the way for me in the early to mid 80s. It is hard to recapture, to describe adequately, the overwhelming shock that came with key movie events of that time like Marker's *Sunless* (1983), Wim Wenders' *The State of Things* (1982), Godard's *Passion* (1982), Akerman's *Toute une nuit* (1982) and Raul Ruiz's *Hypothesis of the Stolen Painting* (1978). Suddenly here were the films playing right outside the maps of 70s' theory: free, lyrical, tender, poetic films, but also tough, savage, cruel, perverse, sometimes violent; films that were open diagrams, unashamed to link up raw fragments of human (or humanist) experience with the most severe or expansive kinds of experiments with form. These discoveries got drawn into a rich historical loop, too: suddenly I and my friends were seeing afresh the films of Jean Vigo, Humphrey Jennings and especially that unique pre-*nouvelle vague* figure, Jean Rouch.

Later, my love for an open cinema, for the ideal of a truly open, inclusive and above all impure cinema form, came to be crystallised in my personal discoveries of Cassavetes and Garrel – the single screenings in my home town of Melbourne of *Love Streams* (1984) in 1985 and *Les Baisers de secours* (*Emergency Kisses*, 1989) in 1994 count as primal scenes in my cinephile life. Cassavetes and Garrel stand for one sort of extreme that I love and cherish in cinema: a kind of *arte povera* fixed on the minute fluctuations of intimate life, on the effervescence of mood and emotion, and the instability of all lived meaning. A cinema which is a kind of documentary event where the energies of bodily performance, of gesture and utterance and movement, collide willy-nilly, in ways not always foreseen or proscribed, with the dynamic, formal, figurative work of shooting, framing, cutting, sound recording. A cinema open to the energies and intensities of life – and perpetually transformed by them.

I have always sought such life-affirming, life-enhancing energies and intensities from cinema. But I am aware that the energies that I like, the energies which feed me, do not come in just one form, from one stream. The *arte povera* of Cassavetes and Garrel gives me a quiet, clear, minimalist intensity. But I get a different kind of energy, no less necessary for the soul's survival, from a completely commercial kind of cinema, a cinema of spectacle decried still today by so many of even a slightly Situationist bent. I mean a kind of pop cinema that includes De Palma's *Mission: Impossible* (1996), Tim Burton's movies, Joe Dante's *Gremlins 2* (1990) – kinetic, sometimes cartoonish, extremely artificial and technologically mutated movies with no small claim on the cinematic language of tomorrow. I have cultivated my own particular, somewhat minor taste (in the sense of Deleuze and Guattari's notion of a troublesome, minor literature) within the halls of contemporary pop cinema – a taste for teen movies, from *Ferris Bueller's Day Off* (1986) to *Romy and Michele's High School Reunion* (1997), films completely comprised of pop quotes, clichés and stereotypes, but blessed with the will and the inventiveness to animate these tokens, to combine and revive and spin them at a dizzy rate.

Jonathan speaks of how the *cinema povera* beloved of us 60s' kids comes in as some kind of reaction or corrective to a *nouvelle vague* legacy oversaturated with filmic and cultural references. But the intimate, minimalist cinema I cherish is really only an interregnum, or an interstice, within a filmic history that refinds its referential, self-reflexive, quotational bent with a vengeance in the post-modern age – which also begins, I believe, in the early 80s. All the proliferating genres and subgenres of pop cinema are part of this movement, as are certain po-mo blockbusters like *Brazil* (1985) and *Blade Runner* (1982), and also seminal po-mo art movies about identities-as-simulacra-in-a-crazy-mixed-up-world, beginning with *Paris, Texas* (1984) and *Diva* (1982). Certain important directors of today – such as Assayas and Leos Carax – find their rich, distinctive, hybrid forms by crossing elements of the energetic American style (the style of Francis Ford Coppola or Martin Scorsese) with miniaturist and minimalist elements from Garrel or Hellman.

I think that I am some kind of product of what was named in the late 70s (by Louis Skorecki) as the new cinephilia. Actually, the first worries about a new cinephilia were expressed as far back as the mid 60s – when youngsters started seeing the great works of cinema for the first (and sometimes only) time on TV rather than cinema screens. But the new cinephilia really gets going with the age of home video – yet another thing that emerged in the early to mid 80s. Video consumption completely altered the character of film cultures all over the globe. Suddenly, there were self-cultivated specialists everywhere in previously elite areas like B cinema, exploitation cinema and so-called cult cinema (and also, of course, a thousand and one campaigns aimed at engineering and guiding such niche market tastes).

Where I live, directors including Abel Ferrara, Larry Cohen, and even far-left-fielders like the forgotten erotomaniac Walerian Borowczyk, figure as video shop directors, to be ferreted out and perpetually rediscovered by termite-like connoisseurs. Video buff culture can sometimes be a strange, nerdish, exasperating and disappointingly limited thing, but I don't think it is a bad thing – because it has opened up new intensities, new streams for the circulation and appreciation of cinema. And this is particularly valuable in an age where – certainly in Australia – the once sacred (and often inspiring) ideal of 'art cinema' has degenerated into the very limited access to world cinema provided by the commercial 'art house' circuit.

So all we need now is a way of rescuing artists like Ruiz, Manoel de Oliveira, Béla Tarr and so many other limit cases from the oblivion to which they have been cast by these merciless art houses – a way of rescuing and then feeding them into the vast, chaotic and slightly democratic video markets whose aficionados only need to stretch their working definition of what is weird and wonderful in cinema. Because what is democratic in this video culture is precisely the capacity (or at least the potential) to suspend normative judgments about cinema – reminding me of one of my all-time favourite critical mottoes, the attitude attributed by Louis Seguin to Ado Kyrou of seeking 'surprise rather than satisfaction' and preferring 'discovery to certainty'.[4]

My own decidedly double taste in cinema (for today I love the hardcore experimental cinema of Martin Arnold as much as the pop cinema of John Hughes, and I never cease looking for the deep and secret connections between them) leads me into the contemplation of several paradoxes. For instance: the films of Garrel and Cassavetes herald some kind of primal, fundamental return to the body, to the body as the only remaining site of authenticity, of lived and verifiable experience, of sensation and desire. This has led film-makers, and film writers, into many eulogies on the flesh, the face, the mortal and vulnerable body fixed within the painfully perishable medium of celluloid. … Yet the cinema of high technological artifice, of special effects, digitalisation and morphing, leads us to contemplate a radically different kind of cinematic body, a body created in and for cinema: the completely synthetic, prosthetic, retouched body, the body of action or horror, the hyper-sensate, super-tensile, immortal and imperishable body. As the Australian cultural theorist Philip Brophy puts it, all cinema's bodies are at some level pornographs[5] – bodies wholly mapped, graphed, by the artifices of the medium – and so all pop blockbusters are (and let us say this without the usual moral condemnation) our mad, delirious, modern pornography.

There is a recourse to the high moral ground – and to a certain lamentable purism – in a lot of film criticism today, even some of the most advanced. We read or hear far too often that there are only half a dozen directors working today who fulfil – or might one day fulfil, if we're all lucky – the potential, the promise of this dazzling medium. We keep getting familiar-looking canons of the greatest Top 100 titles worth preserving, even as we pretend to have gotten beyond all canons, hierarchies and evaluations. We keep looking for the authentic personal voice in film, the true lone poet, the accursed seer and the discarded rebel, decades after the movies let us know that even the sleaziest, most ideologically compromised fantasies of Blake Edwards are also – and who can doubt it? – beautiful, moving, lucidly autobiographical testaments.

As heretical as it sounds, even within this very cabal, I like the sentiment of Deleuze's casual prefatory remark in *Cinema 1: The Movement-Image*: 'The cinema is always as perfect as it can be'[6]. Meaning that its potentiality, its virtuality is, in some way, right here now – if we know where to look for it, how to maximise it, why it matters, and how to make it dance, for us and in us, like Rouch's privileged, shamanic figure of the dancing Socrates.

Your pal,
Adrian

New York, 7 July 1997

Dear Alex, Adrian and Jonathan,
The other day I remembered that the first time Alex and I met we were 'paired up' by a mutual friend who is about twenty years our senior. Her intuition was correct since we are now close friends, but clearly she had us both pegged as younger members of that allegedly extinct species, the cinephile. Now we've been called upon by another older mutual friend to define our own particular version of cinephilia. Jonathan is fascinated not by what he shares with Alex, Nicole, Adrian and myself, but rather by what separates him from us. For many members of Jonathan's generation, cinephilia is as much a thing of the past as the LP record or the dial telephone, an enthusiasm from their fervent and passionate youth that is now gone, spoiled by television and video (and in America, as Jonathan points out, by the demise of independently owned theatres). But as a devotee of Thomas Pynchon and Rivette, Jonathan knows all about practices and rituals carried on in secret, long past the moment when their spark of origin has burned itself out.

I have little time for the mournful predictions of cinephilia's demise from Sontag, Thomson and Godard, all filled with barely concealed rage, but I sympathise with that rage. From 1982 to 1984 I worked in one of the first video stores in Manhattan, and I will never forget the shock I felt when a customer asked me for 'something big and plush that I can really sink into, like the *Godfather* movies'. I realised right then and there that home video was opening up a new form of film appreciation antithetical to any I had ever seen, in which each film could be used as a self-prescriptive therapeutic device. Home video had made each film into a consumer item and potential fetish object which could be stopped, started, reversed, repeated or abandoned at will. This was the beginning of a whole new world, the world we live in today.

It's interesting that in Sontag's death of cinephilia tirade, Quentin Tarantino becomes what is now quaintly referred to as a structuring absence: obviously, the problem for her is not so much that he's *not* a cinephile but that he's the *wrong kind* of cinephile. Tarantino's background as a video store clerk has now become a joke, and I'm afraid that the joke is a snide, snobbish one (when I told an acid-tongued friend of mine that Tarantino was an Eric Rohmer fan he remarked, 'He must have discovered him in the "Foreign" section'). As Adrian points out, home video may have turned films into consumer objects but it has also opened up and popularised film culture – which is infinitely preferable to the most extreme forms of cinephilia, which has a terrible tendency to degenerate into complacent, academic bickering. By now, of course, video culture has been thoroughly infected by corporate culture. But, along the way, the disposable weightlessness of the video experience has opened up the cinema to some very interesting forms of contamination.

The emergence of the rock video and the home video revolution were concurrent phenomena that influenced and reflected back on each other. I've read a lot of useless theorising about rock videos, on the one hand panicky rants about how they have destroyed narrative coherence and on the other hand misguided assertions that their aesthetic had such historical precedents as Bruce Conner, Kenneth Anger and *Un chien andalou* (1928). But it always seemed clear to me that the rock video originated in yet another, earlier technology. One of the key experiences for American teenagers of my generation was driving with the radio on and feeling the intoxicating effect produced by the marriage of rock music and the passing landscape. This poetic, technological ritual of aimlessness, which more often than not was accompanied by dope or alcohol, is celebrated in the Jonathan Richman song 'Roadrunner', which ends with the ecstatic chant, 'Radio on!' It also finds a perfect cinematic crystallisation in Richard Linklater's *Dazed and Confused* (1993), a film that gets better every time I see it.

A secretly manufactured form of virtual reality, producing mysterious epiphanies when the blur from the car window was mixed with the sounds of whatever was coming from the airwaves, the music/movement experience was soon refined by the appearance of the tape deck, thus allowing the music to be chosen and to fit either the exterior or interior landscape (they had a way of mixing together), and henceforth become an actual soundtrack. The Walkman was a further refinement, releasing the whole experience from the limits of the car and giving it the potential for complete privacy and more direct physical impact. Rock videos were an intuitive outgrowth of this new form of experience writ monumentally large by mass production. For someone like Sontag, a truly terrifying proposition.

I think that the feeling of being 'mixed up' with the music (since under supposedly ideal circumstances it should sound like it's coming from the middle of your head – the earliest stops on this journey are the home stereo system and the subsequent addition of headphones), the simultaneous feeling of driving and being driven, has given birth to a new strain of narrative film-making which risks weightlessness in order to build from this new genre of modern experience. It's present in Edward Yang's last two (very unpopular) films, *A Confucian Confusion* (1994) and *Mahjong* (1996); in Wong Kar-wai's *Chungking Express* (1995), *Fallen Angels* (1996) and *Happy Together* (1997); in *Irma Vep*, and in all of Atom Egoyan's movies. In many ways its most extreme manifestation can be found in *Breaking the Waves* (1996), a film that strikes me as a perfect realisation of the music/landscape fusion in Lars von Trier's head, which he guarded preciously from his teenage years through adulthood.

Many film lovers I know have a lot of trouble with these films. If I had to guess why I would say that it's probably because they reflect the infiltration of a womblike subculture by outside forces. For me, the more these film-makers run the risk of complicity with the coreless sense of perpetual motion they are trying to portray, the more exciting they are. But I also understand that these films represent the end of the lovely moment in film culture that began with the *nouvelle vague*, and that when Godard said (introducing his Histoire(s) du cinéma at the Museum of Modern Art during the 1990s) that the cinema, 'at least a certain kind of cinema, the cinema of [Roberto] Rossellini and Rivette', is coming to an end, it's clear that this is the cinema that he fears is replacing it. I only know that this new cinema (if that is, after all, the correct term) speaks to me.

Cinema, cinema, cinema. In front of the TV, or in a theatre, first with our mother or father or brother or sister, then with friends or lovers, then perhaps alone. And for us, the children of 1960, the cinema was already the *art* of cinema: that battle had already been fought and won by our predecessors. So, while I'll never forget the excitement I felt the first time I saw *The Crimson Kimono* (1959) or *Psycho* (1960), it was my subsequent desire to clarify the difference between a cut in Samuel Fuller and a cut in Hitchcock, and then to understand each individual cut as a unique event, that was a generational impulse. If those before us focused on isolating and defining the tools of cinema, we focused on each film as a singular event with a unique logic and set of rules. In that sense, it's impossible to overestimate the importance that Manny Farber held for me as a critic. More than anyone else, he described *what he saw on the screen*: he was illuminating whether or not he liked the film in question because he was so specific. In fact, I think that, in his own way, Farber perfectly described the post-war movement/time rupture so central to Deleuze's books on cinema.

But apart from the fact that we were a new generation in search of fresh discoveries and influences, I must return to audio technology to get to the core of *our* cinephilia. Ours was a generation for whom *listening* to music was a central and obsessive experience – I stress the word listening as opposed to dancing to, playing or singing. And as we listened to the same songs over and over, our ears became attuned to each of them as unique sonic events. In other words, it was not the song but the recording which was the thing. The recording procedures pioneered by Phil Spector and Brian Wilson, advanced by the Beatles after they quit performing to concentrate exclusively on making records, and then sharpened to a fine point and theoretically articulated by Brian Eno, turned the studio itself into a compositional tool. Music was not simply the melody or the structure but the timbre of the voice, the colouring of the instrumentation, the texture of the sound, the slightest idiosyncrasy in the performance, well beyond the boundaries of the term 'phrasing'. A guitar solo was no longer the mere recording of a possible choice among many at a particular moment in time, but a structural component of a singular event.

In its most extreme form, this perceptual/artistic shift incorporates everything that might seem extraneous or accidental into the audio event: imperfections in the recording, even scratches on the record from excessive play (in a lot of current techno music, tape hiss and scratches are put back into the mix). The 'cinematic' organisation of rock music and our obsessive adolescent relationships with that music created a paradigm which now reflects back on film-making, reaching a fetishistic extreme with *Breaking the Waves* (where the grain of the image is exaggerated by correction on video, and endless infinitesimal jump-cuts as well as a relentless hand-held camera become an aesthetic evocation of a common idiosyncrasy in documentary film-making of the 70s) and passing into lunacy with Guy Maddin, whose films perfectly evoke scratchy 16mm TV prints of early 30s' sound films.

I see a reflection of this shift reflected in our mutation of cinephilia, particularly as it was enhanced by video. I believe it's what allowed us to see plastic beauty in a film-maker like Cassavetes. In her essay on *Germany, Year Zero* (1947), Nicole points out that it was not possible for Bazin or Amédée Ayfre to identify what Edmund Moeschke was doing in that film as acting: their priorities were generated by a very particular moment in world history.[7] By the same token, while on one level it seems preposterous that anyone could ever have thought that Cassavetes' films were improvised on the spot, on another level it's understandable. I think that for the previous generation, 'direction' was imagined as an outside, organisational force spread over the action. For us, direction became a matter of engagement with the life of the film – not life as captured by film but the living matter created by the meeting of camera, reality and splicer.

Jonathan has correctly stated that we all feel a special kinship with film-makers like Ferrara, Garrel, Hellman and Eustache. But I would venture to say that the film-maker who really lives in the true centre of our hearts is Cassavetes. In Ferrara, Hellman, Garrel and Eustache there is still a dominant hand from outside of the action. In Cassavetes, the hand of the film-maker feels as though it comes from deep within the action. When Cassavetes recut *Opening Night* (1977) because it was 'too good', I suspect he felt that the flux of action and emotion was not sufficiently foregrounded, that there was too recognisable a structure generated from outside the life of the film. The way that the old Chinaman (Soto Joe Hugh) in *The Killing of a Chinese Bookie* (1978) closes his eyes and mouth tightly, tilts his chin up and shakes his head with an oddly cartoonish sense of disbelief before he is shot by Ben Gazzara is just as much a structural event in Cassavetes as a change of angle is in Hitchcock. For many before us, and many still, Cassavetes is an authentic alternative to cinema. For us, he is *the* essential film-maker because he knows better than any other the difference between real life and cinematic life, and that there is no need to distinguish the latter with artifice since it already distinguishes itself well enough.

It's certain that the warm, communal conditions of moviegoing have vanished forever, at least here in America, and that nothing will ever bring them back. I think that whether or not we all agree about Assayas or Wong is less important than the fact that our respective responses to them are passionate and informed. In the end, that's what distinguishes cinephilia from connoisseurship, academicism or buffery. And now that we have arrived at a moment of Deleuzian multiplicity, in which Robert Fripp's prediction of the 'small, highly intelligent, mobile unit' has come true, we really have become our own islands. Which is why we scan the globe and are heartened to recognise something in others that we, as friends of Jonathan Rosenbaum and admirers of John Cassavetes, recognise in ourselves: real love.

Kent

Vienna, 5 August 1997

Dear Nicole, dear Jonathan, dear Adrian, dear Kent!
I am writing to you in German. You will read this letter in a translation only. I am worried: will you draw from this letter exactly what I have put in? Believe me, I know why I'm worried: in German-speaking film culture, foreign movies are not often seen in their original language. Until a very short time ago, only cinematheques and some art houses in major cities screened original versions. Before I was eighteen, nineteen years old, 95 per cent of all films I saw were synchronised – that's the word for dubbing here: *synchronisation*. This word has a lot to do with how people perceive film culture, which is based on some concurrences and many displacements. The very idea of our generation, of the children of 1960, is a kind of synchronisation. We want to find out the shared aspects of how we were cinematically formed, and with good reason; but in this process the differences will necessarily be brought out as well. The split between the dubbed lines of an actor and the movement of his or her lips.

We share a certain environment where three attitudes towards cinema fight for hegemony: cultural pessimism, affirmation of the market and irony. Roughly characterised, the cultural pessimists believe that 'real' cinema is more or less dead and buried, a hundred years after its birth, and that the few 'great masters' who still exist will automatically rise above the surface of the swamp (according to the nineteenth-century model of genius). The affirmers are mouthpieces of the media industry, redoubling the market's orders in a loud voice. The ironists distinguish themselves from the mainstream by showing off their hipness – they are always one step ahead of the market, only to be caught up with in a matter of months (they have commodified the term 'independent').

I believe that any kind of writing about or working with movies today runs the risk of getting entangled in one of these positions. But I also believe that the kind of cinephilia which has brought us together is well equipped to evade this triangle. Jonathan asks us, 'What were the specific needs of your generation that gave rise to your particular brand of cinephilia?' I think that this was certainly *one* specific need: to become flexible enough, to be able to (re)act quickly and knowledgeably in order to undermine firmly established positions. To become Fripp's 'small, highly intelligent, mobile unit' which Kent talks about.

Mobile in a physical sense, too. We travel a lot, we move toward the films if they are not taken up by the market; we are hunter-gatherers of information (and we exchange it). We try to closely watch the small and the regional in cinema, what

Deleuze calls a minor literature. Jonathan says we are rebels against amnesia. But I think we also try to resist the process of economic and cultural globalisation (another kind of synchronisation) which is a major cause of this amnesia. In the framework of film-cultural globalisation, two fake alternatives to Hollywood have evolved: the Miramax idea of US 'indies' and the reduction of European and Asian cinemas to a few masters who can transcend all national borders and dance on all markets (Krzysztof Kieślowski and Zhang Yimou might be two good examples). I am much more interested in film-makers who speak in concrete words and voices, from a concrete place, about concrete places and characters. I like the image of the Jean-Pierre and Luc Dardenne (*La Promesse* [1996]), standing somewhere in the middle of industrial Belgian suburbia, looking around and saying, 'All these landscapes make up our language.' Next to the film-makers we've often discussed (Ferrara, Assayas, Egoyan, Kiarostami, Wong *et al.*) there are many more, lesser-known examples of this kind of cinema. Their dialects are way too specific to fit into the global commerce of goods. For example, in Austria: Wolfgang Murnberger (today) and John Cook (in the 70s); in Germany: Michael Klier, Helge Schneider. Or in Kazakhstan: Darezhan Omirbaev. And even in Hollywood: Albert Brooks. Each of us could think of twenty others.

At the same time, the need to 'catch up' is quite different from country to country (and so are, therefore, our strategic needs when writing about marginal cinema or programming films). Last year, *Film Comment* published a well-chosen list of the thirty most important foreign-language films not distributed in the United States. In Austria, surprisingly enough, fourteen of those thirty were released on the regular circuit.

I am too young to have witnessed the innovative movements in European cinema as a contemporary. Even the latest of these movements, New German Cinema, was practically over when my passion for movies and my 'research' began (around 1980). But at the same time, I am too old to belong to a later generation, which very 'naturally' grew up with home video, rock video, video games and computers. This might be an important element of how I was (how we were) formed: the aura of movies in the first person singular (as a dominant idea of cinema) was still in the air, like an after-image, and the commodification of film in the context of exploding entertainment industries (as a dominant idea of cinema) was not yet fully tangible. Born into this gap, without a guiding cinematic principle, my perspective was unstable: turning both backwards and forwards. And I share Kent's experience: the only real guiding principle at that time, to define yourself as a young person, was pop music.

For me in Austria, this gap or in-between space lasted from about 1980 to 1986; as a real space in film history, it might have lasted from 1975 to 1983, from *Saló* to *Flashdance*. I can imagine that it was also the formative era for many of the film-makers we cherish today.

(At first, I wanted to continue here with one of the big movie mutations in German-speaking countries: how the ideology of film subsidy has changed in the past ten years, how the state and the market have converged towards the same aim: 'Stop the navel-gazing!' The subtlety of such recent film policies finds an equivalence in the young journalist's rant during his interview with Maggie Cheung in *Irma Vep*. But since 'Newest German Cinema' has not produced a single mutant film comparable to *Irma Vep* in kind and quality, I'll refrain from the digression and spare you the depression.)

I am, however, drawn towards the space of the 70s, the space of that new simplicity, the kind of minimalism you've associated with Eustache, Garrel and Cassavetes, among others. For German film culture, this moment is certainly linked with Wim Wenders, Werner Schroeter and – in a decisive way – with Rainer Werner Fassbinder. In Germany, the endlessly (self-) referential cinema à la *nouvelle vague* didn't have to be broken (as it didn't exist). Wenders and Fassbinder were the first to introduce it, rather quietly (and referring mainly to classic Hollywood movies, only secondarily to the *nouvelle vague*). At the same time they already acknowledged the need for emptying out – their intertextuality never seems playful but like a desperate echo of John Ford, Douglas Sirk or Jean-Pierre Melville, employed to relate a depressive post-68 situation.

Jonathan's description of the world of *Duelle* – 'congealed, under glass, disconnected ... a private and more obsessive world' – corresponds precisely to my experience of Fassbinder's *Chinese Roulette* of the same year (1976). Fassbinder had reached a point where progressive thinking and group action seemed to come to an end (artistically as well as politically); when public discourse became syrupy, stuck in an impasse between terrorism and the police state. Variations of such an emotion are represented in his episode for *Germany in Autumn* (1978) and in *The Third Generation* (1979). The moment is marked by despair (another late 70s' film by Fassbinder even carries that title), and it is surrounded by drugs and suicidal impulses. The great film in this context is the 1978 *In a Year of Thirteen Moons* (where – with Jerry Lewis/Dean Martin on the TV screen – referentiality itself is brought to the level of despair).

I saw most of the films by Fassbinder, Pialat, Eustache, Cassavetes and Garrel five or ten years after they first appeared, but the deep pain they expressed became a moving and beautiful sensation; this pain always seemed to have been experienced firsthand, and it preserved a sense of life even in death or madness. It helped me to finally give up any belief in the historically predetermined improvement of the world. I didn't see myself as unpolitical, quite the contrary, but together with these films I gladly suffered a symbolic defeat. I thought I'd feel more comfortable there than the winners might feel in their greedy, opportunistic victory. Being interested in pain was a kind of advance in knowledge over frivolous friends. And the pain's authenticity (on screen) was guaranteed by the fact that many film-makers of this moment directed their own bodies. When we talk about the importance of the body in these artists' works it might be relevant to note that they often wanted to feel their own flesh in front of the camera – and make us feel it in the moving image (e.g. Garrel, Fassbinder, Akerman, Cassavetes, Jacques Doillon, Nanni Moretti).

To sketch my cinephile formation in a chronologically correct way, I have to go further back. I am, like most of us, a child of popular American cinema. The transition from the naive to the reflective phase is tied to films like *Alien* (1979), *The Shining*

(1980), *Escape from New York* (1981) and *Apocalypse Now* (1979), which put an intellectual spin on my appetite for spectacle. They stand halfway along my path from *Star Wars* (1977) to *Blade Runner*. Maybe Nicole and Adrian's preference for De Palma derives from a similar experience. (Although I agree with Kent and Jonathan about the limitations of De Palma's cinema, I'd probably defend Coppola, Paul Schrader or Scorsese against their objections.)

The start of my university studies in the fall of 1983 (drama and communications – there are no film studies in Austria) was intensely connected with the discovery of European auteur cinema and with a start-up film magazine called *Filmlogbuch* ('film-logbook'). In a very short span of time, cinema exploded for me. I saw Straub and Huillet's *Class Relations* (1983), *Toute une nuit*, Garrel's *L'Enfant secret* (1983), Pialat's *A nos amours* (1983), Rivette's *Le Pont du nord* (1980), *Sunless*, Bresson's *L'Argent* (1983), Andrei Tarkovsky's *Stalker* (1979) and *Nostalghia* (1983); Peter Greenaway's *The Draughtsman's Contract* (1982), Alexander Kluge's *The Power of Emotion* (1983), and *Paris, Texas* soon after; Jim Jarmusch's *Stranger Than Paradise* (1984) – and his *Permanent Vacation* (1980) – and the Godard trilogy *Passion*, *Prénom Carmen* (1983) and *Je vous salue, Marie* (1985) soon after that. The discovery of secret relationships between Straub and Huillet, Wenders, Jarmusch and Nicholas Ray made it possible to also appreciate *The Lusty Men* (1952) and many other *films maudits* from the United States. Godard's dictum about the 'allied exiles' of cinema – Wenders, Akerman, Rivette – legitimised my taste (at some other point he also paid tribute to Straub and Huillet, Pialat and Garrel).

In the magazine, we attempted a kind of new criticism under collective authorship. All members of the group took part in writing huge convoluted hypertexts about important films which we then called 'discourses'. But, pretty soon, two opposing camps became apparent among the editors: those who focused on what they called a 'cinema of film theory', taking their cues from Godard, Kluge, Marker and Gabor Body (their main enemy was Hollywood); and those fascinated by David Cronenberg and David Lynch, who rummaged through the trash (video) scene and American cinema to refertilise it (their main enemy was 'dry' European auteur cinema). For the group – and for the magazine, too – this polarisation turned out to be fatal, but for me it became indirectly quite productive: it seemed absolutely logical and natural to include both of these interests in my relation to movies. The clash of ideologies seemed pointless and almost incomprehensible to me. After all, I was enchanted to the same extent by Peter Kubelka, Godard and *The Texas Chain Saw Massacre* (1974) – mainly because of their 'gesticular' power, which turned my encounters with them into almost corporeal events. I assume that my cinephilia, which is drawn to all cinema beyond the 'High and Low', has its origins in this conscious blending and contaminating of various pure doctrines. To the first of the two camps I owe my reading of Theodor Adorno and Barthes. (Hardcore film theory was no threat for a cinephile disposition in Austria at the time: the foreign-language texts were hardly exploited yet, and German-language film theory was mostly used by semioticians who knew very few films and who had no links to film criticism.) To the second camp in our magazine I owe my reattachment to popular culture. I recall my feverish reading of Alan Moore's graphic novel *Watchmen*, which evokes the whole unrealisable potential of cinema. Like Jonathan's favourite book, *Watchmen* also deals with superheroes. But the metaphor was a different one for me then: the close circle of superhero friends breaks under the weight of contrary utopias and social circumstances (like the *Filmlogbuch* did).

Moore even concurred with my musical tastes: at the very end of *Watchmen*, he quotes John Cale's song 'Santies': 'It would be a stronger world, a strong, though loving world, to die in.' I have still not completely understood this mighty phrase (maybe because some nuances in the English language escape me), but I love it because it contains both the echo of pain and the presentiment of a wondrous future. I experienced this exact blend in the cinema when I first encountered my 'own' film-makers in 1985–6 (those who had not been 'handed down' to me): I discovered Carax and Assayas, and it was as if we discovered everything together – cinema and music and the difficulties of growing up. On both sides, these discoveries were of a romantic, passionate nature. It was a new cinema because it did many things at the same time, it was referential in a cinephile way, it shared in the pleasures and colours of Anglo-American pop music, and it uncoquettishly said 'I' – although it could (like myself) pass on the desperation of an earlier generation only by quotation. I already knew then that Cale would someday write music not just for Garrel but also for Assayas or Carax.

In one of my first letters to Kent, eight years later, I find this emotion still warm; I think it is an important part of our shared enthusiasm. In Cannes 1994, I had seen *Pulp Fiction*, *Exotica*, *Caro diario* and *Cold Water* (and had been amazed by the manifold use of Leonard Cohen songs). I told Kent about these films:

> [Assayas] shows how turntables and records were used during party events, one tune ripped off the soundtrack, the needle screeching, next tune, needle, same tune again to feel the drug-like effects of repeating your high over and over. ... Not because of some nostalgic effect, but because these directors act/move/think in musical and filmic terms *at the same time*. They produce sensations by pushing both together, they do not illustrate, prostitute one for the other; they cannot but feel one in the other.

The music-image in cinema ('L'image-musique'?) has strongly changed the mainstream sector since the early to mid 80s (networking the music and film industries) and it has become one of the most thrilling aspects of auteur cinema. It even surprises us in strange places like the recent comedy *Nothing to Lose* (1997), where sudden non-diegetic music becomes the 'author' of entire scenes, for instance by rerouting a genuine thrill (the spider on Tim Robbins' face) into a lunatic dance performance. In films like *Lost Highway* (1997), *Illtown* (1998) or *The Blackout* (1997) we get an oceanic narrative that seems to be modelled after strategies in electronic music. (And it is exactly there, funnily enough, that Nick Gomez and Ferrara find a renewed 'social relevance', drawing the Dream State America via uncentred tapestry-tales of drugs, identity loss and misty Miami.) Although many in our generation already have to work very hard to get a feel for 90s' ambient and dance music, I think it is an essential component in characterising contemporary storytelling in film. Not only are the 'pop fiction' music artists heavily inspired by filmscapes, but such musical experiences will conversely become more and more important in new cinema.

(I have only one small, Central European thing to add to Kent's precise genealogy of the relationship between pop music, image and movement in America. For lack of our own automobile-highway-teenage culture, we never listened to Creedence Clearwater Revival or Van Morrison while driving through the country. But we've seen and heard how Wenders and Peter Handke postulated this experience as a mythological, imported one from the start, in a little film with the telling title *Three American LPs* [1969].)

A certain obsessive working and reworking of the image texture appears to be another of our generation's mutations – the deliberate alterations of colour, definition and grain which derive from the dominance of electronic media and the contemporary mixing of digital and analogue technologies. Born of visual experiences that stretch from the TV image of the first man on the moon to the hip alienation effects in rock video, a kind of fungus or virus has been eating into the once-transparent movie image. A window on the world has been turned into a fabric which is being woven further by the viewer even if he or she is not interested at all in the world behind it (from von Trier's *The Element of Crime* [1984] to Michael Almereyda's 'pixelegance').

Adrian has already noted the tension between the radically authentic and the radically synthetic bodies in 'our' movies. I have to admit that I perceive most pop blockbusters (which pursue a complete dematerialisation and virtualisation) as genuinely inhuman. *Independence Day* (1996), *The Rock* (1996), *Con Air* (1997) and *Batman & Robin* (1997) celebrate new bodies and new identities only in a fascist sense; they reduce these possibilities to dull and stolid phantasms of a slave society. But I do believe that there are potentially liberating examples of dealing with physicality in today's pop cinema that strengthen and exhilarate me as a viewer – in Asian action movies, in *Babe* (1995), or in Jim Carrey. In John Carpenter's *Escape from LA* (1996), the conscious use of low-tech effects (the 'implausible' illusion) helps to make the bodies more present again. In Cronenberg's vision of a 'New Flesh', finally, the whole potential of our interests seems to be realised: these are multifariously mutated, futuristic bodies, but the movies represent them as radically authentic. (Nevertheless, nobody should be surprised that, as a countermovement, we try to follow the living tradition of neo-realism and passionately promote films like *La Promesse, Kardiogramma* [1995] or *Will It Snow for Christmas?* [1996].)

I almost forgot another significant common interest: avant-garde cinema. Isn't this the place where the weight of the physical, the material/manual use of film are most tangible? With this interest we also, very obviously, turn against specialisation (avant-garde film always suffered from the fact that it had been mined as a field for and by specialists). In the 70s many people lamented the draining of avant-garde cinema and the segregation of film culture – Andrew Sarris, Peter Gidal and Christian Metz had practically nothing to say to one another. I think that my generation in the early to mid 80s (without having suffered this history, or being confronted with a seemingly closed history) could look at the options of the avant-garde with new eyes. The first boom of music video and the blossoming of found-footage films (reworking existing film images) were partly responsible for this. Therefore, I am also a child of Anger-Brehm-Conner-Deren-Gehr-Kren-Rimmer-Sharits-Snow *et al*. (Why do they all have such short, clear, sharp, vehement names? They sound like their films.)

The audience has certainly changed with our generation, with the changes in distribution (and with the films this change brought about). The historian William Paul describes how cinema in the age of video had to be first established as a consumer product next to many others (mall theatres), before it could move towards the centre again (as a new cultural form, a commodity to begin with), where it now rallies other consumer products around itself (theatre malls). Big movies today are made and marketed to fulfil this central function: they are not only responsible for themselves and their audiences but for numerous other consumption processes. (They also often look like they've been directed with their eventual appearance on video in mind.)

Because we visit these places ourselves, because we do see many films on video, because we belong to an in-between generation that shared in earlier rituals as well as new forms of consumption – because of these very reasons we should reject a rhetoric which talks about the audience as a herd of sheep or which assures the audience that it is inevitably part of that herd. (The market says, 'That's what the audience wants.' The cultural pessimist says, 'The audience is a weak-willed mass steered by the system.') The fetishism of big numbers (box office grosses, TV ratings, actors' salaries, etc.) that dominates the popular discourse about films sometimes infects us, too. We dress in mourning if the recent retrospective of classic Westerns attracts only a tenth of the spectators who came fifteen years ago. But is it not most important that these few people still *had* the chance and choice to see the Westerns in a movie theatre?

At the risk of appearing like an essentialist, I ask myself why we still believe in this form of cinema; why it is not enough to see 'our' films on video. To see a film in a cinema means not being able to have it at one's disposal. It unfolds without my being able to access it; it slips through my fingers. On the other hand, the viewer in the cinema is not at the film's disposal either; the film can't make me do anything, it offers itself to me. It is an encounter that I have chosen, but on the same eye level. I pay an entrance fee to make contact with the film. Film-on-video, however, is dominated by the spectator; it is formed, used, worn and torn at will according to the viewer's free scheduling of time and arrangement of space. Film-on-video becomes small – not just in terms of image (screen) size, but also in its relation to me as a viewer. I do not meet it, *I order it into existence*, and go back and forth, fast and slow. I pay the rental fee or purchase price to be able to make it small.

Maybe it was essentialist thinking, too, which had long kept me from visiting an IMAX screening ('all these new gadgets'). A few weeks ago I went to the IMAX cinema for the first time. I saw the film *Mountain Gorilla* (1992), forty-two minutes of simplistic nature documentary. But what I really *saw* was the prospect of a new artistic medium with immense possibilities. If cinema shows moving images, IMAX shows moving slides. I thought of the huge, glowing transparencies by Jeff Wall, one of my favourite artists; and I had an imaginary IMAX movie in mind, directed by Wall and Antonioni, a new category of visual narrative about people in spaces (all the while having seen nothing but a few apes and African rain forests). In front of this wall of images I realise that we may expose ourselves to all kinds of infections. If we believe in cinema, we must also believe that it will always find a beautiful antibody for each virus.

This letter has become very (maybe too) biographical. Schefer writes: 'Subjectivity (my autobiography) remains in it as more than a trace, but as a mechanism.'[8] Therefore a further private footnote about our conspiracy can do no more harm. In my culture, every pupil is required to read a famous eighteenth-century play by Friedrich Schiller. It deals with the power of the state and the absolute resistance of the heart. Its title is *Kabale und Liebe* (in English, *Intrigue and Love*). But Adrian and Kent have already signed their respective letters with 'cabal' and 'love'. So I'll remain the one who has dumped half of his autobiography into your living rooms without asking for permission. . . .

Your Cable Guy,
Alex
(© Alexander Horwath 1997)

Paris, 18 August 1997

Dear Jonathan, dear Adrian, dear Kent, lieber Alex,
After all that you've written about movie mutations – the trauma arising from theorism (as Serge Daney described it), the wonders of video acculturation, the necessity of making certain perceptual shifts to truly see modern films, the structuring role of popular music in contemporary narrativity, a genuinely enormous trust in what cinema is becoming . . . and so many other things about which, with one major exception, we agree – I'd like to return to the origin of these exchanges, the letter from Jonathan, who has gently directed us like Rivette characters, but in reality.

Having lived most of my adolescent cinephilia under the aegis of the 'death of cinema', I believe I understand what Jonathan has in mind when he makes it a touchstone for reflection. But the fact is that, in that period, no one believed it for a moment; for us, the death of cinema merely represented a grand melancholy theme that certain film-makers needed in order to make their films. It was a lovely theme, to be sure: when they abandoned it, Wenders' films became somewhat unwatchable, and when Godard wanted to once again make a film about – or with – youth, a work that was critical but without melancholy, he made to my mind his first and only bad film,

For Ever Mozart (1996). I think I fully understood the dynamic character of the death of cinema only when I had to explain it to someone else. I still remember this very young man (the son of a Marseille movie theatre manager, I note for Jonathan[9]) emerging from an incredibly brilliant presentation by Daney, his idol then and now, with tears in his eyes, asking me: 'Daney has said that cinema is going to die, so what can we do?' I had to console him by saying, even though I was shaken myself: 'No, cinema isn't going to die, don't worry; if you create it, then by definition it won't die.' After which I gathered up my vague memories of *Saturn and Melancholy*,[10] told him the tales and legends of cinematic modernity and, a few lemonades later, his spirits lifted. (The last I heard, he was working in theatre and photography.) In short, the death of cinema lasted a good while as a neat formula, and its productive side became clear once it vanished as an aesthetic theme, to be replaced by dark slick movies of good intention.

By the same token, I would argue that whereas classical cinephilia was no doubt a reason for being, contemporary cinephilia has become a mode of existence. I see my younger friends and students, who think only of cinema, awaiting the releases of films by their favourite authors the same way one awaits a fiancée – with so much love, hope and fever that sometimes they wind up not even seeing them, just as one doesn't dare gaze at the creature with whom one is madly in love. (It's a phenomenon I understood better when I illustrated it myself: having loved *Carlito's Way* [1993] so much that I couldn't bear *Mission: Impossible*, and had to go back in order to discover what the problem was.) They dream about them at night; one of them once dreamed about *The Addiction* (1995) months before it came out, and his dream ('You don't see much of Christopher Walken, and you have to wait a long time before you do') proved to be correct, much as Adrian's premonitory dream of *Planet of the Apes*, which resembles a screen memory, perhaps testifies above all to the intimacy and intensity of the relation of cinephilia to image practices in general: they are like seasoned archaeologists, requiring only the shadow of an image to reconstruct an entire film.

They get up in the morning (around noon), watch films over breakfast (on video), then go to see them in theatres (on film), a few project them at night (on film), then they watch them together (all night long); they make them (on all formats); they comment on them in diaries and private letters, and, above all, they speak only of cinema. (That's why one understands that cinema frees us from speaking about ourselves; the only intimacy we tolerate is imaginary, and the only imaginary we tolerate is shared. Everything else is fiercely secret.) Does this make them consumers? No, there has to be a little curiosity, a virtue quite prevalent among them, so that they emerge from genre films and quickly become experts. Does that make them apolitical creatures, cut off from the world? On the contrary, they immerse themselves in the critical thoughts of history as they proceed past Pier Paolo Pasolini, Fassbinder and Godard instead of past Hegel or Marx (which they discover next), and, in my opinion, that gives them a greater versatility. Christian Metz taught us that the patron saint of film people wasn't Mr Sony but St Augustine, because he had mapped out cinema well in advance of its existence ('A system where the real would be the sign of the real itself'). After Adrian's letter, I have the impression that the patron saint of cinephiles is Artemidorus, ancient author of *The Interpretation of Dreams*: chiefly because of the precision work that understanding images requires, but also, as Michel Foucault recalls in *The Care of the Self*, because 'the analysis of dreams was one of the techniques of existence.'[11]. For this generation of cinephiles, the image in any case does not represent a reflection or displacement of the world. It's a material, a substance, something to subsist on and which one can work on like clay; images are not living, but concrete. (Living images belong to the next generation, that of Tamagotchi.) It's indeed for that reason that we have so much need not only of Godard but also of De Palma: because the former in the mode of the essay and the latter in the realm of fiction have thoroughly explored the economy of images. They show through the medium of images themselves how these images appear limited, how they differ from one another in the context of the same film, then the logical ways one can crack them open, compare, complete, transform, exhaust, convert them. ... In the cases of Godard and De Palma alike, it's neither a referential overload nor an abandonment of reality and life in my view, but the two critical enterprises at work together which, in themselves, are necessary and vital to the understanding of the powers of cinema.

What threatens to vanish in such a culture is, rather, reading. But not so, judging by the example of my friends, who bear a family resemblance to the characters in *Tesis* (1996):[12] before they see *Drugstore Cowboy* (1989), they read the complete works of William Burroughs; and because they love fantasy films above all, they know Edgar Allen Poe by heart; Maurice Blanchot helps them to understand *Body Snatchers* (1994) – one of them underlined in *The Unavowable Community* the same passages as Jacques Aumont!;[13] and I suppose they also read texts without any direct connection to film. On the other hand, one thing that we'd all like to see disappear is home video, that fragile, ugly, cumbersome crutch: we impatiently await the next technology, where films will be reconstituted on shiny, easy-to-handle discs to be exchanged and sent around the world. (That there are great video films, like Michael Klier's *The Giant* [1983], or great works on video, like Bill Viola's, only demonstrates the genius of artists who have overcome mediocre technology.)

Jonathan undoubtedly wrote in a spirit of provocation and as a challenge to be contradicted: I don't share at all his vision of cinema after the *nouvelle vague*. As I gradually discover cinema, I perceive that, apart from the 90s, which promise to be magnificent, there have been three great decades when authors were collectively inspired (we still don't know by what): the 1890s when all films were beautiful, perhaps because of the artisanal quality of the filmic support, but more surely because the long-standing quarrel between Étienne-Jules Marey and Georges Demeny fertilised the history of forms; the 1920s, because of the unsurpassed invention of montage material; and the 1970s, because of the formal liberty that triumphed then. In any case, I can't see the 70s as years of icing-over and a suspension of meaning: historical despair, yes; aesthetic congealing, certainly not. It's with despair that Fassbinder made out of each of his films a sublime treatise on violence, with disillusion that Godard and Jean-Pierre Gorin realised their most beautiful pamphlets, with sadness that Eustache shot his masterpieces, *The Mother and the Whore* and *Mes petites amoureuses* (1975), with disenchantment that Akerman could arrive at the rawness of *Jeanne Dielman* (1975). . . . The 70s, which of course I missed at the time and am now barely starting to discover, were the most beautiful films of Pialat, Garrel, Jean-Daniel Pollet, Jacques Rozier, Bresson. . . . They were (with a little elasticity) Ken Jacobs' *Tom Tom the Piper's Son* (1971), Monte Hellman's *Two-Lane Blacktop* (1971), almost the complete work of Paul Sharits, Malcolm Le Grice's *Berlin Horse* (1970), the most beautiful film of Straub and Huillet (*Too Early, Too Late* [1981]), Jonas Mekas' *Reminiscences of a Journey to Lithuania* (1972), Terrence Malick's *Badlands* (1973), Len Lye's *Free Radicals* (1979), Jacques Doillon's *Les Doigts dans la tête* (1974) and Ferrara's first feature *The Driller Killer* (1979), which is unadulterated Bataille. . . . Last year, Kent put together in New York a festival of American movies of the 70s – twenty films, twenty masterpieces, from *Cockfighter* (1974) to *Dog Day Afternoon* (1975). One could do the same thing with the films of France, Germany, Japan. . . . Last Friday, at the Cinémathèque, I programmed Schroeter's *The Death of Maria Malibran* (1971). In the auditorium, three-quarters full, were almost exclusively young people curious about this legendary and invisible cinema; with few exceptions, they were amazed, overcome, enthused by so much formal freedom associated with such love of beauty. In a way, Schroeter dates today's cinema, appearing newer than most of the self-conscious films of the present. Perhaps they would have loved it less if Wong Kar-wai hadn't accustomed them to the contemplation of faces, chromatic research and narrative destruction. But viewing films by Garrel, Eustache and Hellman invariably produce the same effect, whether at the Cinémathèque or in bad video copies.

Not so long ago, Jonathan and Kent took me aside and explained that Pialat was not at all known in the US; for America, the French cinema stops with the *nouvelle vague* and, necessarily, nothing follows. It wouldn't be hard to prove the contrary: after the *nouvelle vague* came the essential, a cinema which, in its totality, was permeated by a vital need to experiment, to allow authors to exercise their inventiveness to the utmost, to not fall back on any single solution, to formulate every question to the point of total delirium (as in Dennis Hopper's *The Last Movie* [1971]) and the inadmissable. Alex has cited one of the emblematic moments of this, by a coincidence that no longer astonishes but continues to charm me, a sequence that has also been occupying me for months: that of the dance of capitalism in *In a Year of Thirteen Moons*, when, instead of an expected narrative explanation, Fassbinder takes a plunge into the inferno of formal forfeiture, thanks to which he can produce a stupefying theory of human refuse. That which collectively inspired the cinema of the 70s – which I could never call post-*nouvelle vague* because it is so rich and autonomous – is obviously a powerful formal care regarding the figuration of History, and even if all the authors weren't as brilliant as Fassbinder, rare are those who weren't seized by this preoccupation.

The only thing with which I find myself in disagreement with you concerns the theoretical trauma experienced during that period: this is because, unlike Alex, Adrian and Kent, I wasn't a film student. The result is the same but the emotional impact very different. I studied literature; when, saturated (but not so angry), I decided to switch fields and do research in film, the instruments and concepts which were active in this other field seemed very familiar: inevitably they were the same, Barthes, Gérard Genette, semiology and psychology. Thus everything I wanted to learn, which I couldn't study in literature and which interested me in cinema, I had to discover on my own: the figurative dimension of film (in that period, I didn't even know how to name it), the treatment of the body, gesture, acting, effects of presence, speed. ... Unlike Adrian, I wasn't deterred by the theory of the 70s because it didn't please me, but because it seemed very much a thing complete in itself so there was no point going back to it. To broach the cinema as a field of figurative intervention, one needed other instruments that one could elaborate by starting from older texts (Vachel Lindsay, but also Béla Bálazs' *Visible Man*, the critical texts of Jean Epstein, Sergei Eisenstein, Pasolini . . .), and especially from the films themselves – beginning with *The Killing of a Chinese Bookie*, for me the greatest treatise ever on cinematic forms. Since then, the only possible method has been a principled empiricism: always placing your confidence in the film, always presuming that a film can think as well as a theoretical text – which becomes a wonderful and challenging affair when they think exactly the same things. (For the last several months I've been doing work on Lon Chaney, and the connections with psychoanalysis have proven to be intense and quite delicate: how can one explain that the tools of psychoanalysis, such as castration and incorporation, do not encompass the inventions of Lon Chaney, but rather that Chaney opens a new field in matters of understanding the body?) This method is a safeguard: the basic principle is that the cinema is not illustrative but has its own figurative powers, that it's necessary to go with its propositions as far as possible and that these are not 'justifiable' by any other discipline, at least for the moment. Reading Kent's letter, I realised that this principle of 'free analysis', if I can call it that, constitutes no less than the other side of the moment when, as he once wrote, 'the cinema had to be overridden by something outside of it'. But for me the consequence is that nothing clarifies an image like another image, nothing analyses a film better than another film. Many other cinephiles have accomplished the same kind of work, a rupture (more or less painful) followed by a renewal, on questions of history, of aesthetics, of method: magazines like *Meteor* in Austria, *Close Up* in Italy, *Cinémathèque* and *Trafic* in France all echo one another. (Jonathan and Kent could not really think of an equivalent in the United States, which astonished me.)

Therefore, I feel no animosity in regard to the theories of the 70s. On the contrary, the more time passes, the more I see them as protections. Foucault and Adorno remain absolute benchmarks and it seems to me that reading them (I was precocious, but at first I really understood nothing) has kept me from subscribing to bourgeois reflexes (for good, I hope). For example, I am shocked when the majority of film critics, with some happy exceptions, dismiss the most important films. I'm not even talking about the films of Rose Lowder or Cécile Fontaine (which they don't even see), but incontestable films like *The Blackout* or Jean-François Richet's *Ma 6-T va crack-er*

(1997). In both cases, in order to avoid the contemplation of violence, they resorted (as Adrian wrote, who must have had other examples in mind) to a wretched return to moral criteria, to a moralism with absolutely no political or ethical sense (for Richet, who made an indispensable film about misfortune and revolt, without concessions) and with absolutely no formal discrimination (for Ferrara, who made the most beautiful elegy to the image that the cinema has produced in a long time, an elegy that is profoundly gentle). At this moment, I fear that the same thing will happen to F. J. Ossang's *Docteur Chance* (1997), because of its surplus of beauty and poetry, its too-moving imperfections, and its breath that seems too powerful for today's criteria, which are always neat realist constructions. (I too have my limits: it would never occur to me to go see films that many people have assured me are so beautiful. They immediately repulse me, and I would rather go see Tsui Hark's *The Blade* [1995] for the tenth time.)

In the legacy of the 70s, there were also many things that were unacceptable, both great and small – for example, the echoes of sectarian excommunication and never-ending polemics that Adrian recalls in his letter, heard in the rhetoric of our professors. One of mine, for example, compulsively began every sentence with the words, 'I wanted to say that … ' followed by the qualification that, in general, there was nothing to say (on Rimbaud, a genuine achievement). Because of that, I taught myself never to hesitate before making an affirmative statement and never to take the least rhetorical precaution. Better to be wrong than to be safe. On a more serious level, for those people like myself who progressed into their cinephilia through reading *Cahiers du cinéma* throughout the 70s, interest in the American cinema held an aspect of delicious transgression.

One day, in 1978, on the eve of my philosophy exam, my little sister (much hipper than her orthodox older sister) took me to see *Saturday Night Fever* (1977), to 'distract' me. What a complete shock to realise that, yes, the American cinema was just as good at showing people and simple emotions! And one of the most moving cinematic spectacles of my entire life remains the sight of my little sister and her friends dancing the steps of the song 'Night Fever' in the family garage. How many times had they seen the film before they knew those steps by heart? They were dancing for themselves, for pleasure, but it was as beautiful as the funeral processions on the cliffs of Bandiagara. For a long time my prejudices kept me from liking nothing but Bresson, Carl Dreyer and Godard but, all of a sudden, when I defend *Mission: Impossible* against Jonathan and Kent, it seems to me that I'm not doing it blindly. The other consequence was that I started searching out everything that *Cahiers du cinéma* didn't talk about, starting with experimental cinema, whose absence in French cinematic culture remains a fatal misunderstanding.

To put it simply: the 70s were years of divisiveness and 'hard words' (as Adrian wrote), years that put into practice Godard's slogan: 'Television unites people, while the cinema divides them.' Now, and this is for me the most precious movie mutation, today we are witnessing a kind of atonement, not a reconciliation (with due respect to Adorno) as much as a refusal of established limits and a broader sense of what constitutes the cinematic art by cinephiles. Once, a cinephile loved a particular genre or 'field' (as defined by the *politique des auteurs*); today it has become possible to love both Hark and Sharits (two great film-makers of cruelty), John Woo and Le Grice (each of whose work on speed clarifies the other's). I know few precedents, besides Amos Vogel's book *Film as a Subversive Art*.[14] Today, however, it's an obvious fact as much as a desire, one to which our letters testify and which the Cinémathèque Française has put into practice with each day of 'impure' programming from Dominique Païni and Jean-François Rauger, and which new film journals like *101* or *Episodic* reflect every month. At the cinema, I can run into the same guy by chance one night at a screening of Stéphane Marti's work and the next day at *Pazeekah* (1970), a wonderful Indian musical comedy. The same young people make retrospectives of Hark as well as Bresson successes, while others return every Friday to see experimental works as well as exploitation films. A young film-maker whom I had never heard of, Anne Benhaïem, made me curious to see her own films when I saw a list of films that had inspired her, which included Andy Warhol's *Blow Job* (1963), Garrel's *Les Enfants désaccordés* (1964) and Stan Brakhage's *The Act of Seeing with One's Own Eyes* (1971).[15] And yet, for all that, it's not a question of ecumenism, nor of the sudden reintegration of opposing cinemas within orthodox cinephilic culture, nor is it a side benefit of the centenary: it's fundamentally more a question of denying all dominant barriers, of criticising that which we were taught, of never believing a word of standard cultural communication about any given film. And another plus is that this can serve in the creation of a true history of forms.

Over several weeks, I can see Arthur Omar's *The Inspector* (1988) in the Experimental Film section of the Museum of Modern Art's catalogue, and Quelou Parente's *Marquis de Slime* (1997) at an underground session at the Cinémathèque: two staggering films, obviously made under severe financial conditions and yet more sumptuous than anything Cecil B. DeMille ever made. Two films, above all, *that belong to the same formal history*, a kind of history that considers the cinema a heterogeneous, self-perpetuating mélange of theatre, cinema, photography, comic strips, computer art ... in both cases, a cinema that is heteroclite and deliberately wasteful. So obviously the opposing origins of the two films (a political pamphlet for the first, a panegyric to the exploitation film for the second) are less important than the fact of their mingling. Between these two films, which a priori have nothing to do with each other, there is a relationship: comparing them to other works that resemble them, like the researches of Jean-Michel Bouhours or *My Own Private Idaho* (1991), one sees that since Emile Cohl the cinema is above all a set of mixed techniques, and one also sees that morphing is a false movie mutation yet a normal evolution of its system, which exacerbates certain phenomena of artifice without ever resorting to the procedure of actual filming. (According to Alain Bergala, Rossellini invented morphing in the French version of *India* [1958], for the transition passages between the film's episodes, when the animals metamorphose very quickly.)

Jonathan and Alex are perpetually at the forefront and accomplish the most important work: seeing films from all over the world, distinguishing each one from every other, and giving an immediate accounting of them, doing battle against the everyday forces of the industry. Right now, I am sheltered by my university fortress, so the work I do there is of the sort one can do only in a place that is happily cut off from the economic world: watching films without having to make allowances for their industrial origins and their cultural legitimations, not in order to deprive them of their history but to see, as clearly as possible, taking as much time as is necessary (two years for one hour of *Chinese Bookie*, but even then we were going very fast), what it is that they're really saying. To see that Cassavetes is one of the greatest plastic artists of the century. To see that *Body Snatchers*, which comes from the lowest rung of the Hollywood industry, is a more experimental work than the films of those who are mimicking the magisterial films of Jürgen Reble. To see that the same forms of plastically beautiful destruction were achieved at the same time by Sharits and Hellman but to completely different ends. To see how Al Razutis and Godard both thought of creating a history of cinema in its own medium at the same time, each one ignorant of the other. What end does this serve? And, even if I didn't believe in the possibility of an objective formal history (but I do firmly believe in it, since the words 'open work' were endlessly repeated during the 70s and the thought gave form to and released the idea that in a work of art one could say anything and that everything was correct), at least it serves to prove that films are beautiful and interesting, always richer than one thinks they are and not necessarily in the way one thought they would be, to find more pleasure and to find it everywhere, in the bewitching *VW Vitesses Women* (1972–4) by Claudine Eizykman as much as in the very moving *Dans les coulisses du clip 'California'* (1996), a documentary film about the making of a Mylène Farmer rock video by Ferrara.

I don't think it's a matter of eclecticism. I believe that the cinema, for us, is before anything else an ensemble of psychic experiences and that this is how they relate to the real. There is the experience of Kent's client in the video store ('something big and plush that I can really sink into' – personally I find this enchanting); there are the experiences that Jonathan talks about in *Moving Places*, in particular the formidable set of varying descriptions of *On Moonlight Bay* (1951), visited at different moments of his life.

This year, an anxious student asked me a troubling question: 'What do you do in order to analyse a film?' (troubling because the usual question would be 'How does one analyse films?' or 'How can I do it?'). As much as I can figure it out, I do at least two things: first of all, I have confidence in the film (which is easy); then, I try to acknowledge what I don't understand (which is very difficult). So the most important films for me remain the ones that I didn't understand the first time I saw them, the films that demanded a great effort from me before I could love them: Strombolian films, because the first of these was *Stromboli* (1949), initially unwatchable because of my anti-clerical background and because at the time, confusing it with *La terra trema* (1948), I didn't really see how divine grace could resolve the problems of fishermen. ... These are films that resist, that one must surmount just as Ingrid Bergman scaled her volcano, and that change you forever: *Stromboli*, *Mission: Impossible*, de Oliveira's

Nice à propos de Jean Vigo (1983). There are also appetising films, which allow you to unexpectedly uncover an entire world: *Saturday Night Fever* for American commercial cinema, *Schwechater* (1958) for experimental cinema, *Hard-Boiled* (1992) for Hong Kong cinema. There are the films that accompany you through your life (*L'Atalante* [1934], *Francis, God's Jester* [1950], *By the Bluest of Seas* [1936]); the film to which you instinctively compare all others (*Adebar* [1957]); the film that runs through your head like a popular song and in which the familiar images keep coming back in the same way that you hum a refrain (*King of New York* [1990]); those you can't watch again because you've loved them too much (*Contempt* [1963]); those that you understand in fragments, slowly, throughout a lifetime (*Faces* [1968]); those that you hope to understand one day (*Cockfighter*); those for which you must wait to become much stronger (*Epileptic Seizure Comparison* [1976]); those that suddenly offer you everything you needed (*Animated Picture Studio* [1904], *The Killing of a Chinese Bookie*). . . . But I've never encountered a film that made me turn away from cinema. And then, Adrian is completely and absolutely right, there are the films of Jean Rouch, in which one finds all the others. And so many, many other experiences, because, in the end, the cinema seems to me above all inexhaustibly generous.

It should also be said that today there are many other forms and practices beyond those of our (marginal) group in the culture of cinephilia, which is almost always countercultural since it remains a tribe of creatures who are very different from and often unadaptable to the social world; that the idea of a generation is useful in that it can help to define that which determines us *nolens volens*, but that it's also an easy kind of technique that one must contest. Dear friends, pardon me, this letter is much too long: I want you to see here only your reflections and the affectionate attention that they have fostered. Since I've known you, I find myself in the same state as Tom Courtenay, the central character in *The Loneliness of the Long Distance Runner* (1962), who burns the promissory notes that have been given to him in exchange for the love of his father: 'I've learned a lot recently. . . . But I don't know exactly what.' For that and so many other things, I give you all a big kiss.

Nicole

Paris, 25 September 1997

To the Four Musketeers of the new generation, and to my old friend Jonathan, Entering into your letters is a little like breaking and entering into a house. Even if I might at first be your devoted supporter – and in fact the next instalment in the series begun by Jonathan and proceeding through each of you – the letters provoke in me an anguish. The anguish arises from the impossible logic of tastes, feelings and personal positions (once, that is, I begin advancing my own so as better to deal with yours). How can one negotiate, for example, between Adrian's list of his major films of the 80s (*Sunless, The State of Things, Passion, Toute une nuit, Hypothesis of the Stolen*

Painting – this list could be mine, especially with Marker and Godard) and the logical risk that Kent takes in collapsing everything in the end on Cassavetes (where all of a sudden I feel excluded, and this is not a judgment of the work)? How do you locate yourself in the generous and all-encompassing tide that washes across Alex's letters and even more Nicole's, which is disorienting, not because you don't know how to love them, but because it's too much, really, to understand the law or desire (it's all one thing), the politics or artistic credo, that governs these affectionate waves of names and titles?

Like Nicole, I would like not to accord too much to the idea of generations, even if I can't forget the conviction held by Serge (sorry, 'Daney' is too much) that our generation – his, mine – has not really done its work as regards the *nouvelle vague* and the great intellectual works that were its contemporaries. So we're stuck all the same with generations, despite the solitude of each. I think, for example, that I've never entered a video store to buy a film. Only once, actually: several months ago, I ran to a FNAC store to find Kenji Mizoguchi's *Miss Oyu* (1951), which had never been shown on television. I had to present the first sequence of the film at the Cinémathèque Française, and I had to go over it again, patiently, shot by shot, as you do when you sit down to work.[16] But to buy a film in order to simply watch it, never. You buy a ticket, a seat in the dark, but not a film. Even if I was one of the first to decide to study films on video and to buy, at least mythically, one of the first VCRs to arrive in Paris, it was always a pure instrument of work, thus of re-viewing, and of theory. Television is not vision. Marker says it quite well in his CD-ROM *Immemory* (1997), quoting and expanding upon Godard: 'Cinema is that which is bigger than us – you have to lift your eyes up to it. . . . [O]n TV, you can see the shadow of a film, the trace of a film, the nostalgia, the echo of a film – but never a film.' This doesn't mean you can't cry in front of your TV set, but it is first and foremost in the cinema where one cries, in its great shadow. Kent illuminated something about Tarantino for me: his is truly the cinema of the worst amnesia, believing it's being seen for the first time, and not knowing the real weight of an image, which explains its striking ethical irresponsibility.

Another evil in my eyes – and ears – began in the cinema almost from the moment it 'congealed', as Jonathan says apropos of something else altogether, in the realm of music. Here the dividing line Kent traces is unforgiving. I am not speaking, of course, of Straub and Huillet, nor of the intolerably beautiful montages of Godard, nor of Cassavetes, where the music is so alive because it forms part of the body of the image and of the story of the bodies that motivate it. I'm referring to all those films after them in which the title sequence serves as an advertisement for the record companies – a fitting acknowledgment, since the music ends up purchasing the image. I am nostalgic for those films in which sound has dared to be without music (or almost): *La Mort en ce jardin* (1956), where Buñuel made us hear a forest, and *The River* (1997), so bold in that what little diegetic music there is, and which normally imbues the frame, doesn't stop Tsai Ming-liang from making a film brilliantly devoid of exterior occurrences. I confess, however, that I did buy a Mustang in the 70s, in the US, to ride the highways – but it was to act like in the movies, American movies especially, and imitate the music that was situated, sung and given over to the shots, before films took themselves for the actors who breathe bodies in their sound.

Another generation gap, undoubtedly the clearest. Up to the end of the 60s, there was this pure illusion that cinema wasn't so vast, in its history or its geography. In the 50s, an intrepid and obsessed adolescent could still believe, innocently, that it was possible to 'know cinema', to be able to carve out in this finite world an immense province where cinephilia could operate like a conspiracy. Serge said it so well: 'There's American cinema, and then there's all the rest.' He also said: 'The American cinema, how redundant.' He wrote, for example, in the first notes collected in *L'exercice a été profitable, Monsieur*:

> Actors are the flesh and blood of cinema. But they are also the ultimate reality of American society. It is in this sense that the cinema is, in a way, spontaneously *American*, much as all the actors that I just quoted are Americans. It is again their names that one cites today, among friends, as if America had possessed until late in the postwar period *the* definitive secret of our identifications.[17]

French cinephilia was thus from the beginning American. 'How can one be a Hitchcocko-Hawksian?' It's a question of theory, but even more of territory. This is what necessarily divides me from Jonathan, in whom cinephilia was born, like in everybody else, through the *nouvelle vague*, but who, as an American, takes the *nouvelle vague* itself as an object of cinephilia – whereas the cinephile, in the historical and French sense, trains his sights on the American cinema as an enchanted and closed world, a referential system sufficient to interpret the rest. 'When Mel Ferrer leans on the seesaw, it's great!' When I knew Patrick Brion, at the time of our book on the Western in the 60s, he was watching almost exclusively American films. But he saw them all, knew everything about every one of them. Beyond, one might say, love, knowledge, passion, thought, culture of cinema; perhaps cinephilia in the proper sense of the word. But maybe there are at least two cinephilias, much as I have proposed recently (on the occasion of the conference where I showed *Miss Oyu*) that there are two *mises en scène* that ought to be differentiated. On the one hand, there's *mise en scène* that corresponds to both an age and a vision of cinema, a certain kind of belief in the story and the shot, a *mise en scène* that one must carefully distinguish from other modes of organising images that often mingle with and run through it (*mise en plans, mise en place, mise en pages, mise en phrases, mise en images* and especially *mise en plis*, which dissolves the limits of the shot). Then there's *mise en scène* as a general term covering the scenographic world common to all fiction films.

My cinephilia, which has nothing original about it, originally consisted of scouring the Lyons suburbs to find theatres showing horribly dubbed little American films (which also allowed me to discover *L'Amour est plus fort* – as *Voyage in Italy* [1953] was called). This is why I have trouble imagining an entirely open cinephilia, even a cleverly selective one which takes the entire world of cinema as its field, the videocassette as its tool of complicity (at least until something better comes along), television as its space of transit, and the museum as ideal reference. As usual, Godard defined it when he said of the *nouvelle vague*, beginning to end, that it had definitively moved cinema into art history.

But that isn't really the essence of what your letters may say, and of how one might respond to them (taking them abusively as a whole when they are so singular). We should return to the passage by Nicole that Jonathan cited in 'Comparaisons à Cannes' when he first formulated the idea of your cabal, finding there 'a recent formulation of what I think to be the tastes of this group':

> If Fassbinder's *Beware of a Holy Whore* (1970), in spite of certain schemas and motifs in common, doesn't form a link between *Contempt* and *The State of Things*, that is because, fundamentally, it's not really a reflexive film. Closer in that regard to Garrel's *Elle a passé tant d'heures sous les sunlights* (1985), its subject is not the cinema but the body, its material not an image but the actor, its problem not representation but power.[18]

This helps me to understand a certain exclusion, or at least a subordination, across your letters (Alex notwithstanding) of an entire cinema that I don't really know how to name. Let's call it, clumsily, a cinema of speech, of discourse, of critical intent, dissociation, thought, the apparatus, the brain, as Deleuze says (I now have to quote him, as you can see). The great absences (or almost) of your hit parade are, for example, Alain Resnais, Marker (even if *Sunless* is twice positioned well, by Adrian and Alex), Marguerite Duras, Hans-Jürgen Syberberg, Straub and Huillet (Deleuze's exemplary triad at the end of *The Time-Image*). It's striking that of the films of Eustache, one of your elected film-makers, you never choose his apparatus-films, like *Une Sale histoire* (1977) or *Les Photos d'Alix* (1980); you vote instead for his most physical film, *Mes petites amoureuses* (*The Mother and the Whore* playing on a double register). The same goes for Akerman's minimalism; your choices don't speak to her more discursive films. And while you mention so many films and directors, Stanley Kubrick is never one of them, nor João César Monteiro, and barely Tarkovsky, Moretti or Kiarostami. And Godard assumes in your exchange the character of the present/absent God (Nicole notwithstanding ...). In short, it's a little as if you had sliced in two the chapter entitled 'Cinema, Body and Brain, Thought' in *The Time-Image*. If you look closely at the defining feature, as Kent dares to do in the interest of clarity, and if you take as your guide Nicole's phrase, you do touch on a sort of ideal point, that of a cinema of bodies. This would then be the guarantee of cinema, with Cassavetes its hero, and the Chinese bookie its exemplary figure. What I have trouble understanding, or perhaps admitting, is not so much this violent taste – I share it as well, since in our open cinephilia we all share nearly everything – but the tendency to set it up as an intellectual and perceptible reference–preference. I would venture to say, even if it's not immediately obvious, that this accords very well with the oh-so-legitimate and somewhat militant desire to reinsert avant-garde film (Alex) or experimental cinema (Nicole) into the global culture of cinema. Its absence in French cinephilic culture was 'a fatal misunderstanding', as Nicole says. It's shocking, but explicable. It's because this has been demanded so much more in the cinema: a vision of the world and a style of behaviour that are satisfied neither with the appearances of art nor with a too-purified corporeality.

Curiously, the word civilisation springs to mind. A word far greater than cinema, its life or death, but which is itself also interior. There is a name that goes with this word: de Oliveira. You mention him little – Adrian once, in the name of the need to save him as an artist (but what a fate, if it's on video); Nicole too, in the final listing of her indispensable films (but with no real consequence, unless it's to reference the documentary gaze, so little present in your letters). As you know, he is the oldest working film-maker today; at this very moment he's finishing up a difficult film composed of three stories [*Inquiétude*, 1998]. He could be the greatest, if this word had meaning. I remember when we did our interview with de Oliveira for *Chimères*, Serge arrived half-kidding, half-baroquely serious, saying, before giving him the accolade: 'Behold, the greatest living film-maker.' De Oliveira's preoccupation is, to put it banally, the fate of the world, how to live and die, survive in harmony with the logic of an ancient and prestigious country, which was fortunate to discover the world when it was worth discovering, and the strange destiny of having in part escaped the worst conflicts of this century thanks to a cruel and miserable dictatorship. He is, I believe, the only film-maker who knows how to tell, in a single film, the history of his country from its founding through a melancholy myth up to the end of its empire (*No, or the Vainglory of the Commander*, 1990). For de Oliveira is his country; it's enough to see *The Artist and the City*, a short from 1956, to understand what it means to live in a town where one is born (Porto), and to grasp the true limit between the games of art and of life. To know how to make red run with a mad but discreet mastery across some fifty shots of everyday life in a documentary on a minor figure of neo-Impressionism – now, that denotes a formally sure sensibility and humour. Thanks not only to the extreme beauty of the images and a stunning vision of the capacities of the shot and of editing, de Oliveira shows in all his films a profound sense of culture and art, of their place in everyday life as well as in collective memory. In short, he's a great, immense artist, and above all a profoundly civilised man, one who is hyper-conscious, terrified that his civilisation is ending, that his country is succumbing to Europe, that Europe is the shortest route to America (recall the old peasant woman's monologue in *Voyage to the Beginning of the World* [1996], or the comical staging of a representation of the 'Mystery of the Passion' in a small village in *Rite of Spring* [1963]). Where in Godard civilisation is reached through culture, in de Oliveira culture springs forth naturally from civilisation. Incidentally, Godard, the destabiliser *par excellence*, showed himself to be ill at ease in the course of an interview that he had requested with a droll and unshakeable de Oliveira. A stranger to the world of professional intellectual work, de Oliveira does care about it, however, which so many film-makers would deny: our interview had come of his express desire to meet Deleuze (who was already well in decline), in order to understand what he thought about Time, and how that might relate to his cinema.

I no longer know exactly what I'm trying to say in going on about de Oliveira. Simply, it is reassuring that he has existed and exists still in the cinema, and that one feels with him as with most of the great film-makers that the cinema is at once much more and much less than him. One feels in a quite different way the same thing with Rossellini, which explains why he could believe that the cinema was not the height of civilisation, and why he preferred to abandon it for the pedagogy of television.

Unlike real life, the life of the spectator or even the critic doesn't really force you to choose. That's why you can love art more than life, so horrible is it to have to choose. But if I really had to, I would take de Oliveira over Cassavetes, civilisation and its malaise over the body and its desires. Because the body remains at the heart of civilisation – it can't help it – but the inverse is not so.

I was lucky enough to spend three days in the breathtakingly beautiful, authentic setting of de Oliveira's *The Convent* (1995). I thought a lot about what he was able to do there, including making two internationally renowned stars (Catherine Deneuve and John Malkovich) credible in a supremely local film. While there I reread your letters for the first time, which doubtless explains all of this.

I could have gone about it differently. I could have told you, for example (with the cumulative effect of generations and individuation), just how difficult my old love of Hollywood cinema has made it for me to receive the more open American films that succeeded it. The studio period, between the end of the conquest of the West and the beginning of the Vietnam War, has to be the only moment when the US was a civilised country, when it could still affirm itself, despite all of its ideological weight, as one country among others, before becoming insufferably the law for all others. The American cinema today reigns supreme only by virtue of technology and money, despite Hellman, despite Ferrara, despite Burton, despite *Dead Man* (which Jonathan is right to mention). I could have asked you how much and especially how this logic of new cinematic passions that you try to evoke affects (or doesn't) your image of those film-makers that I will call, despite everything, transcendental – those who have reached the level of extreme and unequalled figures, and whom you mention so little, as if they no longer belong to the same world (I myself have often had this awful impression): F. W. Murnau, Dreyer (from *Vampyr* [1932] to *Gertrud* [1964]), Buster Keaton, Fritz Lang, Hitchcock, Josef von Sternberg, Yasujiro Ozu, Mizoguchi, the Bergman of *Persona* (1966), Ritwik Ghatak, Bresson (despite Kent, despite Nicole . . .). I could have told you again just how absolutely linked I have always felt myself to be to the cinema that assumed the duty of speaking the states of the world, like so many slices of civilisation: from *Night and Fog* (1955) to Straub and Huillet, from Marker's essay-films to *Le Gai savoir* (1968), from *Le Camion* (1977) to *Ludwig's Cook* (1974) to *Puissance de la parole* (1988), precisely. I'm thinking here of documentary truth and fiction, which today continually reinvent themselves against the chattering silences of television. We need text as much as image, voice as much as body. Together, they make a figure. Perhaps the image of Rouch, so vividly tendered by Adrian and evoked again by Nicole, will serve across your letters to compensate for that, to reinvest the very body informed in and by discourse. Finally, I could have told you how today I find so incredibly interesting, aesthetically and anthropologically, the entire 'cinema of passages' (which I have called 'between-images'), which recognises not only the essential impurity of cinema, but also a much larger impurity that may go so far as to transform the very idea of it, and that, far from the death of cinema, puts cinema into the future of the past, between photography, painting, writing and music (which is where you find certain experimental works, video art especially, and the technological effects of big American films, such as computer animation – I admit I was touched by Alex's letter almost ending on IMAX, with his reference to Jeff Wall, who bears witness to these uncertain states to come). *Immemory*, as Marker says; all the memory of the world, unendingly and everywhere, always gives more and less than the cinema.

I confide to you these fragments of personal history. It's a way of telling you that your letters touched me as much as they intrigued me. I've known Jonathan for twenty years, Nicole for a long time already, Alex and Kent more recently, and Adrian only through intermittent texts. It is clear that this kind of exercise, in the guise of addressing oneself to others, ends by obliging each of us to himself or herself. Each of us on the *Trafic* editorial committee could have written in his or her way a letter, which would be, I think, both as much and as little considered as mine. With great affection, I thank you for being, through us, 'between-writings',[19] and Jonathan, our faithful trafficker, for having opened this movement.

Raymond

Notes

1. Jonathan Rosenbaum, 'Comparaisons à Cannes', *Trafic* no. 19, Summer 1996, p. 11.
2. Roland Barthes (trans. Linda Coverdale), *The Grain of the Voice: Interviews 1962–1980* (New York: Hill and Wang, 1985), p. 21. The interview originally appeared in *Cahiers du cinéma* no. 147, September 1963.
3. Nicole Brenez, 'The Ultimate Journey: Remarks on Contemporary Theory', *Screening the Past* no. 2, 1997. http://www.latrobe.edu.au/screeningthepast/reruns/brenez.html.
4. Preface to Ado Kyrou, *Le Surréalisme au cinéma* (Paris: Ramsay, 1985).
5. Philip Brophy, 'The Body Horrible', http://media-arts.rmit.edu.au/Phil_Brophy/BDYHRBLartcls/BodyHorrible.html.
6. Gilles Deleuze (trans. Hugh Tomlinson and Barbara Habberjam), *Cinema 1: The Movement-Image* (Minneapolis: University of Minnesota Press, 1986), p. x.
7. Nicole Brenez, 'Acting. Poétique de jeu au cinéma. 1. *Allemagne année zéro*', *Cinémathèque* no. 11, Spring 1997.
8. Jean Louis Schefer (trans. Paul Smith), 'Journey'. http://osf1.gmu.edu/~psmith5/parcours.html.
9. As recounted in Rosenbaum's *Moving Places: A Life at the Movies* (Berkeley & Los Angeles: University of California Press, 1995), his grandfather and father ran a chain of movie theatres in Alabama.
10. Raymond Klibansky, Erwin Panofsky and Fritz Saxl, *Saturn and Melancholy* (New York: Basic Books, 1964).

11. Michel Foucault (trans. Robert Hurley), *The Care of the Self – The History of Sexuality: Volume 3* (London: Penguin, 1990), p. 5. Cf. also Artemidorus (trans. R. J. White), *The Interpretation of Dreams* (New Jersey: Noyes Press, 1975).

12. A Spanish horror-thriller by Alejandro Amenábar set in a film school about the making of a snuff movie.

13. Jacques Aumont, 'Leçon de ténèbres', *Cinémathèque* no. 10, Autumn 1996.

14. Amos Vogel, *Film as a Subversive Art* (New York: Random House, 1974).

15. Anne Benhaïem, 'Le court métrage n'est pas un genre en soi', *Positif* no. 432, February 1997, p. 87.

16. See Raymond Bellour, 'Figures aux allures de plans', in Jacques Aumont (ed.), *La mise en scène* (Bruxelles: De Boeck, 2000), pp. 109–26.

17. Serge Daney, *L'exercice a été profitable, Monsieur* (Paris: P.O.L., 1993), p. 15.

18. 'L'acteur en citoyen affectif', in Nicole Brenez, *De la figure en général et du corps en particulier. L'invention figurative au cinéma* (Bruxelles: De Boeck, 1998), pp. 243–52.

19. The play between 'cinema of passages', 'between-images' and 'between-writings' can best be appreciated if one knows that, in 1989, Bellour curated a show called 'Passages de l'image', based on the connections and contaminations among different types of images, and subsequently published a collection of essays on film, video and photography called *L'Entre-Images: photo, cinéma, vidéo* (Paris: La Différence, 1990); it has been followed by *L'Entre-Images 2: mots, images* (Paris: P.O.L., 1999).

2

Open Spaces in Iran: A Conversation with Abbas Kiarostami

Jonathan Rosenbaum (with Mehrnaz Saeed-Vafa) (1998–2001)

The hero of Abbas Kiarostami's *Taste of Cherry* (1997) is a fiftyish man named Mr Badii contemplating suicide for unstated reasons, driving around the hilly Tehran outskirts in search of someone who will bury him if he succeeds – he plans to swallow sleeping pills – and retrieve him from the hole in the ground he has selected if he fails. Over the course of one afternoon, he picks up three passengers and asks each of them to perform this task in exchange for money – a young Kurdish soldier stationed nearby, an Afghan seminarian who is somewhat older, and a Turkish taxidermist who is older still. The soldier runs away in fright, the seminarian tries to persuade him not to kill himself, and the taxidermist, who also tries to change his mind, reluctantly agrees, needing the money to help take care of his sick child. The terrain Badii's Range Rover traverses repeatedly, in circular fashion, is mainly parched, dusty and spotted with ugly construction sites and noisy bulldozers, though the site he's selected for his burial is relatively quiet, pristine and uninhabited. It's arranged that the taxidermist will come to the designated hillside at dawn, call Badii's name twice, toss a couple of stones into the hole to make sure Badii isn't sleeping, and then, if there's no response, shovel dirt over his body and collect the money left for him in Badii's parked car.

Later that night, Badii emerges from his apartment, proceeds in the dark to the appointed spot and lies down in the hole, where we hear the sounds of thunder, rain and the cries of stray dogs. The screen goes completely black. Then, in an epilogue, we see Kiarostami at the same location, in full daylight, with his camera and sound crew filming soldiers jogging and chanting in the valley below. Homayoun Ershadi, the actor who played Badii, lights and hands Kiarostami a cigarette just before Kiarostami announces that the take is over and they're ready for a sound take. The shot lingers over wind in the trees, which are now in full bloom, and the soldiers and film-makers lounging on the hillside between takes, before the camera pans away to a car driving off into the distance. To the strains of Louis Armstrong playing an instrumental version of 'St James Infirmary', the final credits come on.

Fax sent by Jonathan Rosenbaum to Abbas Kiarostami, 18 November 1997:

Dear Abbas (if I may),

I've been moved to write you this letter because of the distressing news I recently heard that you decided to delete the final sequence of *The Taste of Cherry* [sic] from the version of the film opening in Italy. I've also heard that there is a danger that you may cut the same sequence when the film opens in the United States. I must confess that when I heard this news, I experienced a painful feeling of loss – as if something I loved had suddenly been taken away from me. And I would like to try to persuade you not to touch a frame of your masterpiece.

I've seen *The Taste of Cherry* three times – twice in Cannes [in May 1997] and once in New York [in October 1997] – and although I consider it to be one of your finest works, with or without the video ending, I believe that only with the ending as it now stands does it possibly qualify as your greatest film. I won't attempt to explain all the reasons why I feel this way in a letter – although I will attempt to do so when the film comes to Chicago and I write about it in my newspaper. For now, I can only stress that I regard the ending as a very special gift to the audience – a gift that has complex and profound consequences in terms of how every viewer comes to terms with everything in the film preceding that ending. Without it in any way diminishing the remainder of the film, it allows it to reverberate in a wider, freer world, and allows the viewer to receive it in a fuller way. I should add that I don't think this opinion is merely an 'American' or 'Western' interpretation; [Iranian, Chicago-based teacher, writer and film-maker] Mehrnaz Saeed-Vafa, for example, fully agrees with me about the absolutely vital importance of the video ending. (I just spoke to her on the phone, and she asked me to tell you that she feels as passionately about this matter as I do.)

I realise that *The Taste of Cherry* is a deeply personal work for you, and I wouldn't presume to guess the reasons why the video ending troubles you. But I do believe that many of the greatest artists are capable of producing work that 'understands' more than the artists sometimes do as individuals; that, I assume, is why Gogol destroyed the second half of his *Dead Souls* after writing it – because his novel in some mysterious fashion knew more than he did. Not knowing you, it would be foolish for me to speculate why you've had second thoughts about the ending of *The Taste of Cherry*. But I do feel that I know something about your work, and the wisdom it imparts to me is something I continue to listen to. I humbly ask you to listen to the same wisdom, and to allow it to speak to others.

Sincerely (and hopefully),
Jonathan Rosenbaum

Fax sent by Abbas Kiarostami to Jonathan Rosenbaum, 20 November 1997:

Dear Jonathan (if I may),
I just returned from a long trip and got your fax. I do appreciate your concern and also your feeling on cinema and I . . .

As for the ending sequence, you are quite right and I have to say that I am not supposed to cut or change it at all, neither in my country or anywhere else. I just saw the dubbed version of my film in Italy and decided to play around the screening of the film with and without the video ending in several cities. Some theatres are showing the film with the video ending and some without. It's just a sort of playing, done out of the film . . . a play that you can see the audience reactions after two different endings . . . frankly speaking, I like this play . . . it's very interesting like cinema . . .

Life does worth to experience anything once. If I could ever find a chance to meet you, I'll tell you more in this respect.

Then, assure you again, the ending will be the same.

Thank you for your attention.

Sincerely,
Abbas Kiarostami
with regards to Mehrnaz

A few words about the preceding: my letter wasn't prompted by any thoughts of publication, but simply by my alarm upon hearing, first, that many critics (Iranian as well as American) were trying to convince Kiarostami to delete his original ending from *Taste of Cherry* (which was still sometimes being called *The Taste of Cherry* at its festival showings) and, second, that Kiarostami had done just that in Italy – which implied to me that he might do the same thing when the film opened in the US. It struck me as extraordinary that reviewers who see a film only once or twice could wind up as the final arbiters of works that film-makers spent years working on, yet the recent and injurious recutting of other films prompted by reviews in trade magazines demonstrated that this practice was in fact on the rise.

It's worth adding that Italian screenings of the film without the ending proved to be more popular than screenings with the ending, and after Kiarostami left Italy, despite his wishes to have the film shown in both versions, the distributor opted to show only the cut version. (To the best of my knowledge, this shorter version hasn't been shown anywhere else in the world, but it's difficult to be sure about this.[1])

Prior to our exchange of faxed letters, my acquaintance with Kiarostami was limited. Saeed-Vafa – a film-maker who had known him ever since attending a screening of his first full-length feature, *Report*, in Tehran in 1977 – had introduced us and served as interpreter during a brief conversation at the 1992 Toronto Film Festival, and subsequently we had merely nodded at one another at two or three other festivals, then conversed again briefly – with Mehrnaz again serving as interpreter – at the 1997 New York Film Festival in October. (Mehrnaz and I had worked together, along with a few others, on the English subtitles of Forugh Farrokhzad's only film, the 1962 short *The House Is Black*, which showed with *Taste of Cherry* at the festival.)

On 28 February 1998, Kiarostami presented two pre-release screenings of *Taste of Cherry* at the Chicago Art Institute's Film Center. In between those screenings, when I attended a dinner for Kiarostami, he asked me if my letter to him could be translated and printed in an Iranian film magazine, and I agreed, suggesting that perhaps his letter could be translated and printed as well. I later heard that my letter – though not his – appeared in Persian in *Film Monthly*, and I've taken the liberty of reproducing Kiarostami's letter here verbatim because I believe that what it manages to communicate is far more important than his grasp of English grammar (which is certainly far superior to my nearly non-existent knowledge of Farsi). The fact that we were able to communicate at all in this fashion is fundamental to my sense of what this book is about – in particular the sense of mutual empowerment that can arise from such exchanges.

On 1 March, the morning after Kiarostami presented *Taste of Cherry* at the Film Center, I arranged to meet him and Mehrnaz for a conversation over breakfast recorded specifically for this book, with Mehrnaz translating; Muhammed Pakshir, another Iranian living in Chicago, graciously drove us to the restaurant and joined us in part of the talk. Although it was mainly my intention at the time to discuss general issues about nationality and audiences, Kiarostami wound up explaining a great deal about his working methods – more than I had encountered in other interviews with him that I'd read at the time – and I've decided to retain portions of that material here.

For a book on Kiarostami that Mehrnaz and I subsequently wrote together (published in 2003 by Illinois University Press), we conducted two subsequent interviews with him after this – one in San Francisco about *The Wind Will Carry Us* (1999) in spring 2001, the other in faxes between Chicago and Tehran about *ABC Africa* (his 2001 documentary about the orphaned children of AIDS casualties in Uganda, shot on digital video) the following spring, with Mehrnaz translating our questions into Persian and his handwritten answers – which included his ribbing of the way I signed my name in Persian with a teasing exaggeration of my scrawl – into English. The latter concluded with the following memorable exchange that somehow got squeezed out of our book.

MEHRNAZ SAEED-VAFA: Did the Ugandans that you met know you or your films before you made your trip there? How did they react to you? How do you feel that your presence in Uganda should be read in a non-Iranian context?

ABBAS KIAROSTAMI: I don't think that either I or anyone else who was in that strange atmosphere could remember that he was a film-maker. They didn't know me and I didn't know myself. We were witnessing scenes that made a deep impression on us. It was something like the Day of Judgment. On that Judgment Day, who can remember what he does for a living?

Our hopes of interviewing Kiarostami yet again about his latest feature, *10* (2002) – which we eventually managed to see with his help (a video passed along to Martin Scorsese at

Cannes, whose New York office sent it to us in Chicago) – were ultimately dashed by the increased difficulties imposed by US customs on Iranians entering the US after 11 September 2001, which even went beyond those described in 'Squaring *The Circle*' (see Chapter 7), and understandably convinced Kiarostami to cancel a planned visit to the States in April. It might have made for a nice symmetry, because *10*, also shot on digital video, is set inside a car even more exclusively than *Taste of Cherry*, but I suspect that there are at least a few echoes of his methodology described here in the more recent film.

1 March 1998 (Chicago)

MS: Jonathan is preparing a book, and part of it will be this conversation with you.

JONATHAN ROSENBAUM: Its working title is *Movie Mutations: The Changing Face of World Cinema*. Mutation implies biological transformation, and the basic idea is that there are changes going on all over the world in communications, technology and economics that are altering the ways we think and write about cinema. We want to have sections in the book about Iranian and Taiwanese cinema, and when Edward Yang was in town a few months ago we already began discussing some of the issues I want to bring up here. For me, part of what links Taiwanese cinema to Iranian cinema is a certain resistance to Western values.

AK: Why Edward Yang and not Hou Hsiao-hsien, whose style is more distinctive?

JR: Because he was here. Of course I'd also like to include Hou in our discussion as well.

MS: Jonathan wants to emphasise how audiences are hungry for an alternative – for a different vision.

JR: And it's an interesting paradox that you're perceived in most of the world as an Iranian film-maker, whereas in Iran you're perceived largely as a Western film-maker. How do you feel about this? What are the differences between the perceptions of your films in Iran and how they're perceived elsewhere? I was very much struck by something a Peruvian film critic said to me in Chicago about a year ago: he had recently seen Hou's *Goodbye South, Goodbye* (1996), and he felt it had more to say to him about what's happening in Peru now than any other film made anywhere else.

AK: I feel the same way – that our language, Hou's and mine, is a universal language. And if film doesn't cross geographical borders, what else can? Everything else serves to preserve the borders and separations of cultures, customs and nationalities. Film is the only way of looking down at cultures from a less earthbound perspective.

JR: Yes, but whenever one crosses a border, the idea of nationality appears. Perhaps economic matters are more important than national issues – which is why the Peruvian critic was affected by Hou's film: because people tearing down buildings and other manifestations of capitalism mattered more to him than the national differences between Taiwan and Peru.

AK: I also believe that Taiwan and Iran have many things in common – extraordinary similarities. And the most important of these are economic. Naturally, Iran is related to other countries through its economic situation, which is related to the political situation, and the political situation reflects the social situation. So all the countries with economic similarities have similar problems, which drives them to arrive at a common language. I had a friend in Iran who was supposed to make a film in the US, and he was afraid that if he was given a big budget, he wouldn't know how to spend the money and couldn't make a film according to his own standards. On the other hand, in Iran we sometimes don't have enough money to make films. This kind of difference is the major disagreement between the cinemas of Iran and the US. For example, if they invited me to make a film here and assigned me a big budget and a large crew, I'd have a lot of trouble making my own kind of film in those conditions.

JR: Raul Ruiz hated making *The Golden Boat* (1990) in New York, because so many film students wanted to work with him as assistants and his crew became so large. But part of how that system operates in the US is through unions. Are there unions of the same kind in Iran?

AK: Yes, in every part of the profession, but they don't enforce their regulations so much, so you can still have a crew of less than ten people. I think this changing taste in cinema all over the world partly stems from economic factors, but there are other important factors as well. One of the most important is a participating audience that is active, not passive. The film-makers themselves aren't the only spokespeople; spectators also have the role and the right to create part of the film. Just because they don't have access to the negative and the film equipment doesn't mean that they don't deserve to be regarded as part of the film. I believe the present distance between the film-maker and the audience is immense, and my kind of film-making is interested in reducing that distance. There are definitely people in the audience who are every bit as talented as I am or even more, and they should be given the opportunity to be creative and become part of the film-making.

It seems to me like there is only one audience everywhere I go, and I've learned a great deal from this significant similarity of audiences. I feel like I'm always in the same situation with the audience, and that there's a similarity to their reactions, despite differences in nationality, religion, origin, culture and language. For instance, when I was showing *Through the Olive Trees* (1994) in Taipei, I completely forgot that the audience there wasn't Iranian. I had a similar experience in Rotterdam with *Homework* (1989), an even more local film. I thought at first this was because there were some Iranians in the audience, but when the lights came on I discovered there weren't any. I think all people are impressed by film in similar ways.

MUHAMMED PAKSHIR: I think what he's trying to accomplish is the elimination of the separation between one film-maker and thousands of spectators, and that's a big achievement.

JR: Yes, and part of the way you're achieving this in *Taste of Cherry* is by being multicultural. Someone pointed out at the Film Center last night that the three major characters apart from the hero are Afghan, Kurdish and Turkish, and, as you pointed out, that's because Iran itself is multicultural. This is already a step in the direction you're talking about, because what we're calling 'Iran' is in fact many cultures, not one – just as 'America' is.

AK: And none of these cultural differences interferes with the film being understood. Spectators check their cultural baggage at the door, before they enter the theatre; this is the way that audiences are similar.

JR: It seems that part of what makes your films so interactive is the fact that there are almost always missing parts of the narrative – absences that the audiences have to fill in some way.

AK: My ideal film is something like a crossword puzzle with empty squares that the audiences can fill in. Some people describe films as flawless, without cracks, but for me that means that an audience can't get inside them.

MS: Did you inform the actors in *Taste of Cherry* when you were shooting and when you were just rehearsing?

AK: No. There was no film crew there. They would set up the camera for me in the car, because I was the only one around apart from the actor [i.e., serving as the stand-in for the character the actor was speaking or listening to].

JR: Did the actors have to memorise their lines?

AK: Nothing was written, it was all spontaneous. I would control certain parts and get them to say certain lines, but it was basically improvisation.

JR: So were all these actors speaking as themselves?

AK: Not exactly. The actor playing the soldier wasn't a soldier; I prompted him beforehand about the location of the army camp, for example. It was a combination of real and unreal. For instance, I ordered some guns, so he thought he'd get a chance to shoot one of them later on, when we were filming, and he didn't realise that this kind of instruction was the actual filming. He was even getting anxious and asking when the filming would start. I actually made him believe I was planning to kill myself.

It reminds me of a verse from the poet Rumi:

> You are my polo ball,
> running before the stick of my command.
> I am always running along after you,
> though it is I who make you move.[2]

JR: It seems to have something in common with jazz. Maybe that's why I like your use of Louis Armstrong playing 'St James Infirmary' in the final sequence.

AK: Exactly. Because even though you're following certain notes, you're also following the feeling of the piece, so the performance you're giving tonight will be different from the performance tomorrow.

JR: It's also about playing together.

AK: Yes, but these actors can't have a dialogue with each other because one part is always played by me.

JR: Right – you're the composer and the bandleader.

AK: At one point, I wanted the soldier character to express amazement, but since I couldn't ask him to do that, I started to speak to him in Czech. He said he couldn't understand what I was talking about, and I used that in the film. At another point, I placed a gun in the glove compartment, and asked him to open it for a chocolate, when I wanted him to look afraid.

JR: One thing that *Taste of Cherry* conveys very powerfully is the experience of being alone, and your method of shooting intensifies that sense of isolation.

AK: There are signs in the film that sometimes made me think that the man didn't really want to kill himself, that he was looking for a kind of communication with the other characters. Maybe that's one of the ruses of his loneliness, to engage people with his own emotional issues. He doesn't pick up a couple of workers at the beginning who would be willing to kill him with their spades; he chooses other people whom he probably thinks he can have a conversation with. So that gives us a signal that he's probably not searching for someone who would help him to kill himself.

JR: It's also interesting how your images metaphorically reproduce the situation of the spectator watching the film. In many of your films, the view through a car's windshield represents that situation – of looking for something but also feeling separate from what you're looking at.

AK: That comes from my experience of driving around Tehran in my car and sometimes driving outside the city – looking through the front, rear and side windows, which become my frames.

Notes

1. Several video copies of *Taste of Cherry* purchased from a British distributor showed up in Australia missing the final scene. This seems to be a case not of censorship but a dubbing or laboratory mix-up, as also occurred with *Irma Vep* (1996) on Australian pay TV; both endings were originated on different material to the rest of the film. (Adrian Martin)
2. Saeed-Vafa would like to thank Emory University's Franklin D. Lewis for generously furnishing the authors with this translation.

3

Here and There: The Films of Tsai Ming-liang

Kent Jones (1998–2002)

> That men are men wherever they may be is something we might have predicted; to be
> surprised by it only tells us something about ourselves. [...] If music is a universal idiom, so
> too is *mise en scène*: it is this language, and not Japanese, that has to be learned to
> understand 'Mizoguchi'.[1]

Jacques Rivette began his polemically tinged appreciation of Kenji Mizoguchi with a warning against the dual traps of humanism and specialisation that awaited Westerners dealing with film-makers from 'exotic' cultures. Almost half a century later, the phenomenon of the Western Chinese cinema specialist is very much alive. These are the keepers of the gates to the East, a motley crew that, to the bemused onlooker, suggests a globally scattered variation on the reporters in *His Girl Friday* (1940), only much more frantic in their efforts to protect their turf and more disappointingly sombre in their palaver. With a collective ear permanently and anxiously pinned to the breast of Asia, they listen for the slightest signs of undiscovered life forms, always ready to be the first to announce the good news to their Western friends and competitors.

No one involved in film criticism or programming is exempt from territorial fanaticism – I was once referred to as a 'French cinema specialist', and to the degree that I wrote a lot of articles for American magazines about French film-makers whose work had up to that time (the mid 90s) been either overlooked or ignored, I plead guilty. None of us is immune to the lure of ownership, and many of us have crossed the line from criticism to promotion without even realising it. Not that there's anything inherently wrong with being devoted to the cinema of a particular region, especially when it's as exciting as the various regional cinemas we broadly think of as 'Chinese'.

But I find myself balking at the idea of a critical language that has become mired in regional contextualisation. It strikes me as an outgrowth of imperialist ideas, with a consequent blurring of all value systems beyond the culturally accurate. The old platitude of universal meaning has been replaced by a new platitude of localised meaning, in which reams of national and regional history accompany every film and finally threaten to bury it – at best a matter of critical self-examination, at worst a matter of critical self-validation. This ecstasy of communication has definitely helped lift a few veils of exoticism from

Asian cinema, but it has also backfired by engendering a feeling of anxiety – 'Do I know enough about Hong Kong/Taiwanese/ Mainland history to stay on top of the game?' – and at times it's led to what Asian critic Stephen Teo has dubbed the 'T. E. Lawrence syndrome', i.e. helpful suggestions from Western experts about what film most accurately reflects what particular local, national or regional tradition or historical circumstance.

'The discovery mentality of Western film criticism,' writes Teo, 'may now work against its own progress. It has settled questions of the art of cinema but it cannot settle questions of cultural interpretation.'[2] It's a deceptively simple statement that speaks volumes about the question of writing on any art object from whatever vantage point. The fact is that carefully balanced standards of value nearly always take a back seat in film criticism to staking one's claim like a miner during a gold rush. Just when one imagines that one has extinguished all traces of ill-considered certainty, it creeps back into view. In a sense, this is only natural: certainty is the best position we know from which to address the world. But the fact remains that critical language is infected to the core with imperialist notions, and contextualisation has become its most misused tool.

Let's take the case of Edward Yang's Taiwanese film *Mahjong* (1996). In Taiwan, the film opened and closed in the blink of an eye, and many of my Asian friends were appalled by what they saw as its overall vulgarity. This judgment has always puzzled me. I could see that Yang was pursuing a uniform stylisation among his actors even more aggressively than in his previous *A Confucian Confusion* (1994). And I recognise that there is a certain shrillness in *Mahjong*'s tone. But 'vulgar' was not an adjective that ever crossed my mind. Moreover, many of my Asian friends found the scamming antics of *Mahjong*'s post-adolescent capitalists-in-training wholly unbelievable.

This last criticism put me in mind of many situations I've encountered over the years. A European friend has been excited by an American film like *Little Odessa* (1994), *The Crossing Guard* (1995) or *Hard Eight* (1997), films that, to my American eyes, behaved as though they were cut from the cloth of reality when they were in fact vaguely mythical abstractions cunningly cloaked beneath a synthetically 'real' surface. Perhaps there was something in these films that spoke to European culture, or that filled a void in European cinema – I'm sure it's eternally refreshing for a French cinephile to encounter a truly genre-based, as opposed to documentary-based, aesthetic.

For my own part, I'm heartened by any film that deals unashamedly with late capitalism from a critical point of view, as *Mahjong* did, a point of view that's almost non-existent in American cinema (looking at things from another angle, I have a feeling that *Western* disappointment with *Mahjong* stems from the film's lack of a 'contemplative' sensibility, something that has come to be expected from Chinese cinema in general, and that accounts for the relative Western popularity of Yang's subsequent film, *Yi Yi* (*A One and a Two*, 2000). As I sat in the old Zoo Palast watching *Mahjong* with simultaneous translation blasting in my ears, I wasn't saying to myself, 'Wow, what a startlingly accurate picture of Taipei!' because I've never been there. Perhaps on an unconscious level, I was saying to myself, 'Wow, what a startlingly accurate picture of what Taipei must be like!' More than anything else, I was taken with the film's bold marriage of intellectual distance and cartoonish proximity, and while I can imagine a native viewer looking for something a little more tempered and less in-your-face, I'm sure that even the doubters saw *Mahjong* as the work of a true artist. Would my own judgment have differed if I had come equipped with more firsthand knowledge of Taipei, or if I had been more intimately acquainted with Taiwanese history? I doubt it.

If we are completely honest with ourselves, we should admit that whenever we immerse ourselves in the contemplation of any foreign cinema, we have a vested interest in preserving its foreignness, thus keeping it untouched by the mundane familiarities and certainties of our own everyday realities – I think that all that specialised knowledge among Western experts has the paradoxical effect of preserving and even enlarging said foreignness, as opposed to defusing it. Sensitive viewers may adjust the reality-measuring they habitually bring to their own native cinema in order to accommodate a presumed or posited reality, but I think that they also keep the exoticism of what they're watching carefully intact – if reality is always happening elsewhere, where else could 'elsewhere' be but a 'foreign' place?

In the work of a great film-maker like Tsai Ming-liang, we Westerners have the best of both worlds: we're at home in the strength of the *mise en scène* – and, in Tsai's case, in the cosy self-assurance of his remarkably homogenous universe – yet blissfully abroad with the cultural markers. We're both familiar with and estranged from the on-camera reality, in which we simultaneously recognise similarities to and differences from our own world. In fact, Tsai's most recent feature, *What Time Is It There?* (2001), is all about this all-too-human dialectic of home/away, familiar/foreign.

There is a singular thrill to Tsai's work, resulting from a strange brew of keen observation, clinical fascination and entirely personal mythology. In each of his five features and in his early television work as well, every element is unvarying, and stays in the same fixed relationship with every other element: emotional tonality (greyish unease), range of folkways (cramped, cheaply built apartments; malls; fast-food restaurants; public areas like parks or riversides), psychological backdrop (a disaffected adaptability to urban life, punctuated with sudden, animalistic sexual urges), action (aimless wandering; ravenous eating; time-swallowing activities like masturbation, jumping up and down on a bed or torturing bugs), spatial organisation (a stationary camera positioned in the centre of a room and shooting into a corner from a discreetly low angle; immaculately executed tracking shots of people on motorbikes), sound (quiet audio tracks punctuated with the most obsessively soft sounds, like a masseur's knuckle rapping on his patient's skin, and comically loud ones, like water being sucked down a clogged drain) and favoured motifs (silent wars between fathers and sons, played by Miao Tien and Lee Kang-sheng, respectively; weak, frustrated mothers-as-bystanders; running or overflowing water; sexual triangulation, with one party always left frustrated or unrequited; difficult and heavily fraught passages into homosexual awakening). The only thing that's changed in Tsai's work is the palette, which has naturally moved from the dingy dailiness of the early TV work (*All Corners of the World* [1989], *Youngsters* [1991]) and the first features to the burnished, glowing pockets of light and colour in *The River* (1997) and *What Time Is It There?*.

There is a strange and mysterious unison at work here, not so distant from the perfectly coherent and largely private universe of a Kenneth Anger or a Wes Anderson. But what is odd and quite singular about Tsai is that, perhaps more than any other modern film-maker, he has successfully realised on film something that many of us who live in cities experience but few of us consciously understand, which is the melding of the public and the private. Those of us who walk the same streets, see the same faces, and find ourselves moved from one place to another by the same forms of transportation as we hear the same sounds and feel the same vibrations and breathe the same stale air, day in and day out, cannot help but make private, internalised rituals out of these supposedly neutral but nonetheless important parts of our lives, and key our desires and rituals of discovery and loss to their rhythms. Tsai is the first film-maker to somehow convey the antiseptic poignancy of modern urban life, its multiplicity of circumspect, guarded subjectivities dotting a landscape designed for 'functionality'. It has nothing to do with the old ideas of urban impersonality and alienation. There's no pre-existing, Edenic reality at which Tsai's ordinary people look back wistfully. This is their world, and all that concrete, asphalt and formica is just a regular part of it. Like New York or Tokyo, his Taipei seems to be operating according to a new physics, in which the city itself is set in motion by the private obsessions and biological quirks of the individuals who live within it, and within whom it lives – the reverse of the city films of the silent era.

Since Lee Kang-sheng plays roughly the same autobiographical character in *Youngsters, Rebels of the Neon God* (1992), *Vive l'amour* (1994), *The River*, *The Hole* (1998) and *What Time Is It There?*, it's tempting to imagine him as the 'Asian Antoine Doinel'. But that would be misleading, because the ingredient that puts the finishing touch to this bracingly singular aesthetic stew is the even distance Tsai maintains from each of his characters, Lee's included. The camera seems to gaze at every scene from a distance that is by turns (or, sometimes, all at once) discreet, respectful, empathetic and voyeuristic. Tsai has a knack for dramatising private behaviours that few of his peers would ever dream of filming (such as Lee Kang-sheng jumping out of bed in the middle of the night and pissing into a nearby paper bag because he's afraid of meeting his father's ghost on the walk to the bathroom). Every character is his/her own island, which doesn't make for good conversation: there's about as much dialogue in all of Tsai's features put together as there is in a single Eric Rohmer scene. In this deeply troubling, oddly exhilarating body of work, one has the impression that any life, revealed over a given amount of time, will yield a wealth of pain hidden beneath the surface. Even the fantasised musical numbers in *The Hole*, in which Yang Kuei-mei mouths the words of Grace Chang hits in spectacular sequinned gowns with a tuxedoed Lee Kang-sheng as her sometime partner, feel less like spectacular escapes than internalised extensions of reality. They're a lot of fun, but they're also as melancholy as any other scene of Yang or Lee washing up, watching television, hoarding food, in anticipation of an oncoming apocalyptic plague.

What does Tsai share with the other two indisputable masters of Taiwanese cinema, Yang and Hou Hsiao-hsien? Each possesses a quality that was for a time at the epicentre of Taiwanese art cinema in general: a sorrowful attitude toward the country's troubled past and its harsh, forgetful present. There is a mournful, elegiac tone to existence itself in this cinema – unsurprising, since Taiwan's status relative to the Chinese mainland is so culturally, and emotionally, ambiguous. Perhaps this imbalance is what gives Taiwanese cinema its unique suspension between hard fact and ethereality. Of the three film-makers, Hou remains the most interested in Taiwan's history. Yang is the angriest and most politically trenchant, with an edgy sense of character and an unusual pull toward complex narratives. If Yang is quite close in sensibility to a film-maker like André Téchiné (they both process the world intellectually before dealing with it emotionally), and if Hou is close to a John Ford (both are circumspect elegists looking for just the right pitch between personal and historical experience), Tsai is closest to the tradition of comedy, Buster Keaton and Jacques Tati in particular. Every scene is structured around people and their alternately complacent and disengaged relationships with the world around them.

This impasse accounts for the many moments of apparently unmotivated upset in Tsai's work. The long crying episode that ends *Vive l'amour* – Yang Kuei-mei's character walks the length of an ugly, unfinished public park, sits on a bleacher and begins to cry uncontrollably – is certainly redolent of Jeanne Moreau's famous walk in *La notte* (1961), but there's a crucial difference: the sadness has nothing to do with feeling lost or misplaced in modern society, but rather with feeling all too much a part of it. It's one of the most fascinating, quixotic moments in modern movies, strangely but wonderfully off the track from the rest of the film. *Vive l'amour* is a semi-romantic roundelay, cross-cutting between the mildest, most apparently random actions performed by the three principals, often caught in moments of deep self-absorption. Perhaps this film is the prime example of Tsai's effort to poetically link human action with that of machines (the down escalator that opens *The River*, the video games in *Rebels of the Neon God*, the jacuzzi in *Vive l'amour*) or with inanimate objects, held for so long in the camera's gaze that their movement seems immanent. In the process, humanity, machinery and solid matter become mixed up, resulting in a creepy, clinical overtone. Tsai has been criticised for the *Vive l'amour* ending, but it's a bold choice to end a movie built out of slight, short-circuited actions, most of them indoors and underscored by discomfort, with a long circumambulation around a public park culminating in an unexpected and unforeseen outburst of emotionalism. It creates a doubling effect: we get both a panoramic view of the city itself that has contained all this strange behaviour, and a cathartic release from said behaviour. Yang's is a very good, unsung performance, suggesting in the most trenchant terms possible a person of limited imagination who is still fully aware that she lives a life of cheap satisfactions.

In the same film, Lee's character, with his aggressive politeness, his grudging acceptance of feeling small in the world, his waxy delicacy and his adolescent woundedness, occupies himself in the vacant apartment where Yang and Chen come to tryst by (a) trying to commit suicide and then, after he has slit his wrists, running away in embarrassment when he hears Chen opening the front door; (b) dressing in drag and doing cartwheels; and (c) punching three holes in a melon with a knife (when he makes the first hole, you think he's going to use it to masturbate, so thick is the atmosphere of bottled-up longing), rolling it across the floor like a bowling ball and then eating it. It's a kind of private activity that's common in American cinema, usually part of a moment of self-liberation in a musical montage. But with Tsai, such a moment loses its free-floating vagueness. Idleness and boredom are so thoroughly delineated in this movie that you get a glimpse of something rare in cinema: an incomplete ego in action. As Lee rolls the melon and watches it splat (the sound is perfect), it's like a sudden stab at wholeness, familiar to anyone who has lived through adolescence. I think it's Tsai's profound insight as an artist to render the psychic mix of complacency and unease in a key of comic melancholy. In all the features, liberation, terror and a numbingly complacent truce with life lie within a hair's breadth of one another.

Common to all of Tsai's films is a constant feeling of annoyance shared by each and every character. Everyone is stuck in cramped, closed quarters, and physical space equals psychic space (*The Hole* would be the ultimate expression of Tsai's spatial/psychic discomfort factor). He is especially strong with fathers and sons. In *Rebels of the Neon God* and *The River*, Miao Tien and Lee Kang-sheng silently criss-cross private paths in their tiny family apartment, and grudgingly give up whatever space they occupy before they retreat to their box-like rooms. They each assert different kinds of supremacy: the son is inarticulate, tormented, defensive; the father is silent, retreating, reflexively intrusive, looking for some phantom status quo (the more plaintive *What Time Is It There?* begins and ends with a haunting echo of these painfully closed-mouth interactions). The mother figure is forever on the sidelines, interjecting some crazy superstitious comment, preparing unwanted food or making a suggestion that is instantly ignored. This triangular family configuration seems to occupy the core of Tsai's thinking.

Tsai's is an interesting career trajectory, suggesting a series of underground pathways around a central power station, or the network of arteries leading to the heart. From the acutely observed television work, to the greater abstraction of *Rebels of the Neon God*, where Lee Kang-sheng's homosexuality seems to be latent but ready to flower (a fact that is perhaps more noticeable to us than to him) and where the scenes, while largely silent, are still bound up with standard narrative devices (Lee's revenge on behalf of his father; Chen's problems with the mob after he steals some video-game circuit boards) and less time-wasting; to *Vive l'amour*, in which the parents disappear, Lee has a full if fragile understanding of his sexuality in its first bloom, and the uniformity of the action gives the film a musical structure (it plays like a piece by La Monte Young or Terry Riley); to the even greater abstraction of *The River*, in which every dark corner and every patch of light pulses with desire absorbed from the characters; to the employment of life in cramped, functional spaces as a virtual metaphor for existence itself in *The Hole*; to *What Time Is It There?*, which continues what Tsai started with *The River* by making the dark, ravishing compositions themselves into objects of contemplation, ending with a gorgeous fugue between three lonely, unfulfilled people. If *Vive l'amour* seems to be retelling the story of *Rebels of the Neon God* (in both films Lee is obsessed with Chen, who is having an uneventful affair with a woman), then *The River* takes elements of both films and rearranges them into something disturbingly new; said elements are then reshuffled, and reconfigured against backdrops that are apocalyptic (*The Hole*) and metaphysical (*What Time Is It There?*).

While *The Hole* and *Vive l'amour* are Tsai's most daring films, and *What Time Is It There?* is his most sheerly beautiful and exquisite (while the rhythm is gentler than usual, the perspective on humanity is grander), *The River* is probably his greatest, a movie that looks more impressive with each viewing. The figure of the Woman is now a sweet young girl (Chen Chiyang-chiyi) who has a tryst with Lee, and given the consistency of Tsai's universe, one could say that she later mutates into the unfulfilled and largely ignored Mother (Lu Hsiao-ling). The endlessly backed-up water in *Rebels* becomes a strangely symbolic element here. Chen Chao-jung plays a piece of rough trade cruising the malls, where he is picked up by Lee's father, an extraordinary scene. As the father sits behind a pane of glass in a fast-food restaurant, sipping his soda, he eyes Chen walking by, subtly showing his wares in skintight jeans, then sauntering up the corridor after they've made eye contact. The father gets up to open the door, unleashing the faintest hint of humming conversation from within the restaurant before the door closes. Tsai slowly pans left to encompass the strange dance of avoidance and recognition, and gets a nice bead on the inhuman surfaces of modern malls in the process.

At the beginning of *The River*, Lee is approached by a film-maker (Ann Hui) who's dissatisfied with the dummy she's been trying to palm off as a floating corpse, and dives into the (filthy) titular river to oblige her and make a little extra cash. A little later, he develops a pain in his neck that becomes so severe that he can't straighten it, and he is forced to endure all manner of cures, from a spiritualist (a theme revived from *Rebels*, repeated in *What Time Is It There?* and in Tsai's remarkable DV short *A Conversation with God* [2001]) to an acupuncturist to a masseur to a take-home vibrator. As the pain increases, Lee's need to fulfil his desire increases accordingly, and he wanders into a gay bath-house, where – unbeknown to him – his father also cruises. We've already seen his father in action, but this faintly unpleasant patriarch uses his authority to mask his sexuality, as his wife sits at home unfulfilled, cooking food and watching porn. In the film's profoundly upsetting yet undeniably liberating climax, which stretches out to dramatic infinity, father and son wander into the same darkened room at the bath-house and have uninterrupted sex before they recognise one another and the father smacks Lee across the face. After the fact, the father goes on about his business, trying to pretend it never happened.

The River is far and away the most ominous of Tsai's films, one long, comically uneasy build-up to the Unexpected and Unexperienced. It is also strangely magical, with water a potent symbolic element: Lee dives into the 'dirty' water, surely the cause of his infection, which brings his own desire to the surface and puts his heavily masked father's desire in range as well – because the father's shoddy little room, in which he sleeps alone, is being inundated with water from an overflowing bathtub upstairs (he jerry-rigs an elaborate device to divert the water, i.e. the truth) and then from a rainstorm (this time the mother keeps the water out). Meanwhile, in the bath-house, a river of desire is flowing. The way that Tsai stages and shoots this scene, it is as if he'd been preparing for it his whole life. The naked son lies in his father's arms, their faces and bodies carefully lit in the darkness to evoke a Pietà, and Lee's craned neck is the focal point as he writhes in pain and moans with pleasure at the same time, like a little child. It is a monumental image, its effect even more devastating than the moment in *The Last Temptation of Christ* (1988) when the angel pulls the nails from Jesus' hand and leads him down from the cross: in both cases, centuries of cultural memory erased in an instant. Only here the effect is even more powerful, the moment stretched out in time as well as space. It surpasses sexuality and becomes a communion of two souls unable to ever achieve a real union yet forever on the verge – in other words, the ultimate expression of a father/son relationship.

Tsai is so deft with these symbolic elements that they are not apparent until long after the film is over, and his mastery is total. At first glance, the film's power seems to exist only within the heavily circumscribed limits of Tsai's universe, but once you consider that *The River* is less about the breaking of taboos and more about fathers and sons, it becomes monumental. And in the film's final moments, when the father pretends the event has never happened, the effect is equally monumental – a wall of repression rising up and reforming itself from its own rubble like a piece of trick photography.

What Time Is It There? ends with another monumental image of a father, this time alighting from death into another world that is, at the same time, imagined and real. It's a magically becalmed moment that speaks to something elusive yet fundamentally human: namely, the idea, the *reality*, of 'there' – meaning 'not here'. Meaning wherever one is not: another room, another house, another city, another country, another world. And whatever we imagine about these other places, we know that they contain rules and events and customs which we can't imagine. We can infer what goes on there from what we know of here, but it's ultimately what we don't know that intrigues us and bewitches us most. This final harmonious image pulses with the tension between the knowable and the unknowable. It speaks to that which is common, and that which isn't, between life here and life there. And, somehow, it encapsulates the graceful gesture that is Tsai Ming-liang's body of work.

Notes

1. Jacques Rivette (trans. Liz Heron), 'Mizoguchi Viewed From Here', in Jim Hiller (ed.), *Cahiers du cinéma: The 1950s – Neo-Realism, Hollywood, New Wave* (Cambridge: Harvard University Press, 1985), p. 264; originally in *Cahiers du cinéma* no. 81, March 1958.
2. Stephen Teo, 'The Legacy of T. E. Lawrence: The Forward Policy of Western Film Critics in the Far East', in Alan Williams (ed.), *Film and Nationalism* (New Brunswick and London: Rutgers University Press, 2002), pp. 181–94.

4

Sampling in Rotterdam

Jonathan Rosenbaum (1998)

This year [1998] the Rotterdam Film Festival ran for twelve days in late January and early February. But I could only attend the first half – five days apart from opening night. And thanks to a vidéothèque at the festival with copies of most of the films being shown, including many that were scheduled for the festival's second half, I found myself alternating most days between screenings at the Pathé and the Lantaren, the festival's two multiplexes, where I was always watching something with an audience (between twenty and several hundred people), and solitary sessions with earphones at the vidéothèque (located on the ground floor of the Hotel Central, which served as Gestapo headquarters during the war).

A few other facts: I managed to see about forty films and videos, but only ten of these were full features; I also, for one reason or another, walked out of or only sampled five other features at the multiplexes and wound up fast-forwarding my way through one other feature at the Central – Gunnar Bergdahl's documentary *The Voice of Bergman* (1997), where I went looking for Bergman's dismissal of Dreyer as a film-maker who made only two films of value, *The Passion of Joan of Arc* (1928) and *Day of Wrath* (1943). (As it turns out, Bergman doesn't even bother to support this judgment with any argument, except to insist on the vast superiority of Jan Troell – the director of such films as *The Emigrants* [1971] and *The New Land* [1972].)

I'm bringing up this sort of information in order to clarify a few important considerations.

1. All over the world today, critics, teachers and students frequently watch films alone on video and then write or talk about these films as if they saw them collectively in a cinema. It's a casualty of living through a transitional period, and it often involves a kind of imprecision and a certain imposture regarding our own relation to these films. That is, when we say what a film is or attempt to describe it we generally regard it as an object abstracted from its performance and reception, yet the circumstances of that performance and reception often mould our perceptions of the film as an object.
2. Every spectator at a film festival has an itinerary, whether this is determined by temperamental or professional matters – let's call it a pattern of desire, or at least a line of

inquiry – and my own itinerary at Rotterdam, which takes shape over the first two days, is mainly to trace the differences and the relationships between two periods of experimental film-making, roughly the present (i.e., the past few years) and the past (mainly the 60s and 70s) – using the term 'experimental' as broadly as possible. This, at least, is my conscious line of inquiry most of the time – which largely accounts for why I see so many shorts and so few features. But passing back and forth several times daily between collective viewing and solitary viewing, I eventually decide that I can't completely ignore the consequences of these different modes of viewing either, which also affect the status of these works as objects. And the fact that I'm often seeing videos (as well as films) projected at the Pathé and Lantaren and films on video (as well as videos) at the Central only adds to the complications.

3. It might be argued, in short, that my mode of reception (and perception) has some things in common with 'sampling' in popular music – the way a disc jockey passes between fragments from separate records, using transitions that by cinematic analogy range from abrupt cuts to lap dissolves.

4. A broader consideration: every trip that I take to Europe from the US nowadays affords me the pleasure of experiencing relief from the self-fulfilling and self-serving prophecies of American commerce, especially those relating to cinema and what might be termed 'narrative correctness'. A few of these glib formulas: Hollywood simply gives the public what it wants. (First lie: that Hollywood – or the public, for that matter – knows what the public wants. Second lie: that what the public wants can necessarily be gauged by how it spends money.) The public only wants to see Hollywood genre movies. (See above.) Ergo, everything that can't be described as a Hollywood genre film is of marginal interest and importance.

The worst consequence of 'narrative correctness' as it has entered critical discourse is an identification with producers and distributors rather than film-makers, so that critics are now prone to recommend the same sort of artistically damaging recutting that producers sometimes carry out. I actually know two highly respected critics in the US – one American, one Iranian – who have tried to persuade Kiarostami to remove the final sequence from his sublime *Taste of Cherry* (1997); and in the case of Robert Duvall's *The Apostle* (1997), reviews of its screenings at festivals that suggested it would be 'improved' by cuts eventually resulted in the removal of seventeen minutes by Walter Murch before the film opened commercially anywhere. And even though Murch's recutting was sensitive and thoughtful, the style of the film was altered somewhat; what initially resembled at times a Jean Rouch documentary has been thoroughly narrativised – narrative correctness with a vengeance, all ultimately derived from the mythology of 'giving the public what it wants'.

So for me a particular pleasure of attending the Rotterdam Film Festival year after year – and this is the thirteenth festival I've attended since 1984 – is the pleasure of seeing the received wisdom of American commerce repeatedly confounded. To all appearances, there's a hunger for experimental work that producers, distributors and most mainstream reviewers are completely unaware of, and which gives me a renewed faith in the capacities of spectators.

The late Huub Bals, who founded the festival and defined its spirit until his death in 1988, was certainly open to most kinds of transgressive cinema, but the tradition of non-narrative cinema represented by such figures as Ernie Gehr, Ken Jacobs and Rose Lowder eluded him. A passionate visionary who was not quite an intellectual, Bals resembled Henri Langlois in his reliance on intuition and in his adherence to a French notion of the avant-garde that was, at that time, warmer to Philippe Garrel and Raul Ruiz than to Michael Snow and Hollis Frampton.

Marco Müller, Bals's first successor (1990–1) – a genuine intellectual and scholar with a wider range of reference points, and the only Rotterdam festival director to date with a pronounced interest in publishing books and monographs to accompany his programmes (a project he now sustains at Locarno) – altered this emphasis by inviting to Rotterdam such American experimental film-makers as Leslie Thornton and Laurie Dunphy, but in contrast Emile Fallaux (1992–6), a documentary film-maker with more interest in subject matter than in formal or historical issues, tended to avoid or marginalise 'difficult' works. (Significantly, unlike his predecessors and successor, he systematically excluded Straub and Huillet's films from his festivals.)

Simon Field, who, like Fallaux, has presided over the festival's expansion, combines some of the interests of all his predecessors. But as a specialist in experimental cinema who founded and co-edited the irreplaceable *Afterimage* in London – perhaps the most consistently interesting experimental film magazine England has ever had during its approximately twelve issues and fifteen years of publication (1970–85) – Field this year succeeded in popularising experimental cinema at Rotterdam in an unprecedented fashion. Part of this came about through the opening in 1997 of the Pathé – the largest multiplex in Holland and probably the best designed that I know of anywhere, which quickly became the centre of the festival last year – and Field's decision this year to programme many of the more accessible experimental films there. (By contrast, the Gehr films were shown only at the Lantaren – an older kind of multiplex that used to show nearly all of the festival's films through the mid 80s, until commercial cinemas began to be used more prominently.)

In some respects, the Pathé suggests an airport or a train station where crowds are periodically appearing and disappearing between scheduled departures; in other respects, it recalls superstores like Virgin or FNAC – or, in the US, bookstores like Borders and Barnes & Noble – that have become the capitalist replacements for state-run arts centres or public libraries. The disturbing aspect of these stores as replacements of this kind is the further breakdown of any distinction between culture and advertising which already characterises urban society in general. But a positive aspect may also exist in terms of community and collective emotion.

Paris flashback #1: Thanks to saving my appointment books, I can pinpoint that the 'nuit blanche' devoted to New America Cinema at the Olympia Cinema started at midnight on 4 December 1971, and that I somehow managed to see only three films there: Michael Snow's <———> (*Back and Forth*, 1969), George Kuchar's *Hold Me While I'm Naked* (1966) and Bruce Baillie's *Mass for the Dakota Sioux* (1963–4). I didn't succeed in seeing the films shown there by Ron Rice, Jonas Mekas, Peter Kubelka, Ken Jacobs, Hollis Frampton, Stan Brakhage and Kenneth Anger because the overall experience, as I recall it today, was rather like attending a riot – perhaps the closest thing I've ever witnessed to the legendary premiere of *L'Age d'or* (1930), except that the outraged spectators weren't members of the high bourgeoisie but French hippies, so incensed by the non-narrative rigours of Snow's film that they hooted and whistled all the way through; someone even waved a brassiere in front of the projector, an act greeted by wild applause. Consequently, I had to see most other American experimental films of this era during my trips to New York, most often at Anthology Film Archives, and I wound up missing all the early films of Ernie Gehr.

Paris flashback #2: During the five days I spend in Paris prior to my five days in Rotterdam, I see Noël Burch, who plans to give a lecture in Rotterdam shortly after I return to the US, a paper he's currently working on – 'The Sadeian Aesthetic: A Critical View' – and he gives me an early draft for my comments. The lecture grew out of an invitation to participate in 'The Cruel Machine', a series of films, videos and lectures programmed by Gertjan Zuilhof that Noël has serious misgivings about. Zuilhof mainly defines cinematic cruelty in relation to three films he describes as classics – Michael Powell's *Peeping Tom* (1960), Gualtiero Jacopetti's *Mondo Cane* (1963) and Frans Zwartjes' *Pentimento* (1980) – and Burch's intervention seeks to critique 'what I see as the social relationship central to high modernism, between the demiurgical, megalomanic, ultimately sadistic power of the Great Creative Mind and the stoic masochism of the ordinary devotee, flattered to share the austere tastes of an elite'.[1] A radical and to my mind utopian, even quixotic attempt to reconcile his masochistic sexuality with his Marxist politics and his quarrels with French modernism, Noël's project is clearly mined with booby traps – especially because Sadeian and masochistic aesthetics as Noël defines them are so intertwined with the issues of being French and being American that inform his own autobiography – but I also can't help but see it as a noble and heroic undertaking. (Coincidentally, the modernist elevation of Sade has recently been interrogated in the US – extensively and to my mind persuasively – by Roger Shattuck in *Forbidden Knowledge: From Prometheus to Pornography*,[2] and it's a pity Noël hasn't yet been exposed to this book.) Whatever its pitfalls, it's so ambitious and instructive an undertaking that I find myself carrying out a silent dialogue with it every day I'm in Rotterdam.

On the one hand, I feel that Burch's total rejection of his own earlier formalist writing and his current defence of mainstream masochism (i.e., Sternberg) over what he views as the Sadeian aesthetic of high modernist experimental film-making (Brakhage, Gehr, Snow, etc.) mainly bypass concerns that address my own experience. But on the other hand, no one else is really attempting to reconcile his sexuality, his sexual politics and his aesthetics in quite so concerted a fashion, and whether he intends this or not, I once again find myself stimulated by his arguments as a kind of meta-science-fiction.

Today Noël feels he has to reject his own *Praxis du cinéma* as an elitist validation of everything Sadeian/modernist aesthetics stand for. Yet for me the book was valuable in the 70s (when it was translated as *Theory of Film Practice*[3]) not as any sort of political or social model but as a guide to strains in film-making and formal analysis that I was still learning about; for me, it formed an unlikely but essential dialectic with Andrew Sarris' *The American Cinema*[4] as a sort of catalogue of what I should be seeing and how I should be seeing it. My point is that as a scavenger and *bricoleur*, I have a natural tendency as a spectator to pervert the aesthetic and political programmes of others, and I believe all spectators (Burch included) do this on some level. Consciously or unconsciously, we all compulsively reinvent films and aesthetic programmes in the direction of our own desires, making honest and practical criticism all the more difficult.

As I discovered in college, one can take virtually any line in English poetry, follow it with a particular line from T. S. Eliot – 'Like a patient etherised upon a table' – and confidently expect the two lines to fit together and even produce a coherent meaning. What is it about this line from 'The Love Song of J. Alfred Prufrock' that makes it so versatile and user-friendly? I suspect it's the fact that the etherised patient is none other than ourselves, modernist spectators, committed to following our own divided consciousness wherever it might lead us, which is almost always away from society.

But exceptions to this rule are well worth noting. Included in 'The Cruel Machine' and seen by me on video, Stephen Dwoskin's personal essay *Pain Is . . .* (1997) – a blend of autobiography, investigation and philosophical reflection – is by far the most powerful film that I see in this programme, because it lucidly brings sadism and masochism (among other related topics) into a public arena as something to be examined, not merely experienced or mythologised. Made by an experimental film-maker who has spent most of his life in a wheelchair because of his polio, it has the most complex and nuanced treatment of pain of any film I know because, as Zuilhof notes in the festival catalogue, it does not distinguish between wanted and unwanted pain. The film opens with a point-of-view shot taken from a wheelchair moving through hospital corridors until broad daylight bleaches out the image, and over the last part of this voyage, Dwoskin's off-screen voice begins to ask questions about pain, only a few of which are answered. ('Is it possible to make an image for pain? . . . When you rub your finger on wood, you feel the wood. If you get a splinter, you feel your finger. That's how pain works. It moves from outside to inside.')

The film is full of close-ups of people discussing, experiencing, administering and representing pain of different kinds – aggressive and extreme close-ups that often justify the term used to describe them, 'chokers'. Yet most of the words used to describe the pain in question are relatively detached and dispassionate, distancing one's responses. In the film's most remarkable sequence, Dwoskin films in close-up a dominatrix while she's beating him with a strap, work she clearly enjoys, and then while he calmly interviews her after the session about her work. It's an approach that somehow evokes both Brecht and Montaigne, and for me it provides a precise dialectical (and modernist) response to Burch's attack on the Sadeian aesthetic by moving from inside to outside. Is this achievement enhanced or contradicted by the fact that I'm seeing it on video, alone with my own sexuality and my own phantoms? Not having the benefit of a comparison with how it plays before a full audience, I can only speculate about the answer.

I attend the first programme in the Gehr retrospective at the Lantaren on Thursday evening – *Shift* (1972–4), *This Side of Paradise* (1991) and *Side/Walk/Shuttle* (1991) – along with about twenty other spectators, most of them Dutch people in their twenties, and the response in this case seems fairly bemused and cool; the first question asked Gehr by someone after the films is, 'Are you some kind of 16mm fetishist?' Though I'm taken especially by the camera movements and structural rigours of *Side/Walk/Shuttle*, this is a solitary experience more than a collective one, in striking contrast to what I shared with hundreds of enrapt spectators – again, most of them Dutch people in their twenties – at part of a video programme called 'City Sounds' at the Pathé a few hours earlier.

Having smoked a joint before the previous afternoon programme, it's theoretically possible that I could have been idealising the good vibes at 'City Sounds', but I don't think so. For one thing, the first work in the programme, Jason Spingarn-Koff's >>*Abducted*<< (1996) – a twelve-minute video from Germany, shot in Berlin, Providence and New York – begins in the explicit context of television: one sees a TV monitor over pulsing signals (including some in red and green) located in a panel below, and on the TV screen are silent, faded images of city landscapes. For another, the presence of music (percussive 'industrial' music credited to DJ Fresh Blend) places this in a separate universe from Gehr's work. A full black and white video image fills the screen after the initial television context is established, and a seductive rudimentary narrative establishes itself: a female figure recalling Maya Deren gets up from a bed in a sunny loft and walks over to a window, then subsequently is seen moving through colour-stencilled background images of a city while intertitles in German periodically tell us things about her journey: 'A television tower stands high above the city', 'Did something happen here? Perhaps something terrible', 'At the Reich air ministry?', 'Here stood a Jewish department store'. In effect, the video is recounting a voyage through a dark and unfathomable history that proceeds from the turn of the century to contemporary Berlin, meanwhile resurrecting memories of silent German cinema and the Holocaust that appear like half-remembered dreams, and the overall experience is so bewitching that I wind up seeing >>*Abducted*<< a second time on video at the Central a few days later.

Does this imply that the more solitary pleasures of Gehr's explorations are now a thing of the past? Maybe so, but only for some spectators. When I return to the Lantaren for another Gehr programme on Saturday night, this one consisting exclusively of silent films – *Serene Velocity* (1970), *Table* (1976), *Mirage* (1981) and *Eureka* (1974) – on this occasion there are at least sixty spectators in the auditorium, and virtually no one leaves. So it appears that some sort of education of the audience has taken place between Thursday and Saturday – an induction into a way of seeing and reflecting upon film images that can only grow with experience.

On the other hand, I doubt that an audience for Gehr films can ever achieve the collective rapport that I witness and share when I see >>*Abducted*<< for the first time, and I suspect that the use of music has a great deal to do with it. I experience some of the same difference when I see *Blight* (1996), a video from London made by John Smith in collaboration with the composer Jocelyn Pook – a fascinating work that is simultaneously a documentary about the construction of the M2 Link Road in East London, which provoked a protracted campaign by local residents to protect their homes from demolition, and a treatment of some of these residents' impromptu speech as the basis for a kind of *musique concrete* – the various voices accompanied by piano chords and beautifully orchestrated with the editing, so that I'm inspired to write in my notebook, 'Like Frank Zappa, only better'.

The question is, does the collective audience rapport provoked by *Blight* become translated into any kind of social engagement with the video's subject? Here I become less confident, if only because collective social engagement – including the kind that rejected Michael Snow at the Olympia in 1971, as well as more positive forms of involvement – is much harder to find nowadays at the cinema than other kinds of collective emotion. This is surely in part because the utopian vision of the 60s is no longer available to a contemporary audience; there is too much scepticism about culture and the media, about the plausible gains of revolutionary consciousness, for such a possibility to be considered.

This becomes even more apparent when I attend a David Shea concert on Friday night in which he accompanies Johan Grimonprez's feature-length video *Dial H-I-S-T-O-R-Y* (1997) on a synthesiser, below and directly in front of the screen. The video is a compilation of found footage of TV news broadcasts about terrorist acts (mainly hijackings of planes over the past thirty years) as well as cartoons, commercials and instructional films – a post-modernist celebration of banality, incoherence and fear that reminds me of the similar compilations of Craig Baldwin. It might be argued that Grimonprez escapes the nihilistic framework of Baldwin by including passages of intelligent and suggestive commentary about terrorism from two novels by Don DeLillo, *White Noise* and *Mao II*, but I consider this distinction mainly academic because Grimonprez chooses to import someone else's commentary rather than offer any commentary of his own. Similarly, Shea's accompaniment incorporates echoes of the scores of *Alphaville* (1965) and various Hong Kong films – more post-modernist appropriations that can't always distinguish between text and commentary.

From a 60s' political perspective, this is all highly dubious and clearly 'irresponsible'. Yet I also find myself sympathising with and even partially sharing the quasi-euphoric collective experience being offered by this combination of elements, an experience that combines the pleasures of surprise and adventure with political defeatism in a distinctively 90s' manner. To find pleasure in such sources of pain as 'urban renewal' and terrorism certainly requires a considerable amount of alienation, but it also has to be admitted that this alienation is already produced by the culture and not by the contemplative pleasures derived from reflecting about it. Even if such a perversion of social consciousness represents an ideological impasse, it fully acknowledges that state of affairs, and the pleasure it provides derives in part from that acknowledgment. Is this like the bitter pleasure of a trapped animal rattling the bars of its cage? If it is, maybe the bars first have to be rattled before they can be broken or removed.

On two successive days in the vidéothèque, Sunday and Monday, I see two half-hour American films made in the Midwest, Jill Godmilow's *What Farocki Taught* (1998) and Elisabeth Subrin's *Shulie* (1997), both of them precise remakes of political documentaries made in the 60s: Godmilow's film remakes a black and white German documentary made by Harun Farocki in 1969 about the production and effects of napalm, *Inextinguishable Fire*, in colour and in English; and Subrin's film remakes a 1967 documentary made by Jerry Blumenthal, Sheppard Ferguson, James Leahy and Alan Rettig about Shulamith Firestone, the future author of *The Dialectic of Sex: The Case for Feminist Revolution* (1970)[5] – a book I still recall as powerful – when she was a student at the Chicago Art Institute. *What Farocki Taught* represents itself as a non-fiction film; *Shulie* concludes with the title, 'This is a work of fiction.'[6] Both 60s' films are works of desperate inquiry, and the same can be said of both 90s' films, for all their marked differences in subject and style.

Why did these two remakes emerge at approximately the same time, when neither film-maker knew about the other project being made? The impulse to remake a work of 60s' protest seems to stem from another post-modernist desire to 'bore from within' – to reconfigure the past in terms of a blocked present, to rattle the bars of the cage in a different fashion. Is rethinking the 60s a prelude and prerequisite for rethinking the 90s, or is it perhaps some sort of substitute for that difficult process? In the semi-clandestine reaches of the vidéothèque, I can't be sure.

I have to confess that I prefer Subrin's *Shulie* to the film it remakes, if only because the complex historical pathos produced by her efforts yields far more information about the 90s than the original film could possibly tell us about the 60s, then or now. However, I prefer *Inextinguishable Fire* to *What Farocki Taught*, because the political motivations of the former are more direct and lucid. My preferences have very little to do with the technical skill or resourcefulness of either Subrin or Godmilow, but they have a great deal to do with assessing the value of a political work in its own time.

With some justice, conventional wisdom has it that the 60s were a much freer time than today, so there's a certain boldness in Subrin focusing on a moment in that period when feminist consciousness was still struggling to be defined. The paradox is that even historical hindsight isn't enough to give an actress thirty years later the kind of emotional urgency Firestone conveyed in the original film through her own shyness and confusion; Kim Soss, the actress playing Shulie, projects the kind of contemporary coolness we tend to identify as normal. Yet it's only through this juxtaposition that we begin to see the petrifying fear that describes our present moment – the kind of fear that makes the very notion of a remake seem like a logical response.

On Monday, during my final afternoon at the festival, I attend a screening at the Pathé of the Taiwanese feature *Blue Moon* (1997). Scripted and directed by Ko I-cheng – a member of the Taiwanese New Wave who is best known as an actor outside of Taiwan, particularly for his roles in Edward Yang films – this feature consists of five twenty-minute reels designed to be shown in a separate order each time, so that 120 different versions are possible. All five reels feature more or less the same characters and settings – including, among others, a young woman, a writer, a film producer and a restaurant owner, all living in Taipei and belonging to the same circle of friends and acquaintances – and in each reel the woman is involved with a separate man. One can therefore construct a continuous narrative by positing some reels as flashbacks, as flash-forwards, or else as events that transpire in a parallel universe.

Apart from this unique construction – Ko explains after the screening that he wrote all five parts simultaneously, on different coloured sheets of paper – *Blue Moon* is a conventional, even 'commercial' narrative feature, and one of my American colleagues who saw the film earlier dismisses it for precisely that reason as banal and disappointing. But for me it's fascinating for precisely the same reason: because it demands the creative participation of the viewer at the same time that it pretends to satisfy one's conventional expectations. And there are other beautiful rewards as well: for example, I've always hoped one day to see a feature that unconventionally includes its credits somewhere in the middle, and this particular configuration of *Blue Moon* fulfils that dream by showing the film producer look at a credits sequence in a projection room at the end of the second reel – a credits sequence that I feel sure provides the credits of *Blue Moon*. More conventionally, the very first reel of this screening explains the significance of the film's title.

In short, the possibilities of satisfying some of the spectator's desires and thwarting others are endless, and I completely agree with the film-maker Jackie Raynal, whom I attend this screening with, when she says afterwards that she immediately wants to see the film again, with the reels in a different order. To be sure, not all of the multiple narrative's mysteries can be solved in this fashion, but some fresh clues will undoubtedly emerge, just as additional mysteries will be added. In some ways, it's like the experience of sampling at a film festival condensed into a single feature, obliging each spectator to make his or her own synthesis out of the disparate yet interconnected pieces. Does this make it a political as well as experimental film? Insofar as it addresses and seeks to change the relation of the spectator to the cinematic apparatus, it can't be anything else.

Notes

1. Noël Burch, 'The Sadeian Aesthetic: A Critical View' in Dave Beech and John Roberts (eds), *The Philistine Controversy* (London/New York: Verso, 2002), p. 179.
2. Roger Shattuck, *Forbidden Knowledge: From Prometheus to Pornography* (New York: St Martin's Press, 1996).
3. Noël Burch, *Theory of Film Practice* (London: Secker & Warburg, 1973).
4. Andrew Sarris, *The American Cinema: Directors and Directions 1929–1968* (New York: Dutton, 1968).
5. Shulamith Firestone, *The Dialectic of Sex: The Case for Feminist Revolution* (New York: Morrow, 1970).
6. This title was subsequently removed.

5

Two Auteurs: Masumura and Hawks

Shigehiko Hasumi and Jonathan Rosenbaum

To appropriate one of the categories of Andrew Sarris' *The American Cinema*, Yasuzo
Masumura (1924–1986) is a 'subject for further research'. My first encounter with his
work was almost thirty years ago in Paris, where his *Love for an Idiot* (*Chijin no ai*, 1967),
an updated adaptation of Junichiro Tanizaki's 1924 novel *Naomi*, was playing under the
title *La Chatte japonaise*. (As I would discover much later, there are two other excellent
Tanizaki adaptations in his oeuvre – *Manji* [*Swastika*, 1964] and *Tattoo* [*Irezumi*, 1966].)
Spurred by a twelve-page spread in the October 1970 issue of *Cahiers du cinéma* – perhaps the most extensive critical recognition he's received to date in the West – I found
myself both shocked and intrigued by this depiction of the erotic delirium of a middle-
aged factory worker over the much younger wife he trains, marries and loses. One image
in particular stood out: crazed by his fond memories of crawling around on all fours while
she rode him piggyback, he tries to simulate the same activity alone in his apartment.

Twenty-seven years were to pass before I saw any more Masumura films, and this opportunity came courtesy of a travelling show of a dozen features packaged by Kyoko Hirano
of New York's Japan Society, which arrived in Chicago in 1998. Since then, there are three
specific and separate reasons why I have been drawn towards continuing this research.

1. A curiosity about the mysterious phenomenon of what I would call global synchronic-
    ity: the simultaneous appearance of the same apparent tastes, styles and/or themes in
    separate parts of the world, without any signs of these common and synchronous traits
    having influenced one another – all of which suggest a common global experience that
    has not yet been adequately identified. The series of letters opening this book was
    initially motivated by this sort of curiosity: the fact that a few younger cinephiles whom
    I knew of roughly the same age, from different countries, who mainly didn't know one
    another, shared pretty much the same specialised taste. And it was curiosity about
    another kind of synchronicity that sparked part of my original interest in Masumura:
    how a Japanese director of the 50s and 60s whose films echoed in many respects Amer-
    ican films of the same period by Samuel Fuller, Nicholas Ray, Douglas Sirk and Frank

Tashlin, stylistically as well as thematically, wound up making them without any apparent direct influences running in either direction. Though one could trace a few other glancing overlaps between Masumura's films and American cinema – *Black Super-Express* (*Kuro no chotokkyu*, 1964), for instance, faintly suggesting a Phil Karlson revenge tragedy, or *Ode to the Yakuza* (*Yakuza zessho*, 1970) recalling Hawks' *Scarface* (1932) – it was to these four 50s' directors that I kept returning.

I can't claim to have arrived at any sort of conclusive results in my investigation, except for the perception that I have probably bitten off more than I can chew. The complex relations between the cultures of Japan and the US engendered through the American occupation – including the diverse forms of censorship practised in both countries during this period – is not a subject I feel qualified to tackle in any comprehensive manner, yet any serious study of synchronicity between Hollywood and Masumura films during the post-war period would surely have to factor in this subject. And even a much more narrowly defined inquiry – such as the respective definitions of madness in, say, Ray's *Bigger Than Life* (1956), Fuller's *Shock Corridor* (1963) and Masumura's *The False Student* (1960) or *Sex Check* (1968) – would have to account for some of the different aesthetic strategies at work in these films, such as the role played by allegory in the Fuller film, making it difficult to come up with a workable critical methodology for all four.

2. A desire to pursue a particular experiment in cinephilia. A belief that I encounter frequently nowadays – tied to the more general myth that the cinema is dead – is the melancholy conviction that all the important discoveries in film history have already been made. (One Japanese friend has proposed a variant of this position: that Masumura is in fact the only significant major discovery that remains to be made, at least in Japanese cinema.) Frankly, this belief has always struck me as presumptuous and somewhat arrogant – suggesting a certain capitulation to the mainstream marketing practices that pretend that all the products worth consuming are already known quantities, theoretically accessible if not available. This trait is particularly pronounced in the United States, where it's widely believed by book and magazine editors that readers shouldn't encounter too many references to films that aren't already known and/or readily within reach. So one particular allure of studying a figure like Masumura is that the odds of getting to know his works in the West in any depth would appear to be impossible: an oeuvre of fifty-eight films – fifty-five features and three shorts – not one of which was in distribution.[1]

The challenge of getting to know his work under such circumstances was therefore motivated by a desire to convince both myself and other cinephiles that 'impossible' objects of study weren't as impossible to study as we often pretended, mainly out of laziness and inertia. And, to a large extent, this project was successful. At one point in my efforts to track down videos of some of Masumura's films subtitled in English, for instance, I was delighted to discover that at least a couple of these came from a friend's contact in Israel. In much the same way that a recent conference on Philippe Garrel was held in Dublin and largely planned through devotees of Garrel's work who wrote for an online film magazine in Melbourne,[2] it seemed that email was a potential boon to cinephilia and research that has only begun to be explored. And, meanwhile, it has turned out that my investigation was pretty well timed insofar as Masumura has recently been getting more attention than ever before (see Hasumi's comments in the Epilogue). Like my third rationale for undertaking this study (see below), this suggested that synchronicity was much easier to trace in relation to cinephilia than it was in relation to cinema *per se*.

3. An investigation into certain questions of cultural difference. Reading Shigehiko Hasumi's book on Yasujiro Ozu in French translation[3] shortly after it was published, I was intrigued to see many of the (Western as well as Eastern) clichés about Ozu's essential 'Japaneseness' confounded or at least challenged by some of Hasumi's reading strategies – strategies which were actually quite attentive to specific cultural differences without allowing them to be mystified in the name of exoticism. And because Hasumi was especially enlightening about the ways in which American cinema marked Ozu's films, I began to think that he might be an ideal interlocutor for my inquiry into what was specifically Japanese – or not Japanese – in the work of Masumura. Furthermore, knowing about Hasumi's particular enthusiasm for Hawks, I began to think that it might be fruitful to explore not only what was 'American' about my interest in Masumura, but also what was 'Japanese' about his interest in Hawks.

As it turned out, this latter exploration wound up being pursued only intermittently in our dialogue, and not at all in Hasumi's subsequent essay on Hawks, planned and executed quite independently of our discussion. Yet his essay nonetheless contributes an invaluable dimension to the cross-cultural topic I wanted to address by approaching the international currency of Hawks quite differently, through formal patterns with implications relating to gender, the body and, more generally, principles of inversion.

Highlighting the degree to which formal and stylistic approaches can both straddle and reconcile highly divergent cultural traditions (a project also carried out by Viktor Shklovsky's stylistic commentary on *Tristram Shandy* and François Truffaut's analysis of doubling and rhyming images in *Shadow of a Doubt* [1943]), Hasumi makes it easier to understand precisely why Hawks can communicate *through* classical Hollywood genres rather than simply because of them. Indeed, Hasumi's teaching along these lines at Tokyo's Rikkyo University in the 80s had a decisive influence on a generation of Japanese film-makers known as the 'New New Wave' that includes Shinji Aoyama (*Eureka*, 2000), Nobuhiro Suwa (*2/Duo* [1996], *H Story* [2001]) and Kiyoshi Kurosawa (*Cure* [1997], *Pulse* [2001]). Kurosawa still vividly recalls Hasumi's classroom principle: 'Just as equally in a Robert Aldrich picture as in a Jean-Luc Godard picture, you can find clues to the questions, What is a film? and, What is its place in film history?'[4]

It is largely thanks to this kind of lingua franca that the formal languages of Kiarostami, Panahi, Hou and Tsai – explored elsewhere in this book, and pursued through the very different traditions of Iranian and Taiwanese art cinema (with only occasional references to Western models) – can be readily understood and appreciated across the globe, thereby providing a route into their cultural meanings that would be harder to access through strictly sociological, philosophical or genre-based approaches. The fact that Hasumi's formal training is in French literature seems especially significant in his sensitivity to style and form, developing some of the same traditions that inspired the discoveries of style undertaken by *Cahiers du cinéma* in the 50s (which also defied traditional canons of French film aesthetics at the time in its embrace of traditional and popular Hollywood genres – much as Hasumi has been doing in relation to the traditional canons of Japan, as he notes in our dialogue). One might argue, in fact, that just as attention to form in Hou and Kiarostami communicates both through and beyond their respective national cultures, Hasumi's attention to form in Hawks winds up telling us something indirect about Japan, France and Anglo-American culture as well as something more direct about an international current that straddles these and other traditions.

As luck would have it, my first visit to Japan was in December 1998, to participate in a symposium organised by Hasumi for the University of Tokyo and Shockiku entitled 'Yasujiro Ozu in the World'. Shortly after this visit, I applied to the Japan Foundation for a visitor's fellowship a year later and, after being accepted, used part of my two-week visit in Japan in December 1999 to continue my Masumura research by viewing eight of his films with an interpreter at the National Film Centre, and taping a dialogue with Hasumi at the University of Tokyo about Masumura and Hawks. (During my two visits to Japan, Hasumi was serving in his second and third years in the elected four-year position of president of the University of Tokyo, making his generosity in agreeing to take the time to carry out this discussion in 1999 exceptional.) Furthermore, on my first day in Tokyo, the Japan Foundation arranged a lunch with Sadao Yamane, who had recently published the first book-length critical study of Masumura,[5] and later I was able to photocopy some relevant materials in English at the Kawakita Memorial Film Foundation. During a very enjoyable day spent with Mikiro Kato, an associate professor at Kyoto University, in addition to taking me to the grave of Kenji Mizoguchi, he generously arranged for me to visit a local art museum that housed production scrapbooks for all the Masumura films made at Daiei, constituting about four-fifths of his work.

Further research has been made possible through diverse channels. Chika Kinoshita – a Mizoguchi scholar, former student of Hasumi and graduate student at the University of Chicago – generously assisted me by furnishing me with both videos of Masumura films and detailed, scene-by-scene synopses of most of these, which allowed me to view them without subtitles; she also translated portions of Masumura's film criticism and other materials for me, drawn from an indispensable Japanese book on the film-maker that Hasumi had been kind enough to give me,[6] and in addition has kindly corrected many of my factual errors. In the spring of 2000, I was able to watch nine more Masumura films at the Pacific Film Archives in Berkeley, California.[7] Adding still others I've managed to see on video from diverse sources, I've by now been able to see thirty-eight of Masumura's fifty-eight films, all but a handful of these with some sort of translation. What follows are a few reflections stemming from this work in progress.

Masumura was born on 24 August 1924 in Kofu on the island of Honshu and started going to movies at a very early age, having become friends in kindergarten with the son of a movie theatre owner; in high school he discovered Jean Renoir. After a brief military stint at the tail-end of World War II, he entered the University of Tokyo as a law student who also studied literature – befriending Yukio Mishima, one of his classmates, who would later star in his feature *Afraid to Die* (*Karakkaze yaro*, 1960). After two years he dropped out and found a job working as assistant director at Tokyo's Daei studio, where he earned enough to return to college as a philosophy major, graduating in 1949 with a thesis on Kierkegaard. The next year he won a scholarship at the Centro Spirimentale Cine-matografico in Rome, where Michelangelo Antonioni, Federico Fellini and Luchino Visconti were said to have been among his teachers. (The first of these – and the only one still alive – still remembers him, having recently turned up at a Masumura retrospective in Rome.)

After graduating, Masumura assisted on an Italian–Japanese production of *Madame Butterfly* (1954), then returned to Japan in 1954, where he worked as assistant to Mizoguchi on *Princess Yang Kwei Fei* (1955) and *Street of Shame* (1956) at Kyoto's Daei studio. After Mizoguchi died, he became an assistant to Kon Ichikawa on three more films before shooting his own first features: *Punishment Room* (*Shokei no heya*, 1956), *Nihonbashi* (1956) and *A Full-Up Train* (*Man'in densha*, 1957). Until Daei went bankrupt in 1971, he remained there, often making three or four features a year, most often accepting assign-ments and then sometimes shaping them into his own distinctive forms of rebellion. Afterwards, for the remaining eleven years of his directorial career, he averaged about one film a year – an uneven output that included many of his worst films, but at least two creditable achievements: *Lullaby of the Earth* (*Daichi no komoriuta*, 1976), perhaps his most significant independent production, and *Double Suicide in Sonezaki* (*Sonezaki shinju*, 1978), an adaptation of a Bunraku play. (By contrast, his last two films, which I've seen only without translation, seem to have few defenders: *Eden no sono* [*The Garden of Eden*, 1980] – his only overseas film, an Italian spin-off of *The Blue Lagoon* – and *In Celebration of This Child* aka *My Daughter's 7th Birthday* [*Konoko no nanatsu no oiwaini*, 1982], a detective thriller.) He also wrote extensively for Japanese television – mostly, it appears, after he left Daei – but my knowledge of this work is minimal. And all I know about his personal life is that he married a hairdresser and had no children.[8]

A precursor of the so-called Japanese New Wave that took root in the early 60s, around the same time as the French *nouvelle vague*, Masumura was initially regarded as a major guru by Nagisa Oshima in 1958 before embarking on his own features. Indeed, Masumura, director Ko Nakahita and screenwriter Yoshio Shirasaka – who scripted at least ten of Masumura's features, including *Giants and Toys* aka *The Build-Up* (*Kyojin to gangu*, 1958) and *The False Student* – were all heralded by Oshima in a 1958 essay called, 'Is It a Break-through? (The Modernists of Japanese Film)', and Masumura was labelled the 'possessor of the sharpest sociological perceptions of the three'.[9]

At this point, the release of Oshima's own first film was still about a year away and what he was celebrating in this trio was a taste for youthful irreverence, a conscious methodology and a call for freedom and innovation. In the case of Masumura, part of what this challenge entailed was not an application of the principles of Italian neo-realism – which is what one might have expected from his formal training – but, as I will shortly discuss, something closer to the reverse.

Oshima turned on his role model only two years later, objecting in particular to *Afraid to Die* (not one of Masumura's best films, in my opinion). Essentially he was denouncing Masumura as a modernist – which in Japanese terms meant catering to Western tastes – and he never recanted. Perhaps such a falling out was inevitable given Masumura's own profile as a Western-influenced studio director, though it hardly begins to account for how transgressive much of Masumura's work looks today, especially from an American perspective.

A film critic whose collected articles – published in 1999 in the aforementioned Japanese collection devoted to his work – are almost as extensive as Jean-Luc Godard's, Masumura wrote a major position paper published in *Eiga hyoron* (March 1958) replying to his critics who accused him of making bleak and tasteless films that lacked sentiment and featured comically exaggerated and unbelievable characters without any depiction of environment or atmosphere. Essentially boasting that he was guilty as charged on all counts, Masumura offered a few counterblasts:

(a) 'Sentiment in Japanese films means restraint, harmony, resignation, sorrow, defeat, and escape', not 'dynamic vitality, conflicts, struggle, pleasure, victory, and pursuit ... I buy the straightforward and crude expression, for I believe the Japanese restrain our desire so much that we tend to lose sight of our true mind.'

(b) 'There is no such a thing as non-restricted desire. A person who thoroughly discloses his or her desire can only be considered mad ... [And] what I would like to create is not a stable person who cleverly calculates reality, and safely expresses his or her desire within the calculation. I do not want to create a humane human being. I want to create a mad person who expresses his or her desire without shame, regardless of what people think.'

(c) 'What interests me is a conflict between expressions of naked desires which cannot be mitigated by the environment.'[10]

In Masumura's films, this madness can veer all the way from the hysterical promotional campaigns of three competing candy companies in the Tashlinesque *Giants and Toys* to an army nurse during the Sino-Japanese war in the somewhat hysterical and Fulleresque *Red Angel* (*Akai tenshi*, 1966), dispensing sexual favours to an amputee and a drug-addicted doctor. It's the madness of war itself in *Yakuza Soldier* aka *Hoodlum Soldier* (*Heitai yakuza*, 1965), where the only violence seen in this depiction of World War II is between Japanese soldiers, and desertion is viewed as evidence of sanity and health – or in *Nakano Spy School* (*Rikugun nakano gakko*, 1966), where the personal and sexual betrayals of espionage ultimately rule out even patriotic alibis. One finds this madness in the slow-witted young man (in *The False Student*) who poses as a college student, joins a radical study group, and literally goes nuts after being mistaken for a police informer; and in the tea master who methodically sets about sleeping with his late father's girlfriends (in the relatively lacklustre *Thousand Cranes* [*Senbazuru*, 1969], adapted from Yasumari Kawabata's famous novel). It's very much in the kidnapped model who willingly submits for 'artistic' reasons to getting carved up by a blind sculptor in a warehouse in *Blind Beast* (*Moju*, 1969). (This isn't the only instance of essentialism found in Masumura's eccentric depic-

tions of sexuality – a trait that either compromises his ambivalent feminism or else con-
tradicts it entirely, as in the dreadful *The Tortures of Hell* aka *The Snare* aka *Kung-fu Harikari*
[*Goyokiba-kamisori hanzo jigokuzeme*, 1973], which features a police detective who uses
his iron-hard penis, hammered into shape by an anvil, as an instrument to torture women
suspects.)

Masumura argued that typical social problem films, including those of Italian neo-
realism, foster resignation by giving environment a deterministic force. At the same time,
while insisting that he doesn't regard European society as superior to Japanese society,
he maintains that 'you can actually experience "beautiful and powerful man"' once you
step inside Europe:

> Their museums are filled with paintings and sculptures embodying the human beauty and
> power which the Europeans have spent two thousand years discovering and creating; their
> streets are crowded with people whose daring looks, confident steps and lively demeanors
> convey their pride and confidence as Man. In Europe, 'man' is real. [11]

Critic Tadao Sato, who commissioned this 1958 article – and who takes credit for having
discovered Masumura as a director – told me that Masumura was the first member of his
generation to view such masters as Mizoguchi, Ozu and Akira Kurosawa with a certain
amount of irreverence.[12] A radical whose strategy was strictly to bore from within, working with whatever came to hand (including existing genres as well as scripts and actors),
he can't generally be identified with a specific visual style; reportedly he even disliked the
striking style that cinematographer Kazuo Miyagawa brought to *Tattoo*, with its beautiful
diptych compositions. 'Some believe more in the image, others believe in the story,' he
avowed in one interview. 'Personally I believe in the story. Because images aren't absolute,
one can't express everything with them.' He also maintained:

> I never use close-ups. I detest them. Why do a close-up of an actor or actress' face? I'll agree
> to do a close-up if it's the real face of a peasant, for example ... [but] the performance of
> actors has no interest because it's finally a lie and doesn't wind up with anything beyond a
> certain 'resemblance'.[13]

Lest this sound like an overall denigration of actors, Masumura should also be credited
with developing the performances of Ayako Wakao, one of the greatest and most sensual
of all Japanese film actresses – whom Mizoguchi featured in *Gion Festival Music* (*Gion
bayashi*, 1953) and *Street of Shame* and who appeared in at least twenty of Masumura's
films (and most of his masterpieces) – and with fostering a kind of feminism relating to
the self-determination of his women characters, many of them played by her.

What *is* persistent in Masumura's work, sometimes accompanying his fruitful collaborations with Wakao and other actors, is a certain ethical engagement with the world – and a
set of strategies for pursuing and sustaining that engagement, such as the privileging and
exaggeration of obsessive forms of behaviour. Partly for this reason, many of his films are
deeply erotic on some level. Because sexuality for women has often served as coin of the

realm in Japanese society, the way that these women's 'fortunes' get saved, spent or squandered within that economy remains a profound ethical issue, and I can think of few directors apart from Masumura, his partial mentor Mizoguchi and his partial disciple Oshima who have made as many erotic films in tandem with the frankness of their political concerns. In the US, eroticism tends to be associated more with the right end of the political spectrum than with the left: such figures as Ayn Rand, Josef von Sternberg, Leni Riefenstahl and King Vidor, for instance. But if one wants to understand why Oshima's *In the Realm of the Senses* (1976) is a profoundly leftist (and anti-war) film, Masumura's oeuvre and all it implies points one in the proper direction.

Furthermore, Masumura's desire for an 'exaggerated depiction' of certain aberrant forms of social behaviour arguably stems from the same sort of impulse that led Oshima to systemically exclude the colour green from *Cruel Story of Youth* (1960), his first colour film and second feature. For Oshima, green signified the typical Japanese home including its enclosed garden and tea cabinet, and 'I firmly believed that unless the dark sensibility that those things engendered was completely destroyed, nothing new could come into being in Japan.'[14] For Masumura, the fatality of social realism, suggesting the impossibility of change, was as deadly as the colour green was for Oshima. In its place he wanted to erect a fictional universe where freedom and individuality could take uninhibited flight – in many cases entailing an unsentimental cinema about fanatics. As Canadian critic Mark Peranson has put it, '[Masumura's] movies are about the freedom to do whatever the fuck you want, and the ramifications of taking this attitude when society won't accept it.'[15] This often gets played out in various groupings of features that might be loosely categorised as anti-war films, anti-capitalist films, kinky sex films, youth films, and films with strong heroines – although, as with Fuller's seemingly separate preoccupations with war, journalism and crime, these categories often wind up interfacing to the point where they become indistinguishable.

A case in point is the delirious *Sex Check*, which encompasses all five categories. To sketch out only the first forty minutes, a dissolute former track star (Ken Ogata) fanatically trains and coaches an eighteen-year-old girl (Michiyo Yasuda), who works for an electrical company, to become an Olympic athlete, meanwhile ditching the woman he lives with and ignoring every other female athlete on the team. The ambitious company, yearning for the prestige of an Olympic champion, reluctantly agrees to his single-minded approach, which includes giving her frequent personal rubdowns. Having been advised years ago that athletes have to become beasts to get ahead, he tested this theory during World War II – as we see in a brief flashback – by going berserk with his bayonet on enemy soldiers and raping lots of women, and he tries to introduce the same wisdom to his protégée. At their first meal together, he hands her a razor and says, 'Shave every day so you can become a man; you have to overcome the limitations of female athletes', and before long they're also living together and having sex. (Later on, the question of whether she's a hermaphrodite gets raised, complicating this psychosexual scenario considerably.)

A characteristic note is already struck in *Kiss* (1957), Masumura's first feature, when the young hero and heroine – a bakery delivery boy and an artist's model – meet while visiting their respective fathers in prison; his father is serving a term for an 'election day violation', hers for stealing money to pay her mother's hospital bills. Not wanting her mother to know that her husband's in jail, the model is seriously considering prostitution to raise the money for her father's bail so that he can go visit his wife in the hospital.

Twisted yet subtle moral decisions of this kind become even more prominent in the extraordinary *Red Angel* – one of Masumura's best-known films in the West, although it apparently hasn't yet enjoyed much of a reputation in Japan. The heroine (Wakao), a war nurse who's been raped, subsequently exchanges her sexual services for a pint of blood that might save the life of her rapist; ostensibly she doesn't want him to die because he might think she's taking revenge. And the heroine in *A False Student*, again played by Wakao, has comparable scruples when it comes to dealing with first the sanity and then the madness of the title imposter.

A few more generalisations. Many of Masumura's films fall into a few overlapping categories. To provide a non-exhaustive list, these include: anti-capitalist films (*Giants and Toys*, *Overflow* [*Hanran*, 1959], *Inflammation* [*Tadare*, 1962]), anti-war films (*Yakuza Soldier*, *Nakano Spy School*, *Red Angel*, *A Woman's Life* [*Onna no issho*, 1962], *Seisaku's Wife* [*Seisaku no tsuma*, 1965]), kinky sex films (*Manji*, *Red Angel*, *Love for an Idiot*, *Sex Check*, *Blind Beast*, *Thousand Cranes*, *The Tortures of Hell*), films about strong women (*The Blue Sky Maiden* [*Aozora musume*, 1957], *A Wife Confesses* [*Tsuma wa kokuhaku suru*, 1961], *Manji*, *Tattoo*, *Love for an Idiot*, *Seishu Hanaoka's Wife* [*Seishu no tsuma*, 1967], *Electric Jellyfish* [*Denki kurage*, 1970], *Numbing Jellyfish* [*Shibire kurage*, 1970], *Lullaby of the Earth*), yakuza films (*Afraid to Die*, *Ode to the Yakuza*, *Numbing Jellyfish*, *Turf Wars* aka *Akumyo* [*Nawabari arashi*, 1974]), and youth films (*Kiss*, *The Blue Sky Maiden*, *A False Student*, *Play* [*Asobi*, 1971]).

With some notable exceptions (*Seishu Hanaoka's Wife*, *Tattoo*, *Lullaby of the Earth*, *Double Suicide in Sonezaki*, the war films), Masumura's best films are those with contemporary settings. His least interesting films, in my experience, are generally his crime/yakuza pictures, the absolute worst being *The Tortures of Hell* (ironically the only one available commercially in the US with English subtitles, at least on video, while I was writing this article), though *Japanese Cinema: The Essential Handbook*, with its own characteristic cult and genre interests, treats it respectfully as an entry in the *Hanzo the Blade* series.[16]

A response in part to the post-war and post-Occupation meekness of Japan, Masumura's cinema of crazy individualists straddles a contradiction that might even be said to be built into the Japanese language itself. Having noticed that Masumura's first feature, *Kuchizuke*, was translated variously as *Kiss* and *Kisses*, I asked a Japanese friend which was accurate. She replied there was no way of knowing because distinctions between singular and plural don't exist in Japanese. Apart from radically revising my sense of Japanese film titles – so that, for instance, *We Were Born, But . . .* , *Tokyo Stories* and *We Live in Fear* are just as valid as the titles we know for *I Was Born, But . . .* (1932), *Tokyo Story* (1953) and *I Live in Fear* (1955) – this made me realise that the very notion of individuality in Japanese is linguistically somewhat abstract.

This is no doubt a strength as well as a limitation; Americans who complain that they can't find characters 'to identify with' in some movies – which in my experience Japanese viewers are less likely to worry about – may be suffering from an excess of 'I'. It also points to a complex kind of literary ambiguity that informs the language as a whole. *A False Student* – one of Masumura's best early films, about radical college students who kidnap a naive would-be student with a fake ID, believing him to be a spy – provides a fascinating cross-reference with Godard's *La Chinoise* (1967), a somewhat more sympathetic (if still ambivalent) look at Maoist students seven years later. And the fake student of the title – who eventually winds up in an insane asylum, raving in a manner that parodies Marxist ideologues and recalls Fuller's *Shock Corridor* – is a good example of the characteristically crazy Masumura protagonist. Yet the moment one realises the title could also be *False Students* or *The False Students*, the critique of the Marxists becomes extended a bit further, implicating them more directly.

A promoter of individuality and freedom who paradoxically wound up associating these values with insanity, Masumura was no less contradictory insofar as he was himself the quintessential company man at Daiei. To understand what he was rebelling against, it helps if one regards Ray's *Bigger Than Life* as the closest thing in Hollywood to a Masumura movie, viewing dementia as the alternative to conformity. But it also helps if one considers some of the traits Masumura was challenging in a specifically Japanese context, such as respect for fathers – also undermined in *Bigger Than Life*, to be sure, but not in the same fashion. Most of *The Blue Sky Maiden*, his second feature, resembles one of Sirk's depictions of spoiled, wealthy teenagers – the step-siblings encountered by the young title heroine (Wakao) when she moves from country to city to search out her real mother – in terms of 50s' styling, pastel colours and lighting, behaviour, direction of actors and camera placement. But what gives it a specific Japanese inflection, and a highly transgressive one, is the climax in which Wakao denounces her father in his sickbed and gets him to agree that he's to blame for all the family's troubles. Even more shocking is the rage of the heroine in *Numbing Jellyfish*, a bar hostess (Atsumi Mari) sleeping her way up the corporate ladder, against her alcoholic and philandering father, when she nearly kicks him to death for getting her into trouble with yakuzas.

For that matter, whether *Kuchizuke* translates as *Kiss* or *Kisses*, it was a somewhat provocative title in Japanese at the time (1957) considering that kisses couldn't be shown in Japanese cinema until after World War II (when American Occupation censors actively encouraged them). An excitingly photographed teenage love story that evokes Nicholas Ray in spite of its relative sanity, *Kiss* is more characteristic of Masumura's style to viewers who speak Japanese because of the unusual speed and intonation of the dialogue delivery – though it may have partly been the audience's difficulty in getting accustomed to this manner that accounted for the film's box office failure. Sato's writing about the film faintly suggests that it was the implied content of this manner that was the problem: the film was ignored by critics when it came out because of its presumed similarity to other youth films of the period, and only later did it become apparent that Masumura was rejecting many of the trappings of the genre:

> His hero was neither mild-mannered, romantic, nor especially good-looking, but rather
> audacious and perpetually angry. He was not the first Japanese version of the angry young

man – rich, profligate youths had to some extent raised hell before him – but he was the most significant because he was a poor boy from the masses. In contrast to previous youthful heroes, he gives vent to his frustrations through exaggerated actions rather than through languishing melancholically, for sympathy is the last thing he wants. Thus, there are no atmospheric props or sentimental effects in *Kisses*, and the young hero is going to fulfill his thwarted needs through action alone.[17]

The implications of the manner itself, however, shouldn't be overlooked. According to Yoshio Shirasaka in an interview,[18] Masumura's goal in adapting the novel that was the source for *The Blue Sky Maiden* was to desentimentalise the material. In carrying out this work, Shirasaka – who'd already been working on the script for some time before he met Masumura – had calculated from the dialogue that the film would run about 100 minutes, but once he discovered that Masumura's sped-up style of delivery would reduce this by half an hour, he added some scenes.

Bearing such factors in mind, one should consider to what degree my hypothesis of synchronicity regarding Masumura's films of the 50s and 60s and certain American films of the 50s may be a *trompe l'œil* predicated on my ignorance of certain details regarding language and Japanese social history. Is it possible that my hypothesis reflects the disagreeable American inclination of finding certain traits in other cultures acceptable as well as interesting only when they resemble American traits?

To ward off this potential danger, let me consider a few other ways in which the synchronicity I'm interested in is approximate at best, and therefore potentially misleading. Masumura's third feature, *Warm Current* (*Danryu*, 1957), a remake of a 1939 feature partially set in a hospital, is more generally located in a 'Sirkian' upper-class milieu that resembles that of *The Blue Sky Maiden*. But here the Western elements of that milieu, often viewed in the previous film as a kind of modernist chic (e.g., the stepbrother of the heroine playing Dixieland), more often register as a kind of decadence, whether this happens to be a book of Chagall reproductions or an androgynous French musical number seen on TV. (Another relatively non-Sirkian factor is a line of dialogue in the film, not found in the 1939 version, that became famous in Japan: 'I'll wait for you whether you make me a mistress or a concubine.') It's possible, of course, that I'm misreading the cultural connotations of Western artefacts in both films, but my larger point is that upper-class settings which have a double-edged aspect in both Sirk and Masumura – attractive yet sinister – are obviously not double-edged in the same fashion relative to Japanese attitudes towards the West.

Giants and Toys, the most Tashlin-like of the Masumura features I've seen, differs from Tashlin in the sheer and deliberate ugliness of the garish colour cinematography as well as in the misanthropic treatment of many of the characters, the latter of which seems even more characteristic of Masumura. Though the charge of vulgarity frequently made against Tashlin by his detractors could certainly be lodged against *Giants and Toys* – a film that, like Tashlin's own major film about advertising one year earlier, *Will Success Spoil Rock Hunter?*, was a commercial flop (and according to Masumura, the only one among his early features, apart from *Kiss*) – the film's focus on a poor girl with spectacularly bad teeth being made the mascot of one candy company, then a media sensation thanks to the efforts of a photographer for a porn magazine, aims for a kind of unpleasantness and negativity that would have been minimised by Tashlin, who tended to enjoy many of the cultural and capitalist excesses he satirised. For that matter, one might counter that the 'Tashlinesque' qualities of a mediocre and anachronistic farce in colour and CinemaScope set during the Edo period, *Life of a Don Juan* (*Koshoku ichidai onna*, 1961) – or those of a somewhat better contemporary comedy in colour and CinemaScope, *A Lady Pickpocket* (*Ashi ni sawatta onna*), made the previous year – could just as easily be described as the Japanese equivalent of Bob Hope comedies made during the same era; the Tashlin-like uses of bright colours in the latter, for instance, seem relatively unexceptional.

Even more to the point, the feature I would identify as Masumura's supreme master-piece – an adroit black and white CinemaScope melodrama, *A Wife Confesses* – has no significant parallels that I can discern in the work of Ray, Fuller, Sirk or Tashlin. In fact, confirming the more conventional wisdom that Masumura's most important affinities were to contemporary European film-makers, the film shows the direct influence of Alain Resnais' *Hiroshima, mon amour* (1959) in its startling uses of match cuts to introduce its successive flashbacks. A carefully structured and beautifully directed existential thriller, it centres on the murder trial of a twenty-eight-year-old woman (Wakao) whose husband, an abusive, middle-aged college professor, fell to his death after a mountain-climbing mishap led her to cut the rope binding the two of them together. Complicating her split-second decision – the focus of the entire film – is the fact that the same rope also attached her at the other end to a young, attractive salesman with whom her husband had busi-ness ties and whom she was in love with, and if she failed to cut either man loose, all three would have most likely fallen to their deaths. A powerful metaphor for Japanese inter-dependence, this rope connecting the members of a romantic triangle is also tied, one might say, to Masumura's major theme: the tragedy as well as the necessity of individual choice and desire in a highly interactive society.

Notes

1. After this article was completed in 2001, a company called Fantoma in the US released *Blind Beast*, *Giants and Toys*, *Afraid to Die*, *Manji*, *The Black Test Car* (1962) and *Red Angel* on DVD.
2. www.sensesofcinema.com.
3. Shigehiko Hasumi, *Yasujiro Ozu* (Paris: Editions de l'étoile/*Cahiers du cinéma*, 1998).
4. Quoted in Chuck Stephens, 'Another Green World', *Film Comment*, September–October 2001, p. 68.
5. Sadao Yamane, *Masumura Yasuzo: Ishi to shite no erosu* [*Yasuzo Masumura: Eros as Will*] (Tokyo: Chikuma Shobo, 1992).
6. Hiroaki Fujii (ed.), *Eiga kantoku Masumura Yasuzo no sekai* [*The World of Yasuzo Masumura, Film Director*] (Tokyo: Waizu Shuppan, 1999).
7. For assistance in this work, I'm especially grateful to Mona Nagai, Edith Kramer, Jason Sanders and Nancy Goldman.
8. An essay by Masumura, 'Kon Ichikawa's Method' – translated into English by Michael Raine and included in James Quandt (ed.), *Kon Ichikawa* (Toronto: Cinematheque Ontario, 2001),

pp. 95–103 – shows a great deal of ambivalence towards his mentor. When Masumura notes at one point that 'the assistant director in charge of [the] historically inaccurate costumes' prepared for *Nihonbashi* 'protested strongly but was completely ignored', one wonders if he was writing about himself.

9. Nagisa Oshima, *Cinema, Censorship, and the State: The Writings of Nagisa Oshima* (Cambridge: MIT Press, 1992), p. 30.

10. Translated into English by Chika Kinoshita from Fujii (ed.), *Eiga kantoku Masumura Yasuzo no sekai*.

11. Ibid.

12. Conversation with Tadao Sato at Capitol Tokyu Hotel, Tokyo, 11 December 1999. A previous conversation in Tokyo with Donald Richie at the Japan Foundation (29 November 1999) was also of great assistance, and James Quandt – director of the Cinematheque Ontario and a staunch Masumura supporter – has facilitated my work in numerous ways. Michael Raine also assisted me with advice deriving from his own research into Masumura.

13. Fujii (ed.), *Eiga kantoku Masumura Yasuzo no sekai*.

14. Oshima, *Cinema, Censorship, and the State*, p. 208.

15. Mark Peranson, *Now*, 12 February 1998.

16. Thomas Weisser and Yukio Mihara Weisser, *Japanese Cinema: The Essential Handbook (Featuring Japanese Cult Cinema since 1955)* (Miami: Vital Books, 1998), p. 139.

17. Tadao Sato, *Currents in Japanese Cinema* (Tokyo: Kodansha International, 1987), pp. 210–11.

18. Fujii (ed.), *Eiga kantoku Masumura Yasuzo no sekai*.

PART TWO – DIALOGUE ON HOWARD HAWKS AND YASUZO MASUMURA
(*SHIGEHIKO HASUMI AND JONATHAN ROSENBAUM*: 1999)

Tokyo, 3 December 1999

JONATHAN ROSENBAUM: When did you first write about Howard Hawks?

SHIGEHIKO HASUMI: In 1977, just after he died. At that time, Hawks was so underestimated in Japan that no film magazine wanted an article on him. I published it in a literary magazine.

JR: And is there a particular period in his career that you prefer?

SH: Yes, from *Bringing up Baby* (1938) to *His Girl Friday* (1940). Of course, his two films noirs with Lauren Bacall and Humphrey Bogart, *To Have and Have Not* (1944) and *The Big Sleep* (1946), impress me deeply. But the comedies in this period seem to me the highest accomplishment of his *mise en scène*. For me, Hawks is essentially a film-maker of comedy. In that sense, I could say also that my preference goes to the period between *Twentieth Century* (1934) and *Monkey Business* (1952). And this is a very peculiar point of view, but I also like very much his last three Westerns with John Wayne – *Rio Bravo* (1959), *El Dorado* (1967) and *Rio Lobo* (1970).

JR: It may be more common for Japanese directors such as Ozu to remake their own films, but I believe Hawks is the only one who's done it twice!

SH: We all know that *His Girl Friday* was a remake of *The Front Page* (1931). But, in this case, the copy is much more original than the model!

JR: What were the first Hawks films you saw?

SH: *Sergeant York* (1941) and *Red River* (1948), around the same time, when I was a schoolboy. But I couldn't fit them into a proper context because Japanese audiences weren't able to see the American films produced between 1939 and 1945. And just after the war, it was not those films from the major studios that were selected by the US army during the Occupation of Japan. John Ford's *Fort Apache* (1948), for instance, was prohibited even after the war because it shows the defeat of the American army. *Air Force* (1943) had no chance to be released in Japan because of the presence of some Japanese soldiers. And for some reason *Ball of Fire* (1942) wasn't shown either until after Hawks' own remake, *A Song is Born* (1948). I discovered those films in Paris during my first stay in France from 1962 to 1965.

JR: For me, the most Japanese trait to be found in Hawks is a certain male stoicism, particularly in relation to a group ethic. But then there's also the handling of violence in *Rio*

Bravo – where the violence seems to happen very quickly and is over very quickly – which also strikes me as being rather Japanese.

SH: *Rio Bravo* was an enormous hit in Japan. But, unfortunately, at that time, there was no adequate critical language to appreciate this film, which was judged too commercial. It's strange, because *Only Angels Have Wings* (1939) – the last Hawks film shown in Japan before the war – was highly appreciated by Japanese critics and film-makers.

JR: Is it true that you once said that what you liked most about Japanese cinema was that it was the national cinema that most resembled American cinema?

SH: Yes, Japanese cinema before the 70s was essentially the cinema of major studios, like American cinema. Even Mizoguchi, Ozu and Mikio Naruse were only contract directors. They are closer to American film-makers because they've seen more American films. Not only film-makers, but also cinematographers have learned their skills watching a lot of Hollywood movies. When I interviewed Yuharu Atsuta, Ozu's cinematographer, I was really surprised that, at the age of eighty, he named some of the most eminent American cinematographers like Charles Rosher, Lee Garmes, William Daniels, George Barnes, Gregg Toland . . . as if they were all his old friends.

JR: It seems like what Japanese cinema and American cinema have most in common are the genres and the remakes. And also the series, but in that case the Japanese cinema seems more developed.

SH: Actually, there were so many non-credited remakes of American films. For example, Naruse's *Tsuruhachi tsurujiro* (1938) was an unacknowledged remake of Wesley Ruggles' *Bolero* (1934). This is a typical example of the remake that is much more interesting than the original. Masahiro Makino, during the war period, adapted the detective story of *The Thin Man* series starring William Powell and Myrna Loy for the Edo period in *Kino kieta otoko* (*The Man Who Came Yesterday*, 1940) and *Matteita otoko* (*The Man I Was Waiting For*, 1942). They were both big hits. He also tried to do a remake of Griffith's *Orphans of the Storm* (*Ahen senso* [*The Opium War*], 1943]. He agreed to make this film about the opium wars to satisfy the militarists, but in fact he did a sort of homage to Griffith. The Japanese audience couldn't see this side of the film, but they were excited by the victory of the Chinese people against the English occupation of China. So it's a complicated situation.

JR: In your book on Ozu, you make a very convincing case that he was largely formed by his exposure to Hollywood movies. How aware do you think Masumura might have been of directors such as Nicholas Ray and Samuel Fuller?

SH: Japanese film-makers after the war were less interested in American movies. On the one hand, the impact of Italian neo-realism was really strong. On the other hand, Japanese intellectuals and artists had a somewhat anti-American tendency, and by contrast they idealised European values. Masumura was one of these European-oriented intel-lectual-artists. He wrote a paper on René Clément's *Au-delà des Grilles* (1949) when applying to be a foreign student at the Centro Sperimentale in Rome in 1952, where he stayed three years. I don't think Masumura was interested in Hollywood film-makers of the 50s. I have no idea what kind of films he saw in Italy, but before he left Japan, of Ray's works, only *Knock on Any Door* (1949) and *Flying Leathernecks* (1951) had been shown. And Fuller films like *The Steel Helmet* (1951) or *Fixed Bayonets* (1951) had such limited exposure in Japan at the time, basically in very cheap cinemas, that I doubt Masumura would have seen them.

JR: On the other hand, when I saw *A Wife Confesses*, I was convinced Masumura must have been influenced by Resnais. His match cut from a bleeding hand, moving suddenly from the past to the present, was only a couple of years after *Hiroshima, mon amour*.

SH: Yes, that's certain. *Hiroshima, mon amour* was co-produced by Masaichi Nagata, Pres-ident of Daiei Studio, to whom Masumura was under contract. And Hiroaki Fujii, director of production on all Masumura's films, had been involved in the co-production of Resnais' film.

JR: I was also struck by how close *The Blue Sky Maiden* was to Sirk in criticising spoiled, wealthy teenagers. On the other hand, when the heroine tells her father at the end of that film that he's wrong and he agrees that he's wrong, this is clearly much more of a provo-cation in Japan than anything Sirk was doing in relation to America. But maybe the fact that Masumura wrote film criticism and theorised his own positions at the time also made him more visible as a particular force than Ray, Fuller, Tashlin and Sirk would have been in the US.

SH: Your idea of global synchronicity in cinema interests me a lot. In this regard, some of Masumura's films – especially those criticising capitalism and political power, such as *Overflow*, *Black Test Car* and *Black Super Express* – remind me of a certain aspect of Robert Rossen's *Body and Soul* (1947) and *All the King's Men* (1949). In my opinion, Abraham Polonsky's *Force of Evil* (1948) also has something similar to Masumura's attitude toward social problems. Needless to say, he never saw those films but, as you suggest, the coin-cidence – in theme, in style and in atmosphere – is flagrant. I have to add that, of the Italian films he had a chance to see during his stay in Rome, Visconti's *Ossessione* (1943) was the one he admired the most, as he once pointed out in an interview.[1] It seems inter-esting that his admiration didn't extend to either Roberto Rossellini or Vittorio De Sica, but to this rather melodramatic and American-derived crime story taken up by Visconti. Couldn't we establish a certain parallel between the situation of the wife in *A Wife Con-fesses* – murdering out of necessity her old husband, whom she hated – and James Cain's original story, which *Ossessione* was based on (and, of course, which was later adapted in Hollywood by Tay Garnett), *The Postman Always Rings Twice*?

JR: Yes, you're right. But I'm struck by the generational difference between our reference points: all of mine are in the 50s and yours are in the 40s.

SH: I saw Masumura's first films when they came out, as a high-school student, and I was very surprised by the neutral tone of his *mise en scène*. That was not *new* for me, but it was entirely *different.* You have to understand that for the Japanese film industry at the time, the idea of the good film was Carol Reed's *The Third Man* (1949). That was the model for editing and overall visual effect; all the young Japanese film-makers tried to imitate that, consciously or not ...

JR: I think that would have been the model in the US then as well. Or at least *a* model.

SH: ... and Masumura was entirely free from that influence, using few psychological close-ups. There were no lyrical long shots of landscapes either, which was really exceptional for a Japanese film-maker.

JR: I wonder if the main difference he represented was a kind of *bricolage* – starting with genres and styles that already existed in the Japanese cinema and then boring from within, deconstructing the standard positions and clichés. *Kisses* and *The Blue Sky Maiden*, for instance, were attempts to turn the sun-worshipper films inside out. This wasn't so different in a way from what Ray, Fuller, etc. were doing, although in that period no one in the US recognised their work as radical. With a few exceptions, recognition of what they were doing initially came from France – and I have to admit that I discovered them, and Masumura as well, in the pages of *Cahiers du cinéma*. Was it the same for you and Hawks?

SH: No, not at all. In Japan, just before the war, for example, Mizoguchi was very fond of *Only Angels Have Wings*. And in an interview Ozu said (I'm quoting from memory), 'The film is very good – actually too well done; in the final analysis I don't like it – but I really appreciate the quality of the *mise en scène*.' In my house – I don't know whom they belonged to – there were a lot of collections of movie magazines before the war. I used to read them when I was a high-school student. So I already knew that Hawks was a name to conjure with. And since I'd just seen *Sergeant York*, I couldn't understand why Ozu and Mizoguchi were fond of Hawks, because *Only Angels Have Wings* was not shown in Japan after the war. So it took me ten years to discover Hawks. When I saw *Rio Bravo* for the first time in Japan, I didn't think it was a masterpiece, but I could understand why this kind of *mise en scène* could be appreciated in Japan, even before the war. And maybe I was an exception, but I hated *High Noon* (1952) in that era, and I was very grateful to discover that Hawks felt the same way about it.

JR: Yes. But of course one might say that part of Hawks' hatred had an unacknowledged political aspect. Because *High Noon* was a film about the blacklist, just as *On the Waterfront* (1954) was.

SH: In that political context in Hollywood, the only film I adored was *Johnny Guitar* (1954). For me in that era, the problem was to know how one could be fond of both Hawks and Ray. This question was the point of departure for my career as a film critic. Afterward, I formulated that in a different way, by saying that we like both Godard and Masahiro Makino.

JR: It's interesting how Hawks always seemed to perceive himself as apolitical – which eventually caused a rift with *Cahiers du cinéma* in the 70s, when he told them he was planning a film about the war in Vietnam. Yet if one were to argue that he was a conservative director, *Sergeant York* would have to serve as a prime piece of evidence. By contrast, Masumura must have upset both the right and the left in the 60s by not being politically correct. As a critique of student radicals, *The False Student* makes a fascinating parallel with *La Chinoise* – even though Godard's film was made seven years later and is somewhat more sympathetic to the radical students. And, in fact, my recent discovery that there's no distinction between singular and plural in Japanese opens up a whole new kind of literary irony to me – because the title of that film could also be *False Students*, referring not just to the kid with the fake student ID but to the student radicals in the film as well. This film was made the same year that Oshima attacked Masumura in print, only two years after praising him. Did he remain opposed to Masumura after that?

SH: Yes, I believe he would feel the same way even now. The real point Oshima was making when he criticised Masumura was to view him as a modernist in the Western sense of that term. I don't think that's true, but that's what Oshima thought. For Oshima, Masumura was too distant and sometimes non-engaged when he criticised the Japanese political and cultural situation. And Oshima found this kind of modernism questionable because, after the Second World War, Japanese culture couldn't be explained from such a viewpoint.

JR: It's curious that the two books on Masumura in Japanese have both appeared in the 90s – Sadao Yamane's *Eros as Will* a few years ago and the collection of Masumura's writings and various interviews about him earlier this year. Why did it take so long?

SH: It indicates precisely the poverty of film criticism in Japan. Until the 80s, there was no serious study of contemporary Japanese film-makers. It was our generation – Sadao Yamane, Koichi Yamada and me – who began to write about them. The Japanese audience has by now completely forgotten the name of Yasuzo Masumura after the collapse of Daiei, in spite of our efforts. He was already dead when Yamane wrote his book. For us it's difficult to talk about him because it's difficult to choose a single film. For Kurosawa, regardless of whether you like the film or not, you can always cite *The Seven Samurai* (1954). It's easy. But with Masumura, there's no representative film.

JR: I guess not. But at least there are a few loose categories – the anti-military films like *Yakuza Soldier*, *Nakano Spy School* and *Red Angel*, or the anti-capitalist films like *Giants and Toys*, *Overflow* and *Inflammation*.

SH: I understand your point of view. I like those films and I consider Masumura's *mise en scène* in *Red Angel* extremely radical. But at that time, this film was considered simply like a porno movie. *Yakuza Soldier*, like *Nakano Spy School*, was nothing but an episode in a series. Masumura's most famous film for Japanese people might have been *Seishu Hanaoka's Wife*, but this was only because of the best-selling novel the film was based on. People consumed each of Masumura's films as simply another Daiei production. It was only in 1969 that Yamane and Yamada, both founding members of new quarterly magazines *Cinema 69* and *Film Art*, tried to treat Masumura and Seijun Suzuki seriously for the first time as auteurs. We had the first interviews with them in those magazines. But in 1969, Nikkatsu fired Suzuki and in 1971 Daiei collapsed. During the 70s, they were not as productive as they had been in the 60s. I am very pleased that thanks to the two books on Masumura that were recently published, the younger generation in the 90s has begun to discover his works.

JR: Do you think there's any parallel between Masumura and Suzuki in relation to the studio system?

SH: Yes and no. As you said, both of them tried to deconstruct the genres which already existed in Japanese cinema. In that sense, there is a certain parallel between them. But Suzuki had already been known since the 60s as a cult film-maker. Masumura was not at all a cult film-maker. Masumura's Western experience places his work in a completely different category. Suzuki is appreciated in the West, but essentially he's a traditional Japanese man who regards Western people as barbarians, in the traditional Japanese meaning of that term – you remember the prosaic title of John Huston's film, *The Barbarian and the Geisha* (1958). ... But for Masumura, there's a sort of universality: of course there's a difference, but finally human beings are the same.

JR: It's interesting how, in spite of all his synchronicity with the work of Fuller, Sirk, Ray and Tashlin, Masumura's Western influences appear to be strictly European. I've already mentioned Resnais as one example, and the last shot of *Overflow* is pure Antonioni, just like the shots of the factory in *Love for an Idiot*.

SH: Or the way characters speak in Masumura's films. Especially during his first period, all of them speak with no intonation. And in that regard, there's something similar to Antonioni's films. Perhaps one parallel between Masumura and Hawks is the refusal of a certain dramatic sentimentality. Maybe you could say that sentiment isn't important in their films.

JR: There are certainly social mechanisms one finds in the films of both that aim to avoid sentimentality, such as in *Only Angels Have Wings* and *Yakuza Soldier*. But one might also say that Masumura is more of a dystopian and Hawks is more of a utopian.

SH: Yes, Masumura is a pessimist. He should have considered himself a stranger in his homeland, just like certain Ray heroes, because for him Japanese society wasn't suffi-

ciently modernised, especially on the level of individual consciousness. His male characters accept the falsely modernised system in Japan – sometimes they accept it with absurd
fidelity, as in the case of *Nakano Spy School*. But his female characters refuse instinctively
to be integrated into it, as we see in the solitary violence of the behaviour of the actress
Ayako Wakao in such a major work as *A Wife Confesses*. . . .

JR: The tragic ending of that film is for me the epitome of Masumura's dystopian ten-
dencies. By contrast, one of the most utopian Hawks films for me is *The Big Sky* (1952).
I loved that film as a teenager.

SH: That's right – a beautiful film. Kirk Douglas was not a Hawksian hero, in my opinion, but I very much liked his partner, Dewey Martin.

JR: Maybe that's because Douglas is too much of an individualist; you can't see him as a
member of any group. The collective spirit is so fundamental to Hawks – even in a film
like *His Girl Friday*.

SH: Yes, even when it means sharing the same problem with one's enemies. For example,
the old journalists: they're awful, but they're also some kind of community. In *Red River*,
when they start the cattle drive, Hawks shows everyone in a separate full shot. And in *Air
Force*, when the plane is about to leave the airport for the first time, Hawks shows us
everyone, without singling out the captain or the sergeant. There's no hierarchy.

JR: That's true, but you couldn't say that of *Rio Bravo*. You wouldn't find a cut there of
that kind between Pedro Gonzalez-Gonzalez and Wayne. In fact, even in *Red River* . . .
is Wayne included in that montage of faces?

SH: No, he's separate.

JR: So it's like a king and his subjects, and it's the subjects who are equals. Yet what I find
fascinating is that, even when Hawks is at his most conservative, you might say that aesthetically he's still a socialist. And there's a comparable kind of paradox in Masumura:
even though he favours individuality, he can't help but view it as a kind of hell and tor-
ment. And, paradoxically, Masumura himself is the quintessential company man whose
career started coming apart only after the collapse of the Daiei studio in 1971. In fact,
what I find difficult in *Rio Lobo* is the loss of camaraderie; there's the kind of bitterness
one might associate with *King Lear* that's reflected in the violence. And I was reminded
of that feeling in Masumura's *Ode to the Yakuza* – a kind of political and sexual frustration
reflected in the rage of the escalating violence. Yet even though the brother–sister incest
in that film evokes *Scarface*, I can't imagine any version of *Scarface* that ends with Tony
Camonte having himself killed so that his sister can get married. That kind of abnegation
of self, that sacrificial gesture, becomes a typical Japanese ending.

SH: You're right, the ending of *Ode to the Yakuza* seems to be typically Japanese. But, according to Hiroaki Fujii, director of production for Masumura's films and a real friend of his who established an annotated filmography, it was chief executives of Daiei, disliking this brother–sister incest situation, who imposed the sentimental ending. If Masumura had had complete liberty, the ending of this film would be different. Since we're on the subject, I have to confess that I am not so crazy about *Scarface*. It's true that, compared to the other gangster films of that period by Mervyn LeRoy, Roy Del Ruth or even William Wellman, *Scarface* is absolutely modern, as Henri Langlois described Hawks' works in general. But I feel upset by the effect of the images in some sequences, with too many shadows. And I can't deny my impression that Camonte's will to power and its tragic failure have something anti-Hawksian about them. For the same reason, I don't like Wayne's character in *Red River* very much. His character is entirely different in *Rio Bravo*. For instance, in the sequence where Dean Martin, Walter Brennan and Ricky Nelson sing songs in the Sheriff's office, Wayne watching them with a smile and a coffee cup in his hand is not in a king's position. He is excluded from the scene and shown only twice at the beginning and the end. I think there is something female in his position; he is looking at them as if he was their mother. . . .

JR: Is Hawks still a specialised taste in Japan, or has he become more popular than that?

SH: I could say in any case that there is no Hawksian period in the viewing history of Japan. He is appreciated, but not regarded as a big figure or important film-maker. I hope the Hawks retrospective that the National Film Centre in Tokyo is planning to hold next year will change the situation.

Note
1. Yasuzo Masumura interviewed by Toru Ogawa, *Eiga geijutsu (Cinema Art)* no. 326, 1978.

PART THREE – INVERSION/EXCHANGE/REPETITION: THE COMEDY OF HOWARD HAWKS (*SHIGEHIKO HASUMI*: 2000)

Note: At the Hawks retrospective that the National Film Centre in Tokyo ran in 2000, Hasumi presented this paper as part of a symposium he organised.

Introduction

Over a directing career that spanned more than four decades, Howard Hawks tried his hand at almost every Hollywood genre other than sentimental melodrama. With few exceptions, such as the musical *Gentlemen Prefer Blondes* (1953), he created masterpieces in each genre, including the gangster film *Scarface*, the aviation movie *Only Angels Have Wings*, the film noir *The Big Sleep*, the Western *Red River* and the adventure film *Hatari!* (1962). *Air Force* is unquestionably one of the greatest war films featuring airplanes, and *His Girl Friday* is of course a monumental comedy. In terms of quality, it is thus difficult to prove that Hawks' comedies are superior to his work in other genres. For example, it would be impossible to say which is better, the comedy *Ball of Fire* or *To Have and Have Not*. So, instead of quality, let's take a look at quantity.

From the silent *Air Circus* (1928) through *Air Force*, filmed during World War II, Hawks directed many aviation films. Hawks himself was a pilot, and for a while pilots had a privileged status as the heroes of his films. After the end of the war, however, those aviation films disappeared from his oeuvre, and the settings for his adventure films shifted from the sky to the Wild West. *The Outlaw* (1943) – credited to Howard Hughes but mainly directed by Hawks – set the framework for his Westerns, and his creative peak was reached with *Rio Bravo*. He closed out his career with *Rio Lobo*. Because of the many Westerns he made with John Wayne, Hawks even came to be regarded, mistakenly, as a specialist of the genre.

Thus, in terms of sheer quantity, Hawks' comedies do not outnumber his aviation and Western films among the more than forty works of his career. However, one fact remains undeniable: although Hawks' comedies predominate in neither quality nor quantity, the director did work in that genre throughout his entire career, including before, during and after World War II. In that sense, comedy was the dominant form for him. From his early, silent *Fig Leaves* (1926) to his late *Man's Favorite Sport?* (1964), Hawks directed comedies of a consistently high quality. Today, I would like to look at some characteristics of Hawks' comedies as he shaped them throughout his career. The French film director Eric Rohmer said that you don't understand film if you don't understand Hawks.[1] My position is that you don't understand Hawks if you don't understand his comedies.

1. The trap of similarity

Hawks himself said that adventures and comedies are essentially the same. The only difference, he said, is that the danger depicted in adventures is replaced by embarrassment in comedies.[2] This comment suggests that he regarded the genre of a film as being of only secondary importance. Or it may be that he thought of all of his films as forming a single oeuvre that transcended the individual works.

Hawks' films do contain significant similarities that extend throughout his career and into every genre in which he worked. For example, the last scenes of *Only Angels Have Wings* and *El Dorado* depict nearly identical situations. In *Only Angels Have Wings* the two wounded pilots try to fly their airplanes, each with one arm in a sling. In *El Dorado*, the two wounded sheriffs have to maintain peace in the town while walking on crutches. The viewer may wonder whether pilots who need help putting on their coats would be able to hold onto the plane's joystick, but that doesn't really matter. The handicap of their injuries increases their sense of mission and fills the final scene with a suitable tension. In contrast, the two limping sheriffs in the last scene of *El Dorado* have already defeated their enemies, and that carefree atmosphere is what brings on the laughter.

It's hard not to laugh at the picture of those movie stars limping along on crutches. No other director would dare to put Wayne and Robert Mitchum in such roles. But the similarity between the final scenes of these two films, separated by three decades, is not a coincidence. In fact, it's a reminder of Hawks' repetition of the theme of physical impairment. Beginning with Robert Armstrong's injured finger in *A Girl in Every Port* (1928), Hawks' heroes are repeatedly made to suffer handicaps. In *Tiger Shark* (1932), the ship captain (Edward G. Robinson), who courts a beautiful woman, has an iron hook in place of his hand that was chewed off by a shark. In *Today We Live* (1933), Robert Young climbs onto a torpedo boat even though he is unable to see. Even Cary Grant's thick glasses in *Bringing up Baby* and *Monkey Business* continue this theme of physical impairment. Yet another example is the drunkenness of Dean Martin and Mitchum in (respectively) *Rio Bravo* and *El Dorado*. Even a Western with Wayne playing a paraplegic sheriff is not surprising for a film by Hawks. Thus the last scenes of *Only Angels Have Wings* and *El Dorado* are just another example of the Hawksian repetition of the theme of male weakness.

It is typical of Hawks for two people to share the same weakness. In fact, *Only Angels Have Wings* and *El Dorado* are so similar in this regard that the latter almost seems to have been copied from the former. In *Only Angels Have Wings* Cary Grant is injured by a gun accidentally fired by his girlfriend (Jean Arthur), and soon his colleague (Allyn Joslyn) also becomes unable to use one arm. Once again the theme of repetition through imitation appears, only to be repeated thirty years later. Hawks implements the logic of this repetition as an almost mechanical reversal, the two men with injured arms in the earlier film replaced by two men with injured legs in the later film. The concept is essentially formalist in the sense that the situation remains the same despite the exchange of legs for arms.

But in this exchange of injured limbs, *El Dorado* is connected not only to *Only Angels Have Wings*. There is also a close similarity to *Gentlemen Prefer Blondes*, with the exchange extending across the gender boundary. Instead of the two male sheriffs supported by crutches, we see two dancers (Jane Russell and Marilyn Monroe) deftly wielding their canes. The poster for the nightclub where they're performing shows a photograph of the two of them in tights with canes in their hands. The crutches and canes are similar in that both are made from long, thin pieces of wood, but their function is clearly reversed for the men and the women. For the men in *El Dorado*, the crutches are a symbol of their impairment, while for the women in *Gentlemen Prefer Blondes* the canes are a sign of physical freedom. Male weakness is converted into female strength. Hawks' women are able to respond much more appropriately than men to the repetition of similar elements. Such repeated similarities only confuse men. For example, in *Come and Get It* (1936), Edward Arnold is confused by the similarity between a mother and daughter. Both are played by Frances Farmer. When he hears the young woman singing a song that his old girlfriend used to sing, he yells at her to stop. The daughter looks so much like her mother that he is unable to get his mind off her, and it puts his marriage in danger. Even a successful businessman is unable to avoid the Hawksian trap of similarity.

Almost the identical situation is portrayed with a comical touch in *Gentlemen Prefer Blondes.* Russell dyes her brown hair blonde to pretend to be Monroe, and she sings Monroe's song so that she'll be detained in her place. Even though Russell's dance is full of suggestive movements that only she could perform, none of the men in the courtroom recognises her through the disguise.

Like the businessman in *Come and Get It*, the judge (Marcel Dalio) tries to make Russell stop, but she continues her seductive imitation of Monroe as the men watch in shock. In contrast to the serious, even melodramatic tone of *Come and Get It*, the role-switching between the two women friends in *Gentlemen Prefer Blondes* evolves into a bold musical number that seems likely to enrage the authorities. What makes this reversal possible is the feminine sensitivity to the effectiveness of the similarity trap.

The same thing happens at the end of *Only Angels Have Wings.* When Arthur is given a coin that is the same on both sides, instead of being confused by this similarity, she interprets it correctly as a sign of the man's love. The coin is a token of Kid (Thomas Mitchell), who has been killed in an accident. He used it to trick his friends out of drinking money. The woman plays with it and interprets it as a sign of good fortune; for men, the similarity had been only a trick. This difference in the response of men and women reveals the Hawksian logic of exchange. With adventures and comedies, the exchange is between danger and embarrassment; with melodramas and musicals, it is between the weakness of men and the strength of women. Hawks seems to have believed that he could always come up with the framework for a new film either by inverting one situation to create another similar situation, or by exchanging one element for another similar element.

That is precisely what Hawks did in *His Girl Friday.* In place of the male lead played by Pat O'Brien in Lewis Milestone's *The Front Page* (1931), Hawks made the leading role female and gave it to Rosalind Russell. Hawks' skilful manipulation of such inversions, exchanges and repetitions is most adroit in his comedies. In *Ball of Fire*, he put Gary Cooper into a role modelled on Snow White, and less than a decade later he remade the film as *A Song Is Born* with Danny Kaye in the lead. Inversion, exchange, repetition: these are the keys to Howard Hawks.

I won't go into the many Hawksian inversions of men forced to put on women's clothing or adult roles transferred to children or animals, for the real issue with Hawks is not the results of his inversions and exchanges but the process itself. I should first note, though, that discussing Hawks through the themes of inversion, exchange and repetition is by no means original. Many critics have pointed out these aspects of his work ever since the famous essay by Jacques Rivette published in 1953.[3] There is also a short but insightful essay by

V. F. Perkins on Hawks' comedies.[4] The point I want to make about these themes is that Hawks incorporated them not only in dramatic situations but also in surprisingly small but specific events that occur on the screen. Throughout his films, such inversions and reversals are captured as distinct visual images. This is what I want to demonstrate now.

2. Coincidence and reversal

Hawksian inversions[5] occur with mechanical reliability, but there is nothing in the story that foreshadows them. A coincidence will lead suddenly to an unexpected reversal in the relations of superiority and inferiority, with the action so fast that there is no time to think. But once again the female characters unintentionally come out on the winning side of the coincidence. The best example is the hotel scene in *Ball of Fire*. An unexpected accident forces Barbara Stanwyck to stay at a motel in a small town. When she slams shut the door of her room, the room number 9 flips upside-down and becomes 6. Unaware of that coincidental change, Gary Cooper enters her room by mistake to talk to his colleague who is supposed to be in room 6. He ends up confessing his love for Stanwyck. (I will leave out the great shot of Stanwyck flashing her eyes in the dark as she listens to him, and just point out that the shot of 9 becoming 6 is faithfully repeated in *A Song Is Born*.)

In Hawks' logic, the numbers 9 and 6 are equivalent morphologically. But to realise that equivalence, the screw that is supposed to hold the top of the number to the door must come loose by coincidence, and the coincidence is implemented only by the action of the female character. The coincidence becomes decisive when people are manipulated by it. The beneficiaries of coincidence are Stanwyck in *Ball of Fire* and Virginia Mayo in *A Song Is Born*. In Hawks' world, where inversion, exchange and repetition always ensure the dominance of women, the key issue is who will control the coincidences and not be deceived by similarities. In almost all cases, it is the men who are in the weak position and the women in the strong position. To confirm this, let's consider the ultimate effect of the inversion of numbers.

3. Numbers and bodies

An inversion of numbers plays an important role in *Monkey Business*, in which a laboratory assistant's confusion between young and old monkeys leads to some unexpected consequences. It occurs when Cary Grant and Ginger Rogers, made much younger after ingesting some chemicals, appear in the office where the laboratory heads have gathered. Because the monkey they are holding between them is upside-down, the number 3 on the monkey's back is now inverted. Unlike 9 and 6, the numeral 3 can't be inverted to create another number, but its inversion in this scene does seem to make the transformation of the two adults even more extreme. Rogers' bratty behaviour is especially surprising. But what I want to focus on here is the mechanical phenomenon of something being inverted along its vertical axis. In one Hawks comedy, there's a scene in which a human being performs the same upside-down inversion as the number 9 on the door in *Ball of Fire*. That scene occurs in *Man's Favorite Sport?* when Rock Hudson falls into the water wearing the unsinkable trousers that he has invented. For Hawks, the human body imitates physical matter. In this film, Hudson plays a fishing consultant who has himself never gone fishing. He is invited to a fishing tournament, where he falls into many embarrassing situations. The only way he can get out of them is by standing on his head.

This is a perfect example of the upside–down phenomenon. In Hawks' comedies, men are frequently victims of that phenomenon in embarrassing episodes that expose their weaknesses. Another example is in *I Was a Male War Bride* (1949). When Cary Grant tries to pick up something that was dropped by a female soldier (Ann Sheridan), he is lifted into the air by a crossing barrier and hung upside-down for all to see.

In this comedy, the absurd military regulations oblige a man to dress in women's clothing, so it is only natural that the theme of inversion should be repeated many times. But an abstract concept has an actual effect only when realised as an action visible on the screen. Hawks' morphological formalism is expressed through specific events. A similar physical inversion occurs in *Monkey Business*. The victim is again Grant. His glasses are broken by his now bratty wife, and she chases him out of their hotel room. As he gropes around trying to find the room, he ends up falling head first down a laundry chute into the basement. (Embarrassments like this occur not only to near-sighted scientists. In *Ball of Fire*, the gangster boss [Dana Andrews] is tripped, and his pistol falls out of his jacket.)

Apart from the slapstick comedies of the silent era, no films show men turned upside-down as often as those of Hawks. The men in his films are unable to avoid being exposed in embarrassing situations. In *Gentlemen Prefer Blondes*, the private detective (Elliott Reid) is trapped by two women and dropped head first onto a chair. His trousers are stripped off, and he is left with his bare legs waving in the air.

Let me point out that, for the heroes of Hawks' aviation movies, an inverted posture is used as a sign of courage. In a test flight in *Only Angels Have Wings*, Grant valiantly keeps his plane from turning upside-down. And in *Ceiling Zero* (1936), James Cagney is shown actually flying upside-down to demonstrate his extraordinary skills as a pilot. In *The Dawn Patrol* (1930), a plane crashes behind enemy lines nose first. The shock of the impact flips the body of the plane upside-down. Despite the crash, the two pilots walk away unharmed and are able to escape back to friendly territory. In these cases, the genre of the film is different, so a similar situation leads to a completely opposite result.

Let's turn now to another war film, *Sergeant York* starring Gary Cooper. In one fight scene, you can observe Cooper's upside-down face as he lies with his legs stretched up against the wall. The effect is comic, which is not surprising since this scene occurs at a point in the film when his character is still a tough guy and hasn't yet received religion. In fact, the story of *Sergeant York* itself is an ironic tale in which a worthless young man is inverted to emerge eventually as a battlefield hero.

4. Femininity vs masculinity

Hawks' comedies are full of confusion created by the weaknesses of men who are unable to adapt to the new order when up and down are reversed. Their weaknesses appear most often when their legs are exposed and the women find out about it. Hawks' women almost always aim at men's legs when they trap these men in weaker positions.

The archaeologist in *Bringing up Baby* is an expert at inversion in every part of his life. He falls down everywhere, from his own living room to the garden of an old woman he doesn't even know. In *Rio Bravo*, Wayne seems to have inherited the inferior genes of that archaeologist. When he gets caught in an enemy trap, he tumbles head over heels onto the floor.

What this shot suggests is that women in comedies fulfil, even if they don't intend to, the same function as the bad guys in the adventure films. Depending on the genre, co-operation and interference are of equivalent value. However, the loss of physical co-ordination that the men suffer is seen not only in physical inversion. In *Monkey Business*, Grant also loses his basic sense of forward and backward. One scene depicts a man who cannot perform the simple action of opening a door and stepping outside. This occurs not only because he is near-sighted. He fails precisely because his wife gives him detailed instructions on how to close the door and go outside. Of course, she is unaware that her own attempt to help him is in fact an interference. This is a splendid example of a Freudian dilemma.

A similar scene with Grant appears in *I Was a Male War Bride* when the doorknob to Sheridan's bedroom comes off. He doesn't realise that he can get out by simply pushing on the door, so he spends the night anxiously awake, thinking he is trapped in her bedroom. The key point here is that Sheridan is lying in the bed. She's exhausted and sound asleep so, unlike Rogers in *Monkey Business*, she can't tell him what to do. But her silence still acts as a command to him, so he is unable to get out of the room. Thus even a sleeping woman is able to destroy a man's bodily co-ordination. In Hawks' films, such failures occur only to men. His women never fail. And while inversions indicate inferiority for men, they put women into the dominant position.

This is proven by Katharine Hepburn's amazing inversion in *Bringing up Baby*. Her thin legs tripping over a thick tree trunk are a nearly perfect example of this inversion. But for Hepburn this does not signify failure. In fact, the accident functions to her advantage. Grant has just told her that he wants to break up with her, but now, as he tries to pick her up, he is so surprised that he forgets completely what he was saying. The Hawksian logic wins again: the more women fall down, the stronger position they acquire.

This recalls another scene in *Bringing up Baby* in which Hepburn uses falling down as an excuse to attract a man. As this scene shows, Hawks' comedies do not rely only on men falling down in front of women who remain standing. The inversions happen to both, but the effect is different depending on the gender. In his films, women often perform actions that are very similar to those performed by men. For example, in *Gentlemen Prefer Blondes* Monroe tries to escape through a porthole and gets stuck with her head down and her legs in the air. The young boy (George Winslow) speaks in an adult way, creating a comic touch. But compared with Grant being unable even to open a door, Monroe's escape through this porthole, though not particularly skilful, does clearly show her superior physical powers. Women are skilled at harmonising their bodies along the vertical axis.

Another good example of this is in *A Girl in Every Port* when the female acrobat (Louise Brooks) dives into a tank of water. Like the hero in an aviation film, she easily inverts her vertical orientation and falls through the air completely upside-down. But this is her job; she does it to earn money and to entice men. After Victor McLaglen's jacket gets splashed, he goes to see her backstage. We must be careful not to interpret her attracting him as relying solely on the feminine sexual strategy of exposing her figure through her bathing suit. As in the examples I've cited so far, this is an example of a woman in a Hawks comedy accurately imitating the posture that represents physical inferiority for men. In the female case, though, the repetition of that posture has a completely different effect.

We should use the same perspective to view the famous scene in *Ball of Fire* in which Stanwyck points her bare legs at Cooper. This scene depicts a provocative action as the woman leans back into her chair with her legs exposed and her feet pointing at the dopey man. For men, though, such a posture would be extremely shameful. In fact, it's the same position that Reid falls into in *Gentlemen Prefer Blondes* when his pants are stripped off and his bare legs are exposed. The comic logic of Hawks is consistent: a position of inferiority for a man is one of superiority for women. As Hepburn shows when she falls down in *Bringing up Baby*, women's legs are much more expressive than men's legs. Once a man's legs have been tipped upside-down or reversed, they're no longer of any use. Women's legs, when lifted up high, can become an effective defensive gesture.

A superb example of a woman using her legs to good effect is Carole Lombard in *Twentieth Century* (1934) kicking her co-star. Those legs are too much even for the veteran John Barrymore. Another example is in *His Girl Friday*, in which the shrewd reporter suddenly pulls up her skirt, dashes off faster than any man could run, and tackles a man like a rugby player in order to get her scoop.

For a mature man to pull off such a trick, he would have to take some drug that would restore his youth. In fact, Grant in *Monkey Business* tries just such a stunt, executing a triumphant cartwheel to show that he has lost his clumsiness when he thinks that he has succeeded with his chemical experiment. Of course, this is only a temporary victory. As we have seen, he will soon be plunged deeper and deeper into inferiority. After all, Hawks' comedies are built around men losing their physical abilities due to the helpful interference of women. No one can violate this principle.

5. 'Who are you?'

For men, who are constantly put into inferior positions by the morphological inversion that makes the number 9 equivalent to 6, there's only one way they can maintain their dominance: by talking. That is the source of much of the talkativeness in Hawks' comedies. In fact, the only man who manages to avoid inversion, Grant in *His Girl Friday*, maintains his position as editor by giving a steady stream of orders over the telephone. He uses his speaking skills to try to restore his relations with his estranged wife Russell while making no effort to hide his plan to take advantage of her skills as a reporter. He tells reporters over the phone to use anything short of murder to get their stories.

He knows well that the telephone is a superb instrument for disguising one's identity in order to confuse other people. In *The Big Sleep* the private detective Marlowe (Humphrey Bogart) manipulates the police in a similar way while also trying to attract a woman's interest. In *Ball of Fire*, Andrews deceives the Professor by pretending over the telephone to be Stanwyck's father. Once they hang up the phone, though, men begin to lose their superior position. As we saw earlier, Andrews is attacked by Cooper's old colleagues and put through an awkward inversion. And once the editor in *His Girl Friday* leaves his office, he is faced with a steady stream of wrong people and confused names. He ends up asking the question 'Who are you?', almost as though he wants to start an argument.

Perhaps that question really should have been put by Grant to Hepburn in *Bringing up Baby*. But words like that would have no effect on a woman. In fact, they might make the situation even worse, such as when he encounters an old woman while wearing a woman's bathrobe. Here the question 'Who are you?' is uttered almost simultaneously by the two characters. Imitation creates a mutual, nearly mechanical repetition that destroys the meaning of the question itself. For men who have begun to fear for their own identities and who are overcome by the talkativeness of women, even the barking of a dog adds to the confusion in a subsequent scene. Without realising it, Grant has lost his own name and now everyone calls him by a different name. He is stunned, but there is nothing he can do about it. The more he talks, the more confused the situation becomes. (The same situation reaches a climax toward the end of *I Was a Male War Bride*. This time Grant knows who he is, what position he is in, and what he should say. But even though he explains that he is a male war bride, the situation only gets worse.)

Another example of a situation falling into utter confusion by the repetition of the 'Who are you?' question appears in the scene in the police station at the end of *Bringing Up Baby*. Here, nobody is able to prove who they are, so they get locked up. The only one who is able to get free is Hepburn, who gives an excuse off the top of her head.

So how is it possible to bring an end to the endless cycle of 'Who are you?' questions? Or, put another way, why is that utterance repeated in film after film by character after character without ever being resolved? The reason is that it is not really a question. Instead, it is used to express doubt about a suspicious person, to show displeasure in another person, to threaten a person with arrest, or even to serve as an excuse in order to hide responsibility. Nevertheless, Hawks' men have a hard time coming up with a reasonable answer, and the more they try to explain the situation, the more they just confuse everything.

When Grant goes to a butcher's shop in *Bringing up Baby*, he worries that he looks strange buying so much meat, so he explains: 'It's for Baby.' For the butcher, who doesn't know that Grant's pet leopard is named Baby, it's an absurd, incomprehensible comment. As a result, Grant ends up looking strange after all, and merely increases other people's feelings of distrust. Grant is in a similar situation in *I Was a Male War Bride*: the more he tries to explain his situation, the more he gets confined to the barracks. Not only actions but also words put the men in Hawks' comedies in positions of inferiority. But when woman make similarly absurd statements, they do not suffer in the same way.

Let's look at the scene in *Monkey Business* where Rogers is rushing to the hospital in a taxi. She thinks that her husband has become a small child again because of the chemicals he drank. Rogers' manner of speaking here comes from her being so obsessed with one thing that she doesn't worry about whether other people will understand her. But her hasty mistake that the child next to her is her own husband is a typical Hawksian comic technique. So where is the way out for these men who try to answer the question 'Who are you?' seriously? The solution seems to be found at the end of *Monkey Business*. The chemicals that had turned Grant into a child have worn off, and he wakes up. He puts on his glasses and points at the child sleeping next to him. He asks his wife, 'Who is this?' His wife's answer prolongs the confusion, but the key point here is that their question is now directed at a third party. The husband and wife are finally set free from the endless round of 'Who are you?' questions.

Conclusion

By looking at Hawks' comedies from the angles of inversion, exchange and repetition, we can confirm that women are definitely shown in the superior position. Even when faced with the same trap that has caught men, they themselves are not caught. Even when turned upside-down, they are not made inferior. Even when blabbering on and on, they avoid confusion. They always maintain their advantage over men. But, although Hawks depicts women as never being defeated even when they make mistakes, he has often been regarded as a masculine auteur. In fact, he has even been classified as a misogynist. It is true that Todd McCarthy's biography of Hawks suggests that there may have been some truth in those assertions.[6] However, I would like to avoid interpreting the meaning of Hawks' works from his personal biography. Instead, I want to emphasise that Hawks allots only a secondary role to 'meaning' itself. What attracts him is not meaning but the endless exchange and repetition of elements to create nonsensical situations that do not have any decisive meanings.

Hawks enlivened his works with repetitions that transcended genre boundaries. When we look again at his comedies, we can see a strong formalist desire not so much to tell a story as to play with narrative structure. In each film he tried to apply his story framework anew in order to see for himself how well it could work. Of course, that story framework was the ultimate in simplicity. On one side is a person trying to achieve a goal. On the other is a person trying to prevent that. And in the middle is a vague category represented by a woman in an interchangeable role. In Hawks' adventure films, typified by Lauren Bacall in *The Big Sleep*, the woman is an interfering helper who ultimately assists the protagonist in achieving his goal. In almost all of the comedies, however, the woman's function is not to offer interfering help but helpful interference. She draws the man into a shadow zone of action that is neither interference nor co-operation, a place where his initial goal becomes fundamentally meaningless. Without exaggerating the meaning of that meaninglessness, she varies the process in many ways based on the principles of inversion, exchange and repetition, and thus prevents the formation of any meaning. One often hears discussion of 'Hawksian transparency'. The source of that transparency is the absence of meaning. As an auteur, Howard Hawks disappears behind the stories that he creates. He is like an invisible hand manipulating the stories, a hand whose structure and function cannot be analysed.

Notes

1. Maurice Schérer [Eric Rohmer], *Cahiers du cinéma* no. 29, December 1953. An English translation is available in Eric Rohmer (trans. Carol Volk), *The Taste for Beauty* (Cambridge University Press, 1989), pp. 128–31.

2. Jacques Becker, Jacques Rivette and François Truffaut, 'Entretien avec Howard Hawks', *Cahiers du cinéma* no. 56, February 1956. Available in English in Andrew Sarris (ed. and trans.), *Interviews with Film Directors* (New York: Avon Books), p. 236.

3. Translated into English by Russell Campbell, Marvin Pister and Adrian Brine in Jim Hillier (ed.), *Cahiers du cinéma: The 1950s – Neo-Realism, Hollywood, New Wave* (Cambridge: Harvard University Press, 1985), pp. 126–31.

4. V. F. Perkins, 'Comedies', *Movie* no. 5, December 1962, pp. 21–2.

5. As I mentioned earlier, many critics have treated the theme of inversion from various points of view. To name only two: Jean A. Gili, *Howard Hawks* (Paris: Seghers, 1971), p. 31; and Noël Simsolo, *Howard Hawks* (Paris: Edilig, 1984), p. 108.

6. Todd McCarthy, *Howard Hawks: The Grey Fox of Hollywood* (New York: Grove Press, 1997).

PART FOUR – EPILOGUE (SHIGEHIKO HASUMI AND JONATHAN ROSENBAUM: 2002)

Email exchange between Chicago and Tokyo, Summer 2002

JR: In the two and a half years that have passed since our original dialogue, the National Film Centre (NFC) in Tokyo has held substantial retrospectives devoted to both Hawks and Masumura, and I'm curious whether these have brought about any noticeable changes in the Japanese understanding and appreciations of these directors. It seems significant to me that Hawks was not really recognised in the US by film critics until the early 60s, when Andrew Sarris began writing about him as an auteur; prior to that time, as Peter Bogdanovich and others noted, almost everyone had seen and valued some of Hawks' films, but critics hadn't really viewed them as a coherent body of work – unlike, say, Ford and Hitchcock, both of whom I was quite aware of in the 50s. As for Masumura, recognition in the US is only beginning to become a possibility due to the release of a few of his films on DVD. The ones released so far are *Blind Beast*, *Giants and Toys*, *Manji* and *Afraid to Die*, all in colour; still to come at this point are two titles in black and white, *Black Test Car* (another industrial espionage film, like *Giants and Toys*) and *Red Angel* (to my taste, the best in the lot, though the second, third and fifth films on this list also have their strong points). One possible distinction between Japanese and American perceptions of Masumura that I can already detect is the overlapping of exploitation films and art films as a loose generic category in the US, especially applicable to *Blind Beast* and *Manji*, and complicated still further by the unfortunate notion that any foreign language film (with a few rare exceptions, such as *Crouching Tiger, Hidden Dragon* [2000]) automatically becomes regarded as an art film in terms of its marginalised distribution.

SH: The Hawks retrospective in Japan, held by the National Film Centre in Tokyo from December 1999 to February 2000 and co-organised by *Asahi Shinbun* was, as far as I know, the most complete, comprising all thirty-eight features. *Asahi Shinbun* is a quality Japanese newspaper and the tendency of its film pages has been rather conservative. Consequently, for this newspaper, co-organising the Hawks retrospective was a really new and surprising initiative. It would have been absolutely inconceivable two decades ago to see the two names Hawks and *Asahi Shinbun* joined together. So, it is clear that something is changing in Japan. Even two different versions of *The Big Sleep* – a release version and a pre-release version recently restored by the UCLA film archive – were shown. The round-table organised on this occasion, entitled 'Rethinking Howard Hawks', bringing together Geoffrey Nowell-Smith, Peter Wollen, Anne Friedberg and myself, attracted more than 300 people. Personally, it was a real pleasure for me to be able to rediscover in Tokyo some of his early works, such as *Fig Leaves*, *Paid to Love* (1927) and *Fazil* (1928). For these rare films, the big hall of the NFC (310 seats) was always full. In conjunction with the retrospective, Todd McCarthy's book *Howard Hawks* was published in a Japanese translation (*Hawks on Hawks* by Joseph McBride had already been translated into Japanese in 1986). So it was an exceptional opportunity for the younger generation to discover Hawks' oeuvre in its entirety. Unfortunately, there was no positive reaction from the young film critics. Statistically speaking, the Jean Renoir retrospective held in 1996 by the NFC attracted more spectators. Compared to Renoir who is officially recognised as an auteur, Hawks, I am afraid, still isn't considered an artistic auteur in Japan.

I remember, in this regard, that in the 60s and 70s there were two famous art movie theatres in Tokyo, where principally European films – Bergman, Bresson, Buñuel, Godard, Joseph Losey (his films shot in the UK), Truffaut, Andrzej Munk, etc. – were shown. It is significant to note that only three American films were released in these prestigious movie theatres: John Ford's *The Sun Shines Bright* (1953), Orson Welles' *Citizen Kane* (1940) and John Cassavetes' *Shadows* (1960). That was the typical image of art films in Japan, when I began writing on cinema. Neither Hitchcock nor Hawks was regarded as an auteur. That is why I decided to put a still from *Bringing up Baby* on the cover of my first book on film, *Eizo no shigaku* (*Poetics of Image*, 1979), as an act of provocation. These art theatres, called the Art Theater Guild (ATG), also co-produced and distributed Japanese films, mainly the works of independent film-makers such as Nagisa Oshima, Kiju Yoshida and Shuji Terayama, among others. The only Masumura film distributed by the ATG was *Ongaku* (*Music*, 1972). He shot this relatively weak adaptation of Mishima's novel right after Daiei collapsed. Masumura was essentially a film-maker of the studio system, and almost all his films were adaptations of novels. That is why, compared to Oshima, Yoshida and Terayama, Masumura was never regarded as an auteur in the 60s and the 70s.

The Masumura retrospective was held, not by the NFC, but by Daiei – whose rights were taken over by a publisher, Tokuma, that played an important role in co-producing Zhang Yimou's first films – in a small movie theatre called Euro-space (120 seats) from November 2000 to January 2001, comprising fifty films. This movie theatre is known as one of the most important art cinemas in Tokyo since the 80s, after the collapse of the ATG, and is principally frequented by students and young cinephiles. Godard's *For Ever Mozart* (1996) and *JLG/JLG* (1995) are currently being shown there. So, I can say that the Masumura retrospective was held in a prestigious venue and, fortunately, was a real success. Because of this, Euro-space immediately decided to hold a second retrospective straight after the first. Important municipal museums and libraries throughout Japan are now welcoming the Masumura retrospective. And at the same time as discovering Masumura, the younger generation also discovered the outstanding actress Ayako Wakao, who had never appeared on television. Thanks to the unexpected success of the retrospective, major Masumura films have been released on video and DVD. Any important video rental shop in Tokyo now has a Masumura corner, where you can easily find at least twenty of his works, which was inconceivable ten years ago. Young and influential film-maker Shinji Aoyama (*Eureka*, 2000) declared that Masumura is the most important film-maker in the history of post-war Japanese cinema. Masumura is now becoming a mythic director for Japan's younger generations, fifteen years after his regrettable disappearance at the age of sixty-two. I would say that this time lag is not exceptionally long, because in Japan, Ozu also took this long to be recognised as an auteur. Ozu's first complete retrospective was held by the TFC only in 1981, eighteen years after his death.

6

Musical Mutations: Before, Beyond and Against Hollywood

Adrian Martin (2000–2002)

1. Overture

The film has a beauty that is brash and pathetic, like splintered coloured glass, fragments that somehow compose a picture while refusing to hold together: musical, sad, uproarious, definitely frail. It is this simultaneous celebration of beauty and its frailty, of gaiety and its ephemerality, of the transient nature of all emotion, that reveals in *Une Femme est une femme* (1961) a peculiar romantic attitude, reserved and self denying, which is perhaps the only possible romanticism for a contemporary sensibility. (Edgardo Cozarinsky, 1969)[1]

Jacques was not a radical filmmaker. What was radical was his desire to bring music, song and dance to things that seemed outside that realm – like the class struggle. (Agnès Varda on Jacques Demy, 1993)[2]

In a single day, I expect to cry, laugh, dance, sing. I may even be locked up in jail. A film should contain all those things. (Youssef Chahine, 1997)[3]

ANDRÉ LABARTHE: You like jazz?
JOHN CASSAVETES: Yeah, I like all music. It's good. It makes you feel like living. Silence is death.
AL: You feel like making a musical?
JC: Yeah.
AL: Yeah? With dance and everything?
JC: Yeah, one musical. Only one.
AL: Only one? You wrote the story already?
JC: No, I didn't write it. Dostoevsky wrote it: *Crime and Punishment*. I would like to make that a musical.[4]

The bitter musical which I would dearly love to see remains unmade. (Raymond Durgnat, 1973)[5]

Although she regularly bursts into song, Björk's character, a beleaguered factory worker, suffers horribly in *Dancer in the Dark*. (Karen Durbin, 2000)[6]

And anywhere that Judy Garland mingles with Jean-Luc Godard is sure to leave some scorched earth. (Geoff Pevere, 2000)[7]

2. Same old song

If proof of American imperialism – not only over popular culture, but also the critical thinking about it – was ever needed, the vast mountain of literature devoted to that film genre known as the musical offers depressing evidence. This claim may seem odd or perverse, because the phenomenon has been so totally naturalised within film culture globally that it is scarcely ever noticed. However, the truth remains: 'the musical' essentially means, in discussions of the genre all over the world, 'the American musical' – an assumption usually made without the slightest consciousness or commentary. Rick Altman's influential anthology *Genre: The Musical* uses the terms musical, Hollywood musical and American musical interchangeably; its concluding editorial list of 'areas which need to be more fully explored' does not suggest any geographical extension of the terrain.[8] His later book, *The American Film Musical*, is more specific, but unforthcoming as to why the topic needs to be geographically constrained in this way.[9] The 1981 survey *Comédie musicale* by Alain Masson – who himself criticised Altman's seemingly patriotic fix on *homo americanus*[10] – is only about Hollywood musicals.

And the beat goes on. An essay by Marc Miller on the movie musical in the 90s in the anthology *Film Genre 2000* mentions a mere handful of musicals, all American, all high-profile, high-budget productions – and, unsurprisingly, he finds the genre to be in a dismal state.[11] Richard Barrios' informative *A Song in the Dark: The Birth of the Musical Film*, while acknowledging 'outstanding works from France, Germany, and Britain' in the years 1931–2, candidly frames itself as 'chauvinistically pointed toward the Yankee progenitors'.[12] Even when musicals from other countries are discussed, they are invariably marginalised in relation to the American model. For instance, Brian McFarlane finds it necessary to remark at the beginning of the *Oxford Companion to Australian Film* entry on *Star Struck* (1982): 'The musical is a film genre that the USA has made peculiarly its own.'[13] Peculiarly, indeed.

Within the context of such a myopic world film culture, it is a shock to come across a comment like this one by Paul Willemen at the end of a 1980 essay on screen porn: 'Perhaps there is material here for a comparative study between Egyptian, Hindi and US musicals?'[14] Over two decades later, this fact is even more staggering: there is no available reference book that even begins to sketch a properly international history of the musical. Occasionally, a revival, restoration or documentary compilation – like Edgar Ulmer's independently produced Yiddish musicals of the 30s, the Communist musicals showcased in the international festival hit *East Side Story* (1997) or (for non-Hindi viewers) the wild doco-fiction collage, *Cinema Cinema* (1979) – makes us pay attention to an aberrant strain of the musical genre. But even speaking of alternatives to Hollywood is not always pertinent, since that gesture ends up, despite itself, reinstating the dominance of the American model.

And yet, probably every country that has a cinema has a very local and often very popular history – whether great or small – of musicals. Our understanding of musicals and, before that, our most basic, material access to them is hampered by a simple fact: of all the genres, musicals travel least well abroad (since they respond well neither to subtitling nor dubbing) – except to ethnic video and DVD stores for diasporic communities all over the world.

A true history of the musical – if it can ever be written, or more likely collated in a collective, international project[15] – would have to recognise, once and for all, that the model taken as the dominant paradigm of the genre (those Hollywood musicals made in the 40s and 50s, mainly those associated with MGM) is far from being an absolute and determining reference point. There are musicals beyond Hollywood (the Hindi tradition, supremely, being much larger and more enduring), and also before it – in America as much as anywhere else. Ernst Lubitsch's or King Vidor's musicals of the 30s are now as foreign to many students of the genre as independent musical productions of today like *Manhattan Meringuez* (1995). There are also plenty of odd cases right inside the Hollywood studio system itself, such as all those films with song and dance elements like the Dean Martin/Jerry Lewis comedies or Elvis Presley's vehicles, rock'n'roll exploitation films like *Twist All Night* (1961) with Louis Prima, or fantasies for children such as *The 5,000 Fingers of Dr T* (1953). . . .

Theoretical speculation (in several languages) upon the musical – which takes as its focus those canonical American films of the 40s and 50s – has itself narrowed down to multiple variations upon a small number of postulates derived from a handful of texts: Altman's *The American Film Musical*, Richard Dyer's brilliant essay 'Entertainment and Utopia' and Jane Feuer's *The Hollywood Musical*.[16] From these texts – whose seminal contribution to cinema studies I have no wish to belittle – have come a restricted series of elements that now constitute a veritable dogma of the musical genre: song and dance as emotional release and utopian imagining; the syntactical relationship of song numbers to the plots that contain them; self-reflexive entertainment. Taking this constellation on as doctrine inevitably leads, in many cases, to a dismissal of anything that works outside these very particular rules.

One of the surest signs that we generally work with an exceedingly narrow model of the musical comes at the most basic level of plot premise and dramatic or comic situation. We casually expect musicals to concern themselves with either fantasy worlds (*Brigadoon* [1954]), show business (*Singin' in the Rain* [1952]) or cosy, nostalgic, small town communities (*Meet Me in St Louis* [1944]) – hardly anything, in short, related to realism. When a musical does broach naturalistic elements (as in that great limit case, *West Side Story* [1961]) or borrow from an action-based genre (as in the Western reference of *Seven Brides for Seven Brothers* [1954]), they must be sufficiently heightened and abstracted to pass muster as proper subjects or settings for a musical. It thus becomes an instant, camp joke to imagine absurd forms like the horror musical (*The Little Shop of Horrors* [1986]), the espionage musical (*Awesome Lotus* [1981]), the sci-fi musical (*The American Astronaut* [2001]) or the holocaust musical (hence the celebrated incongruity of the 'Springtime for Hitler' number in *The Producers* [1967]).

But this reflex immediately cancels out many actual manifestations of the genre: supremely, Jacques Demy's quasi-tragic musicals that touch on matters of suicide, industrial dispute, serial murder and incest, and moving through all those modest, whimsical musicals which are about everyday life and work environments – a form that defines the second, cheaper tier of Hollywood musicals (films such as *I Love Melvin* [1953] or *Give a Girl a Break* [1953]) as well as, for example, British musicals featuring Arthur Askey (*Band Waggon* [1939]) or Cliff Richard (*Summer Holiday* [1963]).

The standard critical approach to the musical tends to be relentlessly normative: having narrowly defined the glossiest, slickest, most perfect American form as the model, it is able to judge deviations from that norm only as bad, clumsy, try-hard, laughable. This net of gloomy ungenerousness casts itself far and wide, damning everything from Deanna Durbin musicals and *Guys and Dolls* (1955) to *Yentl* (1983) and *Popeye* (1980), from *The Wiz* (1978) and *Pennies from Heaven* (1981) to *Absolute Beginners* (1986) and *Jeanne and the Perfect Guy* (1997). Of course, one must admit and take due account of the importance of the Hollywood musical as a reference or touchstone for film-makers all over the world – as Youssef Chahine, for example, has lovingly testified, and as his films including *Silence . . . on tourne* (2001) show.

All the same, what are classed as the deviations from the American model ultimately comprise most of the musicals made in the world. Against Pauline Kael's judgment that Demy's films demonstrate 'how even a gifted Frenchman who adores American musicals misunderstands their conventions', Jonathan Rosenbaum prefers to encounter them as 'inspired appropriation[s]' of certain 'golden age' Hollywood elements[17] – and, as in all cultural appropriations, what is taken is also changed, customised, combined, geared to specifically 'local' intensities and sensibilities.

In this light, one way to gauge the multiplicity of regional musical forms is to approach these cinematic manifestations via their roots in theatre. Cinema has never ceased absorbing a wide variety of theatrical musical forms (opera, operetta, sprechgesang, the Brechtian epic, theatre restaurant or café-theatre, the school eisteddfod, etc.), each of which has specific national histories and inflections. Whether we are speaking of the Maoist opera *The Red Detachment of Women* (1970); Arnold Schoenberg's ironic drawing-room musical *From Today Until Tomorrow* (1997) as filmed by Jean-Marie Straub and Danièle Huillet; Fritz Lang and Kurt Weill's audacious social musical *You and Me* (1938); or Australia's *Bootmen* (2000), a transplanting of the theatrical Tap Dogs phenomenon – we are at many degrees of separation from a Broadway-defined model of musical spectacle.

In a telling gesture, many critical or theoretical accounts of the musical come to rest upon a dramatic exclusion of certain neighbouring cinematic forms that are deemed not-musical, such as the concert film, or the so-called MTV movie. Rick Altman, for instance, declares:

> If the musical is to survive very far into its second half-century, rather than succumb to its first cousins, MTV and the concert film (as in a monarchy, first cousins are always the most dangerous rivals), then it will have to look to its past – and to the American musical tradition as a whole.[18]

This is, finally, not terribly helpful. Why would we want or need a theory of the musical that disdainfully excludes *Phantom of the Paradise* (1974), *Purple Rain* (1984), *Flashdance* (1983), *Sign o' the Times* (1987) or *The Year of the Horse* (1997)?

The fact is, we have hardly begun to map the larger aesthetic terrain of which the musical is really only a subcategory: the *music-film*, which I define as any film which feels as if it is *driven* by its music (instrumental or lyrical), where the guiding role of music in relation to image is especially foregrounded. This is a very open area which must include everything from films in which songs are prominently overlaid on the action (which is what is generally meant by the term MTV movie); to the films of Martin Scorsese, Emir Kusturica, Federico Fellini, Terrence Malick, Miklos Jancsó, Michael Mann, Glauber Rocha, Werner Schroeter, Sergei Paradjanov or Jon Jost, where musical scores or collages very theatrically seem to direct, dictate or suggest the rhythms of montage or *mise en scène*; to ballad films where a song soundtrack becomes the essential narration, as in *The Tracker* (2002); to modern, animated features from Disney or DreamWorks where songs jump mid-verse from being voiced by characters to external lyrical commentary (as in *The Road to El Dorado* [1999]); to remarkable and unique works weaving a hybrid between musical documentary and musical fiction, like *Latcho Drom* (1993) and *Buena Vista Social Club* (1999); and experimental films such as *Alone. Life Wastes Andy Hardy* (1998).

One particularly large, modern-day family of musicals is simply too noisy to be overlooked. These are the movies that take the Hollywood model, in diverse ways and to diverse degrees, as a totem to be mocked or defied or attacked: obvious musical mutations like the militantly gay musicals (*Zero Patience* [1993], *Highway of Heartache* [1994] and *The American Astronaut*); the post-modern anti-musicals (*Pennies from Heaven* [1981], *All That Jazz* [1979]); the wicked pastiches (*To Die For Tano* [1998] and *South Side Story* [2000]); the avant-garde experiments (*Haut bas fragile* [1995] or *The Long Day Closes* [1992]); the relentlessly eccentric, discombobulated takes on the genre (like *Popeye*); the musicals that are deliberately homely and amateurish (*Awesome Lotus*) or ugly and disconcerting (*Dancer in the Dark* [2000]). . . . Why can't these films, for a change, sit at the centre rather than at the periphery in our thinking about the musical?

3. Bursting

Today, reference to the musical – or rather, what Jean-Luc Godard once specified as 'not a musical' but 'the idea of a musical'[19] – is ubiquitous within popular culture. On television, situation comedies including *Ally McBeal* regularly feature song and dance break-outs, and series from *Taxi* in the 70s to *Buffy* today have featured all-musical special episodes. Bret Easton Ellis boasts of the unused ending he scripted for the film adaptation of his novel *American Psycho* (1999) – a musical sequence featuring yuppies atop the Empire State Building. Vincent Gallo announces he is about to make a 'Charles Manson musical'.

Even mainstream cinema has its unusual and sometimes inventive musical stylings: in the incessant put-on numbers of pastiche comedies (such as *Life Stinks* [1991]) or John Waters' high-camp teen-movie satires; in high concept pieces like *Little Voice* (1998) or *Duets* (2001); in Baz Luhrmann's grandly theatrical, post-modern work (from *Strictly*

Ballroom [1993] to *Moulin Rouge* [2001]); in the increasingly music-oriented films of the Coen brothers (*The Big Lebowski* [1998], *O Brother, Where Art Thou?* [2000]); and in the sophisticated farces of romance and manners structured around Gershwin or Porter standards (*Everyone Says I Love You* [1996], *Love's Labours Lost* [2000]).

Art cinema, too, dreams its musical dreams. Ang Lee is planning an Americanised remake of Alain Resnais' masterpiece *Same Old Song* (*On connaît la chanson* [1998]). *Magnolia* (1999), possibly in homage to stylistic predecessors including *Welcome to LA* (1977), *Last Chants for a Slow Dance* (1977) and *Light Sleeper* (1992), is constructed in relation to a running commentary comprised of songs by Aimee Mann, building to the central moment where every character, in his or her separate situation, sings a few lines. *Water Drops on Burning Rocks* (2000), adapted from a Rainer Werner Fassbinder play, contains a show-stopping musical interlude. *Caro diario* (1994) first announces director Nanni Moretti's running gag – or is it a fonder, more serious wish? – regarding a musical he wants to make about a Trotskyite pastry chef; *Aprile* (1998) concludes with a lovely snippet from this dream-film. And, a decade and half before this current upsurge, John Cassavetes did get to film not a musical of *Crime and Punishment* but an extraordinary fantasy insert of ballet and song at the emotional height of *Love Streams* (1984).

We can risk staking a claim to the universalism – as opposed to the imperialism – of the musical form: as Masson puts it, the musical can be grasped 'as sovereign art and fulfillment of the cinematographic genius'[20] – not the genius of any one film-maker, but the genius inherent in the medium itself. The musical, as Platonic ideal, embodies everything that is theatrical, artificial and purely expressive in cinema as aesthetic language, as artistic gesture. Anything goes; everything sings. Here, in the realm of broad but essential concepts, the musical aligns itself with melodrama and expressionism in defining one essence of the cinema as a medium. Godard most certainly had this essence in mind when he mused (in the course of a review of *The Pajama Game* [1957]) that the musical 'is in a way the idealisation of cinema'.[21]

The musical depends on artifice, and also on the magic of a certain uncanniness. The central spring of any musical number in film is that the music is not quite outside the film (extra-diegetic) since people move to it, and not inside it (diegetic) either, since no one physically hears it in its full flowering. Rick Altman calls this the realm of 'transcendent, supra-diegetic music'[22] to which, as Tom Gunning remarks, 'the world itself responds', in a 'gradual enchantment of the diegetic world [...] as if infected by rhythm or melody, given over to pure expressivity'.[23]

Here again we touch the notion of the music-film, greater and vaster than the musical *per se*. Whenever the stylistic elements of cinema – colour, movement, rhythm, sound, bodies – are joined in synchronous intensity, we feel on the verge of a musical, almost a musical. This sudden, sometimes fleeting flowering of sight and sound in magical fusion can occur in the least likely places: in the overhead shot of brightly coloured cars taking off from a crossing in perfect orchestration, Demy-like, in *Carlito's Way* (1993); when Barney Wilen's breathy soundtrack saxophone harmonises with Brigitte Sy's casual singing, twice over, in a sequence-shot of *Les Baisers de secours* (1989); or the haunting moment where Jeremy Irons calls out over and over, in a plaintive tone, the name of his twin brother over the swelling and disappearing chord clusters of Howard Shore's score in *Dead Ringers* (1988). Perhaps the greatest sequence of this sort, deliriously stylised, is the morning wake-up of an army of bouncing women in *The Ladies' Man* (1961); between Walter Scharf's music, Bobby Van's choreography and Jerry Lewis' *mise en scène*, it is a dazzling declaration of the power and elegance of artifice, and its expressive freedom.

There is a supreme threshold, a point of no return, at which the almost musical passes over into a real musical – and also, inescapably, enters into a dialogue with the genre's history. It is the moment where characters, as is so often said, burst into song. It is this precise moment – with its promises, its potential, its connotations, its burden of history – which is at once the most attractive and the most difficult for contemporary film-makers. The attraction is in the thrill of the ideal – the possibility of going to the very end of cinema's expressive, intensive energies. What is difficult to negotiate, however, is the contradiction between this felt, aesthetic thrill and the awesome, constraining weight of cultural taste that prefers, and proscribes, more realistic or naturalistic codes and protocols. Tellingly, it is only in the field of feature animation for children – where all-over artifice poses no problem for anyone, where taste barriers are lowered for the very young – that the musical can really march unfettered as a popular genre.

Beyond the pressure of cultural taste, history also implacably intervenes. Between enthusing over *The Pajama Game* in 1958 and making his third film, *Une Femme est une femme*, three years later, something profoundly changed in Godard's attitude towards the promise of musicals; disenchantment had at last set in.

> In any case the musical is dead. *Adieu Philippine* [1963] is a musical in a sense, but the genre itself is dead. It would be pointless even for the Americans to remake *Singin' in the Rain*. You have to do something different: my film says this too. It is nostalgia for the musical.[24]

This is a historic turning point, for such disenchantment is not felt by Godard alone. Between 1958 and 1961, the French *nouvelle vague* began in strength, and a sense swiftly spread that a whole classical era marked by the Hollywood studio system had ended, or was at least in its death throes.

It is at this moment, all around the world – with the seeming birth of a new cinema and the seeming death of an old one – that a complex nostalgia for the musical is born. It becomes like the romantic comedy, the melodrama or the Western: one can no longer make them the way the old masters used to. The naturalness and innocence, the professionalism and fluency are all gone; a secret has been lost. Thus the horrified and melancholic reaction of Terence Davies – all of whose films are mutant musicals – to the suggestion that he make a 'real' musical: 'The touchstone is *Singin' in the Rain* which I saw when I was seven. Nothing is as good. No matter how hard you try, you can't do it.'[25]

4. Two traditions

Once the musical became, for many film-makers since the early 60s, a lost dream, a quintessential modern gesture arose: that of citing or pointing to the musical within their own works. What is at stake in this gesture is always the marking of an interval between, on the one hand, the world of the fiction lived in by the characters – invariably signalled as drab, weighty and miserable or simply mundane and earthbound – and then, on the other hand, the world of the musical, which is somewhere else altogether, usually locked up in a Hollywood-induced dream.

Rosenbaum exactly locates the fault-line at which this socio-cultural drama of nostalgia, longing, bitterness and loss takes place: those moments that Rick Altman calls audio and video dissolves which negotiate the shifts 'back and forth between story (spoken dialogue) and song-and-dance numbers' – often giving rise to 'queasy transitions just before or after these shifts, when we're uncertain where we are stylistically'.[26]

To handle or negotiate that queasiness is the great aesthetic and professional challenge of the classic Hollywood musical and all those films in other countries which seek to emulate it to any significant degree. For musical mutations, that queasiness is also the central issue, but it gives rise to different responses and solutions. There are essentially two forms of this modern response, giving rise to two traditions.

The first response is to harden and make absolute the distinction or the gap between the real world of the fiction and the musical world. Only a direct cut, a disorienting leap that is variously wishful, agonised or ironic, can take us into the song or out of it. This mutant musical tradition flourishes under the sign of Dennis Potter, writer of the TV series *Pennies from Heaven* (1978), *The Singing Detective* (1986) and *Lipstick on Your Collar* (1993), among others.

The second formal response is to abolish, as far as possible, the distinction between the real world and the musical world, or between song and story. This tradition occurs under the sign of Demy, whose full and long career of musical making (seven in all) deserves to be better known around the world beyond the inaugural milestone of *The Umbrellas of Cherbourg* (1964).

Let us look more closely at the first of these traditions. Potter used relentlessly in his television work the device of mouthing: characters mime pre-existing songs, usually popular standards of a previous era. The gap between Hollywood, Broadway or music-hall dreams and miserable British realities is total, and usually devastating. It is always an ironic juxtaposition: people sing 'We're in the Money' when they're broke; they sing about love when they're mired in frustration and despair; they sing about happiness and dreams when they're marching to the gallows. Potter, and the directors he worked with on TV, invented new, abrupt cues for musical numbers: a coloured light suffuses the scene, and the song suddenly begins. The settings remain depressingly solid and grimy, before, during and after the songs: a bedroom, a diner, a pub. The world conjured in these songs is not only unreal and unreachable, it is also hollow and narcissistic: a realm of desperate wish-fulfilments. Almost every song in a work by Potter is a fantasy in the bad, negative sense.

A scene from the film version of *Pennies from Heaven* based around the song 'It's a Sin to Tell a Lie' encapsulates the model style of Potter's musical interpolations. In this scene, the salesman (Steve Martin) has just returned to the wife (Jessica Harper) to whom he has been unfaithful. Herbert Ross' *mise en scène* works masterfully with an almost Brechtian notion of visual framing: once the wife slips into her fantasy of marital revenge, the very borders of the screen are marked as the pure, cartoonish space of an unreal fantasy; utopia can exist only within these paper-thin artificial boundaries, these narcissistic bubbles. Ross' close framing tracks Harper's movement and lays the ground for the shock moment when she will suddenly bring up a knife from below screen; needless to say, the entire portrait of gleeful vindictiveness evaporates in a split second as the scene abruptly restores this woman to her original, passive position on the bed.

Is it too facile to take away the glamour, energy and art from a typical musical scene, and then declare it, rhetorically, to be empty and false? This is the trap into which much of Potter's television work falls. The equivocality and ambiguity – of mood, emotion, meaning and association – which I sometimes find lacking in Potter's oeuvre is restored by one of the most extraordinary films indebted to his legacy: Tsai Ming-liang's *The Hole* (1998).

This film uses a specific corpus of old pop songs by Grace Chang, a star of glamorous Hong Kong musicals of the 50s, popular throughout South East Asia. These songs are mimed within fantasy sequences by the two principal cast members, Tsai's regulars Yang Kuei-mei and Lee Kang-sheng. If one were to subtract these scenes, *The Hole* might be rather like Tsai's previous work, *Vive l'amour* (1994) and *The River* (1997): minimalist films, very silent and bleak, in the Antonioni mould, about emotional repression, disconnection and social breakdown. But *The Hole*, made for a series of films about the year 2000, possesses an extra, futuristic, transformative element. It narrates, essentially, the millennial apocalypse, with Taiwan overrun by a deadly virus that is carried by rainwater (the rain never stops pouring down), reducing people to an insect-like state before they die. Beyond this bare plot context, what we mainly see are two separate people in two apartments, one atop the other – and the hole in the floor that might in some way connect these young professionals presumably living out their last days. As Robin Wood asked: 'Is this the first – and perhaps last – musical about the end of the world?'[27]

Are the songs really fantasies? Tsai never gives us that much solid information. But two things are clear. First, that Tsai has found the perfect point of intersection between the form and content of a musical and his own cinematic universe: both of them (as Rosenbaum says of *Haut bas fragile*) seek to explore 'the joys and sorrows of being alone and of being with someone else'.[28] Second, that these superficially sunny songs and dances – staged with such zest and invention – contain many bleak echoes and reversals of everything else we see in the film's story world. The ambiguity of this juxtaposition of incommensurable worlds is wrenching for the viewer, and is capped off by a final postscript in the end credits signed by the film-maker: 'The year 2000 is coming. We are grateful we still have Grace Chang's songs with us.'

In one scene, Yang Kuei-mei lies in her bath and sneezes – a sign that the virus is upon her, and also a signal that a wry song is coming on, a wonderful tune called 'Achoo Cha Cha' (by Yao Ming, choreography by Joy Lo).[29] In this number, Tsai ingeniously reinvests the elements of the Potter style. The place – here the apartment block – remains *in situ* for the duration of all the songs; we never leave this physical world for another. Here, however, the grim, worldly stage is at least dressed and prettified. But what is it dressed in? All the objects – such as hanging, fluttering material and rolls of fabric – recall motifs and props back in the story world: the tissues with which the woman endlessly tries to mop up her space, or the paper peeling off her walls.

Richard Dyer's seminal 1975 essay 'Entertainment and Utopia' proposed that musical utopias conjure abundance – physical, material abundance – where, elsewhere in reality, there is only scarcity. Both Potter and Tsai give this aspect of musical form a vicious new twist. As in *Pennies from Heaven* or Chantal Akerman's *Golden Eighties* (1986), problems, worries and obsessions relating to money are everywhere, underwriting all flights into fantasy. The world is a pinched place. So, in *The Hole*'s songs, everything is abundant, overflowing, a fantasy of consumption: surplus, wasteful materials, plus chorus lines of adoring, interchangeable men and women, so different from that other, real world in which not even one man and one woman can connect.

Tsai's way of staging, framing and cutting 'Achoo Cha Cha' is all his own: neither sympathetic (as in Donen) nor antipathetic (as in Godard's musical numbers in *Pierrot le fou* [1965]), the *mise en scène* is full of life and performance energy, but also sparse, diagrammatic, almost geometric in its reversals of direction (shooting up the stairs, then down the stairs), isolated camera movements, and sudden changes of locale (such as when the hero enters a tatty field of white streamers). Once again, the frame borders carve out a static unit of fragile, ephemeral magic.

How does Demy, and anyone who works in the second mutant musical tradition, abolish these deadly, pessimistic distinctions between song and story? In *The Umbrellas of Cherbourg*, this entails making a total, non-stop, feature-length musical, in which the music never stops and every single line, every scene, every interaction, is sung. Other takes on this fanciful desire explore different paths. In *Haut bas fragile*, Jacques Rivette takes that suspended moment of transition or dissolve just before a song begins or just after it ends and turns it into the guiding principle of his *mise en scène*, spreading it through the entire movie: the film is full of walks, gestures and movements that are almost dance-like – and you have to get an hour into the film before the first actual song appears.

In Akerman's *Nuit et jour* (1991), Julie (Guillaine Londez) is forever strolling through Paris and singing to herself about her daily life – whether or not her reverie is in sync with the notes on the soundtrack at that moment. The film plays a hide-and-seek game in which, just occasionally, there is a magic moment of synchronisation or coincidence between this character, her world and the realm of supra-diegetic music. In *Same Old Song*, a project which brilliantly combines the legacies of Potter (to whom it is dedicated) and Demy, Resnais has characters, when they are not miming songs, sometimes speaking in song lyrics.

In *The Young Girls of Rochefort* (1967) Demy uses, between the big song and dance numbers, a lot of humming, people singing to themselves, fiddling around on musical instruments – so that the act of music making is everywhere in the everyday, just as, in *The Tango Lesson* (1997), dance permeates everything (as for instance in the lovely sequence where Pablo Verron dances in the kitchen as he prepares a meal). Extending Minnelli's technique in *Meet Me in St Louis*, where overlapping amateur renditions of the title tune ease us in to its full-blown musical world, Demy's film begins with distinct little outbursts of music and dance (visitors arriving, piano and dance classes) rather than flowering immediately into a full-scale number. On the technical plane, these gestures towards the total musical often give rise to completely or largely post-synchronised soundtracks: that way, speech and song blend beautifully, with no queasy transition between them for the ear or for the actors. This overall post-synchronisation is the case in *Golden Eighties*, and in most of Demy's films.

In *The Young Girls of Rochefort* everyone walks and walks – a delirious extension of what Eric de Kuyper (critic/theorist and screenwriter for Akerman) once called the 'step by step' principle.[30] Around half of Demy's film is set out on the streets, between rendezvous involving the many and various characters. The spatial, architectural, design principle of the film is the open plan: everything is courtyards, town squares, huge windows and vistas. Everybody is constantly in transit, circulating, colliding with or just missing a predestined partner. For Demy, the world – here, the whole town of Rochefort – is truly a stage, in a radical elaboration of the Minnelli ethos. And this stage has no limits, neither in space nor time. The widescreen camera movements and framings are astonishing; this may be the only musical that fits André Bazin's pet film theory of the film frame as a mobile window onto an abounding reality, since dancing constantly shoots in and out of the frame, traverses this rectangular window, like it's going on everywhere all the time, whether we can see it or not. Lastly, Demy intermingles walking with dancing, with some participants gliding almost imperceptibly into the foreground action from a long way in the background.

Some walk and others dance, but all are equally enchanted, recalling Rosenbaum's idea about those musicals (by Demy, Lubitsch/Mamoulian and Milestone) which partake of a 'metaphysical impulse to perceive the musical form as a continuous state of delirious being rather than a traditional story with musical eruptions'.[31] This continuous state can accommodate an enormous stretching of stylistic liberties – an unpredictable freedom with regards to the concept of cinematic address, for instance, so that during Gene Kelly's first appearance (a magical musical mutation in and of itself) a highpoint of delirium arrives when, unprepared for, he begins singing directly into camera, without the alibi of a point-of-view shot. *Golden Eighties* similarly switches in jest between various modes of address – to the point of having a duet in which one character flirts to the camera and her interlocutor merely looks about, puzzled and disturbed.

5. The dark

At the turn of the millennium, Lars von Trier's controversial *Dancer in the Dark* (2000) exploded through global film culture. Here is an example of a musical mutation so bold and brazen that, virtually overnight, it galvanised critical discourse everywhere, disturbing casual, cosy assumptions, and forcing people to ask themselves the question: just what is a musical, anyway?[32]

Dancer in the Dark has enjoyed the paradoxical honour of being hailed as a work in the tradition of Potter – for David Jays, von Trier seeks to 'accentuate the contradictions, to slip spanners into Busby Berkeley's gleaming works'[33] – while being publicised by its Australian distributor as a 'part-homage to the Euro-musicals of Jacques Demy'. In a sense, both claims are true. On the one hand, the film insists on the bleak separation of escapist musical fantasies from the grimy, murky realities of the quotidian, via the standard Potter stylistic device: the shock cut before the song is fully over, dropping us back into the everyday, framing scenes in which these fantasies have arisen. But, on the other hand, the musical numbers themselves have an intensity and virtuosity missing from the Potter tradition.

The real interpenetration of the songs and the drama in *Dancer in the Dark* occurs at the level of an ingenious and carefully wrought formal logic of complementarity. It is easy to take the non-musical scenes as the usual, non-rigorous free-forming beloved of von Trier in his Dogme phase: hand-held camera, incessant jump-cuts, muddy digital images, loosely improvised performances, open (even sloppy) *mise en scène*. But – for once in his career – this mode exists only in a strict counterpoint to another mode that reverses it in almost every detail.

Like *The Hole*, *Dancer in the Dark* opposes a fantasy of abundance to a reality of miserable, economic and material scarcity. But its most brilliant step is to locate that abundance on a formal and stylistic plane. As was widely publicised, the musical sequences were filmed in single takes by a hundred digital cameras, these views then edited in rapid succession. This is not mere capriciousness, exhibitionism or perversity on von Trier's part; the mode of filming chosen has three powerful pay-offs. First, where the dramatic scenes are relentlessly discontinuous in their formal rendering, the songs are almost magically continuous – match cutting (editing on movement) has rarely carried such a palpable thrill. Second, where the dramatic scenes have a cramped, heavy feel, due to the single, hand-held camera shuttling back and forth monotonously between the actors – as if the actors are insects shoved under glass for morbid or sadistic inspection – the musical scenes are seemingly limitless in their spatial extension. As the singers and dancers cover ground (especially in the train number), it is as if their movements, in any direction whatsoever, trigger a static camera to capture a specific segment of the choreography. Third, there is the exhilarating, plastic effect guaranteed by those one hundred cameras, many set at extremely odd, non-classical angles: in a veritable orgy of formal abundance, this multiplicity of views ensures that no angle is ever used twice.

In all these ways, von Trier has taken literally and made explicit the subtle aesthetic at work in Hollywood musicals such as *Singin' in the Rain* in which, as Masson demonstrates, '[t]he space is transparent, the filmic area unlimited [. . .] inaugurat[ing] an abstract vision of space defined only according to its own rule, as if it were independent of any position'.[34] More integrally, these formal devices work in concert to build an expressive world picture: Selma (Björk) never sings to us, never liberates herself from the diegesis to that extent, like Gene Kelly in *The Young Girls of Rochefort*; rather, her musical fantasies constitute fragile, desperate attempts to weave around her an inter-subjective community of harmonious, compassionate souls – and the hundred cameras enclose the bubble of this dream.

This is a radical approach to musical *mise en scène* – one that belies the complaints of those who find the numbers in the film lazily or half-heartedly staged, as if merely mounted in the spirit of an ironic, post-modern, quotational joke, or simply recycling an MTV aesthetic. Too much evident work has gone into the conceptualising and planning of these scenes and into the tight intermeshing of all their elements (staging, song production and choreography) for this to be so. It is true to say that von Trier experiments with what could be called an aggressive approach to the rendering of Selma's songs – as Paul Willemen accurately complains, 'camera positions are consistently divorced from narrative logic' and 'cinematic space and time are destroyed'[35] – but are we so far here from the sort of scenographic fracturings explored by Godard in *Une Femme est une femme* and *Pierrot le fou*? Robert Altman performed a similar experiment in *Popeye*, where the typical elements of his style – extensive use of long shots, a floating babble of voices and sounds, incessant and disconcerting cross-cutting between scenes in separate spaces, and what Leonard Maltin regards as 'cluttered staging' – were used upon the 'alleged songs by Harry Nilsson'[36] as much as on the normal scenes, with some remarkable and exciting disorientations resulting.

Another formal difference between the dramatic and musical scenes in *Dancer in the Dark* occurs on the level of the sound design. The former use a thin, sonically restricted range; the latter explode in multi-speaker Dolby. This is an index of von Trier's attention to sound and its formal logic throughout the film. Each song is composed and produced around a specific kind of audio dissolve – a real sound (such as that of the factory machinery) that provides a rhythm leading into the start of the music proper. Björk's music, however, pushes the envelope of the audio dissolve, since sampled treatments make up so much of the texture of each song. Von Trier, for his part, stages the dances, in their spatial extension, so as to allow the incessant filtering in of non-musical sounds that instantly become musical within the mix, such as the bike wheel spun by Gene (Vladica Kostic) or the metallic ring of the wind-blown flagpole in the resurrection number following the murder of Bill (David Morse).

The film moves towards the magisterial point at which the corny injunction from Kathy (Catherine Deneuve) to 'listen to your heart!' assumes its full formal logic: at that moment, in direct sound, Selma will sing to the beat (amplified for us) of her own heart, the only music left to her once all external audio-dissolve prompts have been cruelly taken away (prison, we are told, is a hellishly quiet place). A course of musical disintegration, leading to this moment, has been charted: its key phase is the disquieting rendition of 'My Favourite Things' from *The Sound of Music* (1965), sung by Selma (the first of two songs recorded in direct sound) in her cell over a sampled loop of the choral singing emanating down the pipes and through the grill in her cell. Prior to this disintegration, all Selma's music has been like an inner music writ large, projected onto the external world – this is the conjured sensorium of her sightless world, akin to Juliette Binoche's condition in *Les Amants du Pont-Neuf* (1991); now she is reduced to the merest scrap of sound, like the steps taken that lead her to the gallows. *Dancer in the Dark* thus takes apart not only the inside and outside of its songs, but even the inside and outside of its heroine – her experience of psycho-acoustic plenitude embodied, then stripped bare, and finally suspended in the moment of non-closure heralded (casually at first) by the film in its dream of the eternal 'second last song'.

Among the reasons that von Trier's film wields such cultural force is because of the severe way it denaturalises the American provenance of the musical genre. In this American story, no locations and few actors are authentically American; instead, the film gives

the impression of (as John Caughie once put it) 'playing at being American' for our troubled and fascinated amusement.[37] And it is a grim game, because, on the dramatic plane,
the film evolves into an unstinting critique of the American system of capital punishment
– a bold extension of conventional generic content that, once again, acknowledges a debt
to Demy's legacy.

Definitions and depictions of nationality inform another major, beguiling element of
Dancer in the Dark. Much is made of the existence of a character who is a star of Czech
musicals that are beloved in his nation's popular memory – so beloved that, in Selma's
fantasy, he is cast as her imaginary father. In a final, dizzying twist of anti-verisimilitude,
this Czech star is ultimately incarnated by Joel Grey from *Cabaret* (1972).

Von Trier's perversity here is inspired. What makes this surreally foreign character at
once so bizarre and so magical is the utter alienness of his conception: only within such
a completely fantasticated, desperately wishful world would a non-Hollywood musical
star hold such enormous sway over sentimental and social destinies. But maybe that is,
after all, a real world for many spectators in far-flung lands and subterranean pockets of
world culture – or a musical utopia actually worth having in the future.

Notes

1. Edgardo Cozarinsky, '*Une Femme est une femme*', in Ian Cameron (ed.), *The Films of Jean-Luc Godard* (London: Studio Vista, 1969), p. 27.

2. Quoted in Judy Stone, *Eye on the World: Conversations with International Filmmakers* (Los Angeles: Silman-James Press, 1997), p. 229.

3. Quoted in Jonathan Rosenbaum, 'Echoes of Old Hollywood', *Chicago Reader*, 2 April 1999. http://www.chireader.com/movies/archives/1999/0499/04029.html.

4. *Cinéastes de notre temps*, television documentary, 1966.

5. Raymond Durgnat, 'Film Favourites: *Bells Are Ringing*', *Film Comment*, March–April 1973, p. 49. Reprinted in Gregg Rickman (ed.), *The Film Comedy Reader* (New York: Limelight, 2001), pp. 230–6.

6. Karen Durbin, 'Every Dane Has His Dogma', *Good Weekend*, 17 June 2000, p. 32.

7. Geoff Pevere, 'Naive Revisionary', *Cinema Scope* no. 4, Summer 2000, p. 41.

8. Rick Altman (ed.), *Genre: The Musical* (London: British Film Institute, 1981), pp. 216–19.

9. Rick Altman, *The American Film Musical* (Bloomington: Indiana University Press, 1987).

10. Alain Masson, 'Notes de lecture', *Positif* nos 329–30, July–August 1988, pp. 124–5.

11. Marc Miller, 'Of Tunes and Toons: The Movie Musical in the 1990s', in Wheeler Winston Dixon (ed.), *Film Genre 2000* (New York: State University of New York, 2000), pp. 45–62.

12. Richard Barrios, *A Song in the Dark: The Birth of the Musical Film* (New York: Oxford University Press, 1995), p. 10.

13. Brian McFarlane, Geoff Mayer and Ina Bertrand (eds), *The Oxford Companion to Australian Film* (Melbourne: Oxford University Press, 1999), p. 468.

14. Paul Willemen, *Looks and Frictions: Essays in Cultural Studies and Film Theory* (London: British Film Institute, 1994), p. 123.

15. A recent attempt in this direction is Bill Marshall and Robyn Stilwell (eds), *Musicals: Hollywood and Beyond* (Exeter: Intellect Books, 2000).

16. Richard Dyer, 'Entertainment and Utopia', in Altman (ed.), *Genre: The Musical*, pp. 175–89, originally published in *Movie* no. 24, 1975; Jane Feuer, *The Hollywood Musical* (London: British Film Institute, 1982).

17. Jonathan Rosenbaum, 'Not the Same Old Song and Dance', *Chicago Reader*, 24 November 1998. http://www.chireader.com/movies/archives/1998/1198/11248.html.

18. Altman, *The American Film Musical*, p. 363.

19. Tom Milne (ed.), *Godard on Godard* (London: Secker and Warburg, 1972), p. 182.

20. Masson, 'Notes de lecture', p. 125.

21. Milne (ed.), *Godard on Godard*, p. 87.

22. Altman, *The American Film Musical*, p. 70.

23. Tom Gunning, *The Films of Fritz Lang: Allegories of Vision and Modernity* (London: British Film Institute, 2000), p. 265.

24. Milne (ed.), *Godard on Godard*, p. 182.

25. John Boorman and Walter Donohue (eds), *Projections* no. 6 (London: Faber and Faber, 1996), p. 174.

26. Rosenbaum, 'Not the Same Old Song and Dance'.

27. Robin Wood, 'Singin' in the Rain: *The Hole*', *Cinema Scope* no. 2, Winter 2000, p. 29. Originally published in *CineAction* no. 48, December 1998.

28. Jonathan Rosenbaum, 'Ragged But Right', *Chicago Reader*, 26 July 1996. http://www.chireader.com/movies/archives/0796/07266.html.

29. This song is sometimes identified as 'Sneezing (Da Penti)'.

30. Eric de Kuyper, 'Step by Step: Reflexions on the "Dancing in the Dark" Sequence from Vincente Minnelli's *The Band Wagon*', *Wide Angle* vol. 5 no. 3, 1983, pp. 44–9.

31. Rosenbaum, 'Not the Same Old Song and Dance'.

32. See José Arroyo, 'How Do You Solve a Problem Like von Trier?', *Sight and Sound* vol. 10 no. 9, September 2000, pp. 14–16; and the dossier of essays in *Cinema Scope* no. 4, Summer 2000, pp. 38–41.

33. David Jays, 'Blues in the Night', *Sight and Sound* vol. 10 no. 9, September 2000, p. 19.

34. Alain Masson, 'An Architectural Promenade', *Continuum* vol. 5 no. 2, 1992, pp. 164–5.

35. Paul Willemen, 'Note on *Dancer in the Dark*', *Framework* no. 42, Summer 2000. http://www.frameworkonline.com/42pw.htm.

36. Leonard Maltin, *Movie and Video Guide* (New York: Signet, 2000), p. 1091.

37. John Caughie, 'Playing at Being American: Games and Tactics', in Patricia Mellencamp (ed.), *Logics of Television: Essays in Cultural Criticism* (Bloomington: Indiana University Press, 1990), pp. 44–58.

7

Squaring *The Circle*

Jonathan Rosenbaum (2000)

Note: The following article was written in 2000 for the Chicago Reader, *to coincide with the release of Jafar Panahi's* The Circle – *although a differently edited version was published – and several traces of these journalistic origins have been allowed to remain.*

Last month, I was taken aback by an email from a colleague – not a cranky stranger – waiting for me at my office computer one morning. It said, 'I thought, as an apparent defender of the Islamic Republic of Iran, that you should read this.' Before I even accessed the link – an AP story about a woman stoned to death by court order for appearing in porn movies – I wrote him back that I felt insulted by the implication that regarding Iranians as human beings meant supporting a totalitarian regime. He promptly sent back an apology, but added, 'It's just that sometimes it sounds as if you regard their regime as "better" than ours. Perhaps I'm misreading you.'

One might ask, 'better' for whom? And why put quotation marks around that word but not around 'their' or 'ours'? But I'm getting ahead of myself. To tell the truth, his second email upset me even more than the first, and not only because it was a misreading. If the first email could be rationalised as a sick joke – a bit like being called a 'nigger lover' when I was an Alabama teenager (an epithet sometimes followed by, 'Just kidding!') – the personal pronouns in the second chilled my blood, carrying me back to the either/or, us/them mentality that is surely the most primitive as well as the most dangerous of all our Cold War legacies. It scares me even more when I reflect on where this country's current isolationism may be leading us, and what those pronouns may wind up doing to live bodies as well as developing minds.

I guess this must sound like an excessive response. But I have to admit that those words and what they suggested haunted me for the rest of the week. They echoed in my ears like a tribal directive, implicitly telling me that my colleague and I – along with Timothy McVeigh, Janet Reno, Jeffrey Dahmer and every other American who might be construed a mass murderer – shared something irreducible in terms of our identities that couldn't be superseded by anything I had or felt I had in common with anyone else in the world. They were implying that even though I had no choice about being born an American, a white male, a Jew or a southerner, these were nonetheless the very attributes that entitled me to use the personal pronouns 'my' and 'our' – unlike the more existential attributes I chose for myself, such as remaining an American but not a southerner, remaining a Jew but not a practising one, or, most importantly, regarding myself as a member of the planet. Like it or not, we – my colleague, I, and those others mentioned – were all members of the same club, and other folks need not apply.

But what did my colleague actually mean by 'their' regime, anyway? Could it honestly be called a regime belonging to the woman who got stoned to death? If it was, how could one account for her appearing in porn films, which isn't 'their' sort of thing at all? Even the Iranians I know in Iran are people I wouldn't dream of insulting by identifying them with the oppression they all have to cope with, just as I'd feel slimed if someone insinuated that George W. Bush was 'my' personal leader. *That* twerp, whom I and most of my fellow citizens didn't even vote for? After all, it's him and his sponsors, not 'us', who are breaking all those international treaties and polluting our planet for coin – or would it be more appropriate at this point to call it 'their' planet? One reason, in fact, why I like remaining an American is that there aren't so many laws here obliging me to take the blame or the credit for someone like Bush.

The only time I've been in Iran – last February, to serve on a film festival jury – I was treated with a great deal of warmth and hospitality by people I didn't regard as totalitarian, maybe because Iran and Islam are far from the same thing. But my hosts and I were still subject to totalitarian laws, this being a country where, for instance, it's illegal for men and women who are unmarried to touch one another in public, even to shake hands. This doesn't mean they don't touch one another in private; the parties I attended in people's homes were pretty relaxed. But it does mean that I can't tell you everything I saw and heard in Iran without getting some friends into trouble – and I can't even say this much without giving a false impression that I'm lewdly winking about something. One of the big problems with totalitarian societies is how cramped they make everyone's communication in general – tribal personal pronouns and Cold War paranoia included. During the single afternoon I spent in East Berlin before the wall came down, the most disturbing aspect of the bars and cafés I visited was how deadly quiet they all were, with voices seldom rising much above whispers.

This wasn't the case in the Iranian cafés and restaurants I visited (there are no Iranian bars). But one does worry at times in public places about being observed, and film-maker Béla Tarr, a fellow juror in Tehran, told me that the city reminded him of his childhood in Budapest. It's part of the singularity of Jafar Panahi's *The Circle* (2000) – and indicative of the courage and perceptiveness of the man who made it – that this is almost certainly the first Iranian movie that depicts this everyday fear and makes it part of an overall emotional texture. It's a far cry as well as a quantum leap from *The White Balloon* (1995) and *The Mirror* (1997) – Panahi's previous two features, both of them relatively light-hearted films about little girls – though it also makes me want to see those pictures again, because it clearly has certain stylistic as well as thematic links with them. All three features, for starters, present unaccompanied females on the streets of Tehran and play with notions of real time. But it's with *The Circle*, in any case, that Panahi fully establishes his credentials as a master, a man who clearly knows film-making like the back of his hand.

Perhaps the most talented of all of Kiarostami's disciples – he worked as an assistant on *Through the Olive Trees* (1994) and got Kiarostami to write the story of *The White Balloon* – Panahi can be credited with going well beyond his mentor in at least one major respect: by giving a particular political thrust to the same kind of narrative ellipsis and deliberate formal construction that Kiarostami is famous for. Showing how formal and political radicalism can work together is itself a sizeable achievement given the way such projects are commonly viewed as being at loggerheads with one another, especially in this country.

As one example of what I mean, some of the central women characters in the film are fresh out of prison, but we never find out why any of them went to jail in the first place, and our understanding in some cases of whether they escaped, got out on parole, or simply reached the end of their sentences is either delayed or remains incomplete. We gradually come to realise that none of this information matters, given the story that Panahi has to tell, and that our lack of certainty about these details even adds a particular edge to the viewer's engagement with the storytelling. It's an edge that qualifies as an ideological inflection once we realise that this is a movie that refuses to allow us to rationalise the way these women are treated by their society with any excuses or alibis. The film lacks villains or heroes in the ordinary sense, because the protagonists all have their lifelike mixtures of strengths and weaknesses. But it's obvious from the beginning that what these women have to put up with is intolerable, and Panahi refuses to allow us to say at any point, for any reason, that any of them is 'getting what she deserves'. As with Kiarostami, the narrative gaps constitute a form of respect for the viewer, but in this case the respect is not merely for the audience's imagination but also for its ethics, its innate sense of decency. It's a sensitivity we wind up sharing with Panahi and therefore feel entitled to call 'ours' – meaning, in this case, 'his and ours', not 'ours' in contradistinction to 'that Iranian's'.

The point at which *The Circle* really kicks in for me is when a teenage character named Nargess keeps trying and failing to board a bus that would take her back to Raziliq, her home town. We know she wants desperately to go, but something keeps preventing her. Panahi and Nargess Mamizadeh, the wonderfully expressive and spontaneous non-professional playing the part, create a virtual symphony out of all the things we know and don't know about her, adroitly dovetailed with all the things she knows and doesn't know as well as the schedules of the various buses leaving. Like the wedding party that keeps re-entering the movie at separate stages, her character is both consistent and unpredictable, and her disorientation in the terminal as she wanders about soon becomes ours. She sports a large bruise under her right eye, and we never learn its source; she's convinced that a reproduction of a Van Gogh landscape that she sees on the street depicts her home town, though the painter forgot to include certain details. We also suspect but can't confirm that her older pal Arezou (Maryiam Parvin Almani), whose name means 'hope', turned a trick in order to raise money for her bus fare, and we aren't told why Arezou eventually decides not to go with her either. What we gradually discover is that Nargess' failure to board may be a phobic reaction, and assuming that we ever learn its cause, it may not be until very late in the picture – when we see another woman boarding a police van – that we can figure out its source.

In fact, it's part of the overall risky strategy of this poetically interactive movie to have the story of one woman continued or 'completed' by the story of another – a highly artificial procedure that the film miraculously brings off by making all the fragments we glimpse both extremely lifelike and congruent with one another. This method may constitute a kind of shotgun wedding between formalism and realism, poetry and agitprop, but Panahi stages the match with such natural grace that it sometimes feels like a marriage made in heaven.

This is the first Iranian noir I've seen[1] – and I'm using 'noir' here to denote a style that isn't 'ours' but the world's. After all, the term itself is French, and it's worth adding that France has probably influenced Iran as much as us. (The most common way of saying 'thank you' in Tehran, audible in *The Circle*, is 'merci'.) Fear and noir typically go together – and the most frightening of Val Lewton's noirish B films, *The Leopard Man* (1943), has a somewhat similar narrative structure, a narrative relay passing from one character to the next (though so do Luis Buñuel's *The Phantom of Liberty* [1974] and Richard Linklater's *Slacker* [1991], among other art-house examples).

Other mainstream movie counterparts come as readily to mind. In more ways than I can count, *The Circle* is also like a punchy Warners proletarian-protest quickie of the 30s, with salty convicts, a hard-nosed, self-accepting prostitute who could have been played by Joan Blondell, snappy extras, and a kind of narrative pacing – the way characters drift in and out of the plot – that evokes the way traffic moves on a busy city sidewalk. (Parenthetical query: are American movies made before we were born 'ours' or 'theirs'? Answer: I think they can become ours if we decide to adopt them.)

The movie begins and ends with two virtuoso long takes, both 360-degree pans that define the poetic and metaphoric limits of Panahi's universe and are so overloaded that they threaten to explode the film's structure. In the first, a baby is being born off-screen in a hospital, her mother howling with pain, and when a nurse reports through a window in a door that it's a girl, the grandmother, speaking on the other side, is clearly upset – 'But the ultrasound said it would be a boy!' – and continues to worry about the expected anger of the in-laws as she goes downstairs and speaks to another daughter. The latter leaves the hospital, passing three women beside a phone booth – all former prisoners who quickly take over the narrative. In the last shot, a prostitute enters a jail cell where virtually all the major characters in the film, excluding the grandmother, are revealed over the course of one lengthy circular pan. When a nearby phone rings, and a guard appears at a window on the cell door asking for a woman who isn't there, but is apparently in an adjacent cell, the name is that of the mother whom we heard giving birth in the opening shot.

Simply put, Panahi's film is about Iranian women who aren't free – free to ride on buses or stay in hotels without IDs, free to walk down the street alone or enter some places without chadors or hitch rides or smoke cigarettes in public (a running gag as one character after another tries to light up) or have abortions or function as single mothers or be let off easily by the cops (unlike some men we see). And for all the artificiality of the bookend shots, and the many circular paths in-between that are charted (and doors with windows that are peered through) – not to mention a narrative comprising a catalogue of abuses – the surface textures of this film are every bit as real and as immediate as those in *The White Balloon* and *The Mirror*. Moreover, the fact that it's so blunt and effective makes some people furious, Iranians and non-Iranians alike – because it's axiomatic that political provocations tend to put us all on the spot and make us angry or defensive, sometimes both.

To hear Panahi tell it, *The Circle* isn't political at all and this story could be set anywhere; that's what he insisted when I met him at the Toronto Film Festival last September, and what he has said on several other occasions. For me, calling *The Circle* apolitical is tantamount to insisting that pork is a vegetable, but considering all that Panahi has had to contend with for having made it, it's hard to fault him for saying such a thing, and it's even likely that he believes it.

It may only be a matter of semantics – a question of whether or not humanism qualifies as a kind of ideology. 'A political filmmaker commits to a certain ideology, tries to propagate that through his work, and attacks opposing ideologies', Panahi has said:

> In *The Circle*, I am not attacking or supporting anyone. I am not saying who's good and who's evil. I am trying to look at everyone from a humanistic point of view and hold a mirror that reflects social realities. It's up to the audience to interpret those realities in political terms if they wish to do so. I have made an art film with a message of protest, not a subversive political film.

One thing that's pretty clear about both Panahi and his movie, regardless of whether you think they're political or not, is that both are unreconciled, perhaps even irreconcilable. Panahi fought for years before receiving script approval from the Iranian government, and it seems likely that he never would have gotten it without the prestige of his two previous features. The film still doesn't have a screening permit for showings in Iran, and reportedly has been shown there only once – at a secret screening planned for twenty-five students, though according to Panahi, 'Four hundred students showed up' and 'their reaction was very positive'. He rejected a proposal last year to show it at the Fajr Film Festival in Tehran with the final eighteen minutes removed, but wound up showing a video of the uncut version in his house to foreign guests. This has encouraged some Iranians – including many liberal-minded ones – to accuse him angrily of tailoring his film for the West and reinforcing the stereotypes of Westerners about Iranians.

This is part of the gist of an attack by two Women Studies professors writing last March in the *The Montreal Gazette*[2], Roksana Bahramitash and Homa Hoodfar, who define 'three distinct kinds of problems for those of us intent on familiarising people with the realities of women's situation in the Muslim world':

> First, it ignores completely the multiplicity of women's acts of resistance to and subversion of oppressive practices. Second, it presents the story of Iranian women as one of continuous defeat. As a result, they seem in dire need of a white knight to ride in from the West, much as the Crusaders did, to rescue them. Third, it compromises Muslim women's position and

poisons the atmosphere among family, friends and community. When one of our teenage daughters saw the movie, she whispered: `I will never go back to Iran' because of her shame about being Iranian.

This sounds like another form of the 'them' and 'us' discourse alluded to earlier – some of which may seem unavoidable, though I must say it still gives me the creeps. But if people are going to make charges of this kind against Panahi, they might as well be more precise and say that *The Circle* is tailored specifically for Westerners who tolerate cigarettes and abortions, and find virtue in unhypocritical prostitutes. But how seriously would we take anyone who charged, say, William Faulkner with tailoring *Light in August* for Yankees and French intellectuals? I assume it must cater to Iranians, because I'm told it's easier to find several Faulkner novels in Persian – including this one – than it is to find any Iranian novel in English. Since it's my favourite novel in any language, I harbour the fantasy that some Iranians, some other Americans and I might like it for similar reasons, regardless of all our other differences – and that's an 'our' unlike the one proposed by Bahramitash and Hoodfar that I can fully endorse and respect.

I hope they'll forgive me for saying that the problematic responses to *The Circle* they cite are precisely the sort of thing that complex works of art tend to foster; I'd hate to hear the shellacking *King Lear* might get from critics who point out how unfair it is to grateful children and humble patriarchs, among the types that Shakespeare overlooked. Obviously, there's always a price to pay for expressing negativity about the state of things. But it strikes me as unthinkable that Panahi himself would ever express shame about being Iranian, whatever his quarrels with the Islamic Republic, and highly unlikely that any white knight – a stereotyped version of my ethical self-image that I find abhorrent, whether it applies to other Western white males or not – could offer the blazing light provided by Panahi's measured detachment as well as his anger. Furthermore, to suggest that the women he shows are all 'defeated' is a reductive summary of a story where solidarity between women, shown in varying degrees throughout, surely counts for something, along with highly visible signs of pride and defiance. (One of the first things we see in the film is a woman aggressively berating a passing male on the street for asking her and a friend, 'You two alone?' – not exactly the behaviour of a passive victim.) And I'm afraid these academics give the game away when they add, 'Interestingly, the movie was made by a man, evidently seeking Hollywood success.' I'm not holding my breath while DreamWorks offers Panahi an exclusive contract; but given that he doesn't speak a word of any language except Farsi, I can't imagine what he'd want to do with one if they did.

'There are many other Iranian movies, technically and aesthetically of higher quality,' they continue, 'which present a far more accurate picture that have received no acclaim in the West.' Since they refuse to divulge a single title, thereby making their argument impossible to refute, I'll be presumptuous and cite one myself that happens to be showing for free on the Northwestern campus this Wednesday – *Divorce Iranian Style* – and tied for fourth place on my ten best list for 2000. I wouldn't call it 'technically and aesthetically of higher quality', and it may be further disqualified by having received at least a modicum of acclaim in the West. But since it's a masterful documentary made by two women, one of them Iranian, I see no point in ranking it alongside Panahi's masterful work of fiction as if the two were comparable. Suffice it to say that it's wonderfully attentive to 'the multiplicity of women's acts of resistance to and subversion of oppressive practices', presents the story of Iranian women as one of frequent – if not continuous – triumph against impossible obstacles, and beautifully complements *The Circle* without in any way challenging or negating what it has to say.

Of course Panahi doesn't give the whole picture of women in Iranian society. Who could, and who would want to? *Light in August* doesn't begin to offer the full range of Mississippi society, either, and its own rage about racism – which must give a certain amount of unwarranted solace to glib Yankees – also has to be judged for the emotions it stirs in the rest of us. Southerners who call those feelings defeatist, provoking embarrassing shame in their children, are being just as parochial as everyone else – including me, who finds it both exalting and tragic, beautiful and caring, measured and unreconciled. Like many works of art, it can and should affect many people differently.

Since we're no longer living in a Cold War, I hope it's still possible to criticise this country's government without being labelled a potential terrorist. That must sound hyperbolic, but only because I'm lucky enough to not be an Iranian. According to our State Department, simply being an Iranian automatically makes one a potential fundamentalist terrorist, regardless of whether or not one is critical of this country – and even regardless of whether or not one is a fundamentalist. In this respect, at least, one has to concede that 'their' regime may be better than 'ours', because even though Iranians hear about Americans such as McVeigh and Dahmer, not to mention countless trigger-happy teenagers with handguns, 'their' officials are sufficiently trusting and respectful – that is to say, civilised – not to fingerprint and take mug shots of American visitors to Iran.

But that's what US custom officials routinely do to all Iranians crossing our borders. When a movie by Majid Majidi was nominated for an Oscar, he was fingerprinted and photographed *en route* to the Academy Awards ceremony he was invited to attend. (Maybe they were afraid he might shoot Billy Crystal if he didn't win.) The same year, Darius Mehrjui, one of the pioneers of the Iranian New Wave, met the same humiliation with his Harvard-educated wife and their two-year-old son, *en route* to a retrospective of his own work at Lincoln Center, where he'd been invited jointly by the Human Rights Watch Film Festival and the United Nations. Still in a state of shock, he and his wife decided they'd rather fly back to Iran instead – only to be told that they couldn't do that unless their fingerprints and mug shots were taken first. Why? Because, it was explained to them, they were already on American soil and thus subject to American laws.

Why do our customs officials – or more precisely, the blowhards dictating their policies – insist on being so obnoxious? I can't believe it's always been this way or that it hasn't been a coarsening of behaviour brought about by the increased and largely market-imposed isolationism of American culture. Lately, as Gore Vidal wrote in *Vanity Fair* in 1998:[3]

I have been going through statistics about terrorism (usually direct responses to crimes our government has committed against foreigners – although, recently, federal crimes against our own people are increasing). Only twice in 12 years have American commercial planes been destroyed in flight by terrorists; neither originated in the United States. To prevent, however, a repetition of these two crimes, hundreds of millions of travelers must now be submitted to searches, seizures, delays.

And it appears that Iranians and Cubans get treated with particular callousness. The Iran hostage crisis during the Carter administration is probably a major reason for this behaviour – a crisis that, in keeping with Vidal's point, was partly a response of fundamentalists to the CIA-orchestrated coup ousting Prime Minister Mohammed Mossadegh in 1953.

In any case, Panahi got so sick of being treated like a criminal every time he came here – and he's been here many times with his films – that he finally chose to stop coming if he had to go through it all again. This led to special waivers of this practice when he attended the New York Film Festival with *The Circle* last fall and the National Gallery somewhat later, but not any more since George W. has assumed office, even if Panahi's only changing planes. I kid you not. When Panahi was recently flying from Hong Kong to South America to attend a couple of film festivals, and had to change planes at JFK, United Airlines assured him that he wouldn't have to submit to the usual insult 'we' dish out impartially to all Iranians, regardless of race, creed or colour. But United was mistaken, and when Panahi refused to co-operate, he was shackled to a bench for over a dozen hours in a room full of illegal aliens, not allowed to phone anyone, and then sent straight back to Hong Kong with his hands and feet in chains, even after he showed evidence of who he was and where he was going. After all, the fact that *The Circle* won the Golden Lion in Venice last year doesn't mean he might not have managed to sneak a hand grenade through the metal detector in Hong Kong.

One can argue that Panahi, a man with an evident martyr complex, should have put up with the minor nuisances and not been such a diehard – though if he'd done that, it's unlikely the rest of us would have ever heard any of the above stories (recently reported by Stateside teacher and film-maker Jamsheed Akrami). I can't imagine Bahramitash and Hoodfar condoning what happened, but it does seem ironic that the man who allegedly caters to American prejudices about Iranians and 'is evidently hankering after Hollywood success' suddenly gets treated like a dog when he passes through one of our airports. Yet it also seems terribly consistent, because those who condemn Panahi for raising a ruckus, either through *The Circle* or in American customs, are essentially saying the same thing: 'Sit down, you're rocking the boat.' Or, 'Who do you think you are, an American?'

So what should we do? Should we applaud Panahi for protesting injustice wherever he finds it? Or should we call him an asshole for protesting when he finds it over here? And how should we feel when he forces us to become aware of a practice that most of us know less about than the chadors Iranian women have to wear? Maybe this man is a terrorist after all – an emotional terrorist whose project is to upset us, and whom most of us are determined to ignore as a consequence.

I realise that the referents for 'we' and 'us' in the above paragraph keep shifting, meaning something different with every usage. But I'd argue that's what often happens when we use those words, especially when they have national, racial and ethnic referents, and it's only when boat-rockers like Panahi come along that we even begin to notice some of the problems and impostures involved. If we're all simply Westerners looking at Iranians in *The Circle* – 'us' looking at 'them' – we can't be paying much attention to what the film is doing, which also has something to do with an Iranian looking at Iranians, among other things.

One of the festivals Panahi had been heading for, which he never reached, was one I was attending in Buenos Aires, and when his own account of his ordeal went out in English on the Internet, I spent some time with Mark Peranson, the editor of the Canadian magazine *Cinema Scope*, in the festival's cybercafé, trying to find what American newspapers, if any, had bothered to report the incident. At that point, none had, though the *LA Times* and *Village Voice* ran stories a bit later. Typically, the *New York Times* decided around that time that the jokey putdowns of Otto Preminger's *Exodus* (1960) by Miramax's Harvey Weinstein were what its urbane readers who followed movies really needed to know.

Getting back to personal pronouns, it's worth asking, finally, whom *The Circle* belongs to. Although it may have been authorised in part (and with difficulty) by the Islamic Republic of Iran, one clearly can't claim it belongs to them, especially if 'they' won't allow it to be shown. And one can't say that it belongs to 'the Iranian people' either – not if many of them are so vociferous about disowning it. Does it belong to the Westerners whom some Iranians (and Westerners) claim it was tailored for, most of whom haven't seen it? Or does it belong to the Iranians who can't see it, some of whom wouldn't like it if they did?

The problem, however, isn't nearly as acute as I'm making it sound. In fact, there are many people all over the world who feel passionately about *The Circle*, and their numbers become even more apparent once we drop this antiquated nationalist jargon and silly tribal chant and recognise that some of them are in the West, some are in the East, some are in the Middle East (including Iran), and some are even in the Midwest. I also know some Iranians in North America who like it. We might even constitute a community of sorts, though some of us may not know this yet. I daresay there are a significant number of us on the planet who would be happy to call this lovely and mysterious object *our* film, at least if other people let us. In fact, though I don't speak a word of Farsi, I can't think of a movie I've seen anywhere over the past year that speaks to me as directly or as powerfully. I certainly haven't seen any shot as breathtakingly beautiful or as dramatically satisfying as the long take of the prostitute (Mojhan Faramazi) sitting alone in the police van after a male prisoner has successfully offered cigarettes to the two cops riding in front, one of whom had previously told her to put out the cigarette she was starting to light. (It's apparently easy to smoke in most places in Iran if you're a man.) Taking a furtive glance around her, and coming to the realisation that she can finally light her cigarette in peace because no one will mess with her now or even notice, she looks out the dark window and takes a drag while the night rolls past.

Maybe there's something important about the fact that Panahi, I and several others have a film and certain emotions about it in common, even though we don't share a country, a government, a language, a set of laws, a definition of politics, or even the same treatment at the hands of American customs officials. At this particular moment in history – when this country, according to some of 'our' leaders, is supposed to be the only one that truly exists or matters – I'd say that's a meaningful start of something, even if the middle or end of it still isn't in sight.

Notes

1. Postscript: as of 2002, I would add another title, Ebrahim Golestan's remarkable and beautiful *Brick and Mirror* (1965) – though it qualifies equally as neo-realism and New Wave.

2. *The Gazette* (Montreal), 15 March 2001.

3. Gore Vidal, 'Shredding the Bill of Rights', *Vanity Fair*, November 1998; reprinted in *The Last Empire: Essays 1992–2000* (New York: Doubleday, 2001), pp. 399–400.

8

The Future of Academic Film Study

Adrian Martin and James Naremore (2001–2002)

I think the problem is one of having too much information, excessive knowledge. There is no longer enough doubt about artistic modes of operating, doubt concerning what the painter or filmmaker is searching for. It's terrible that a certain language and capacity to make judgements come so easily. It should be hard to write on these films. Whatever the film, we are told endlessly, shot by shot, scene by scene, what's good or bad. It's crazy, totally crazy. I'd like to see that mode of criticism applied to Cézanne or Mozart, saying what does and doesn't work at every step. I'm not even talking about Hitchcock or Hawks. In short, the resistance posed to criticism by artistic material has vanished; it's turned into a pie that critics quickly slice into pieces. (Manny Farber, 1982)[1]

Q: What is the role of evaluation in your critical work?
MANNY FARBER: It's practically worthless for a critic. The last thing I want to know is whether you like it or not: the problems of writing are *after* that. I don't think it has any importance; it's one of those derelict appendages of criticism. Criticism has nothing to do with hierarchies. (Manny Farber, 1977)[2]

15 August 2001

Dear Adrian,
Perhaps like you, I have mixed feelings about these Farber quotes, which nevertheless go to the heart of all writing about movies. My first reaction to his statements is that they seem disingenuous, because everything I've read by Farber seems to me to be evaluative; in fact, it's precisely his quirky value judgments and ongoing battle with a certain kind of middlebrow taste that makes his reviews of the 50s and 60s so much fun to read.

But I'll get back to him later. I think it's partly the case that criticism (and maybe even film) has been in a bad state over the past decade or so because of a lack of evaluation. As I see it, we've been caught in a situation where at one extreme you have frumpy academics who for one reason or another think it isn't their job to make value judgments, and at the other extreme you have popular reviewers who operate purely as guides to the consumer economy and who think of their jobs as a matter of sticking their thumbs up or down. The best writing has always been in-between these extremes, where a certain historical perspective and an openness to experiment are joined with a manifest love of the thing one is discussing.

Actually, I don't think it's possible to write any kind of film history, theory, or criticism without engaging in value judgment on some level. The very choice to write about 'x' instead of 'y' entails a decision about value. And I think that writers need to be honest about this situation. But they also need to be aware of the important question: what's 'good', anyway? Some answers to this (for instance in your own work) involve matters of formal skill and emotional complexity. But of course there are other ways (some more political) of answering the question, and that's where the problems arise.

You and I occupy slightly different worlds as writers because I'm an academic and you're truly a practising critic who does a fair amount of journalistic work. In my own sphere, I feel very unhappy with the tendency of academics to think they are doing something more detached and theoretical than mere criticism. Whether they know it or not, they are always evaluating and always setting or confirming canons of taste.

I can prove this thesis with my own history. When I look back over the intellectual movements that have shaped my career and that still operate in my consciousness like a kind of palimpsest, I find that each of them implicitly valued certain genres or types of art (even though I didn't know it at the time). Here they are, in the order in which I discovered them.

1. *New Criticism*. This type of literary training has gotten a bad rap as far as I'm concerned because it is often described as elitist and right-wing. Actually, the original New Critics worked in public universities and they created a type of criticism that was empowering to kids who had never read anything but a Sears-Roebuck catalogue. Their basic idea was that, in Eliot's phrase, you should study literature as literature and not another thing. (That begs the question of what literature is.) To do this, you just had to closely look at the art object and its inner workings – in other words, any ordinary person had the ability to comment on the text if she just gave it serious attention. Of course the New Critics always picked a certain kind of text. What they most valued was linguistic complexity, irony, ambiguity and verbal skill. Their ideal was lyric poetry and literary modernism.

2. Related to the New Critics and somewhat less influential to me was *F. R. Leavis* (who had a powerful influence on Robin Wood). Leavis and his group at *Scrutiny* believed in a traditional, agrarian, Protestant England that was being damaged and destroyed by industrial modernity and cosmopolitan modernism. (Eliot shared some of these views, but was Catholic instead of Protestant, and more right-wing politically.) What Leavis valued above all – and he often wrote like a passionate and brilliant preacher – was the nineteenth-century realist novel plus the novels of D. H. Lawrence.

3. *Auteurism*. This I don't need to explain. I encountered it outside academia (I never took a film course in school), and it exerted the strongest influence of all. It was relentlessly evaluative. What it valued was classic Hollywood and the international art cinema.

4. *Screen theory*. I give this name to the critics who wrote for *Screen* in the 70s, in the heyday of French high theory. This sort of writing was often impenetrable but was always against both Hollywood and social realism. What it favoured was the 'counter cinema' of Godard and the political avant-garde.

5. The *cultural studies* movement. This critical formation, which is initially left-wing, reacted against the leftist theory of *Screen* by advancing a somewhat populist notion of movies and TV. It paid more attention to audiences than to the formal qualities of films, more attention to reception than to production. In practice it often seems 'above' evaluation, operating like science or anthropology. It debunks most established forms of criticism (including those listed above) by suggesting that they are 'top-down' and class based. It avoids making essentialist claims about the media, but it tends to favour or to give emphasis to certain kinds of things rather than others. Its canonical texts are slasher flicks, soap operas and kick-ass action movies.

Where does Farber belong in relation to all these things? Well, in the 50s and 60s he's pretty much an auteurist, advancing populist but formally quite sophisticated claims about uses of space in directors like Hawks, Walsh, Wellman, Fuller and early Godard (meanwhile ceaselessly putting down the mostly left-wing Tradition of Quality in America, represented chiefly by John Huston, whom he hates). His sources of reference and taste, however, come from the New York art world rather than from the literary background that I (like Sarris and Wood and Rosenbaum) bring to the movies. In later decades he's influenced more by the structuralist and political avant-garde, and eventually he more or less stops writing about movies.

I can understand why Farber downplays evaluation, because it can sometimes get in the way of the more subtle analysis of forms. But the sense of something valuable at stake is exactly why he's such a compelling critic. And one can admire or enjoy critics with whom one doesn't agree. In Farber's case, I don't agree with him about Wellman vs Huston, but I think what he says about them is fascinating and valuable and worth debating. To choose a more extreme example from outside the movies: I despise T. S. Eliot's politics (which strongly influence his literary judgments), but I think he's one of the most interesting critics who ever lived, and greatly enjoy reading his critical essays.

How can a critic (or a film-maker for that matter) be 'good' in my opinion even when I don't agree with his/her values? That's a key question. I have more thoughts about it, but I'll stop this foray into intellectual history until I hear what you have to say.

Best regards,
Jim

30 December 2001

Dear Jim,

In looking for possible futures for academic film study, I think it's intriguing that both of us feel a need to trace certain fault lines that either connect or divide – sometimes it's hard to tell which – the various schools, movements and eras in this field. In the same way that you have traced a palimpsest of tastes in your own intellectual formation, and the preferences in cinema that are favoured by each successive movement, I am interested in what might be called the different social spaces of film culture (the academy being one of these), and the kinds of cinema they promote or limit in their practices of evaluation.

Here's a good example of what I mean. In the mid 80s, the celebrated Australian cultural historian and critic Sylvia Lawson wrote a searching piece called 'Pieces of a Cultural Geography'.[3] It offers an account of a month or so in which Sylvia attended a number of different public forums that piqued her interest – one was a film conference, another an art world seminar, and the last a political forum. Sylvia records her impression that, while some of the faces in the crowd – and even some of the speakers on the panels – recur, there is a strong sense of non-overlap between these pieces of the cultural terrain: they simply don't communicate with each other. Each one becomes a kind of box, with its own history, its own language, its own concerns. They each become tribal centres, massively self-generating and self-sustaining – like all institutions, I guess. And even when individuals with wide interests and open, synthesising minds like Sylvia travel from one to the next, they experience a kind of alienation, as if they have to reorient, reconfigure, even reinvent themselves upon entering each new space.

I find myself thinking a lot about how this relates to the lay of the land in film culture today. Academia doesn't seem to have much (or indeed any) relation to either the realm of film reviewers – by which I mean people whose attention, by necessity, is riveted upon what the mainstream exhibition–distribution system puts before them to cover – or the realm of a certain kind of worldly film critic, who tours the globe chasing the latest in international cinema at film festivals and writing for various, serious journals and magazines.

It seems to me that each of these three activities can be defined by a particular relation to a symbolic home base, a settled turf of activity. Reviewers are, whether they like it or not, relentlessly local and home-bound: what matters to them is what film opens next week in their home city. That's the entirety of the cinema to them at any given moment, which is fatally limiting. The touring, festival critic, on the other hand, often exists in a stateless reverie: most local, national cinemas (even in those countries hosting the festivals to which the critic travels, or their own country back home) are boring or meaningless to them, a mere twentieth-century throwback. They chase the manifestations of a certain borderless cinema that is led by the latest and greatest names (Hou, Kiarostami, de Oliveira, etc.). We know that many progressive critics of this sort spend much of their time pining (and publicly complaining and militating) for what they (and, by extension, the community they represent) cannot see at home, the riches elsewhere that they are deprived of, and which they hence romanticise a little. . . .

Academia is a strange hybrid of (to cite the title of a popular Australian TV soap!) home and away. The international circuit of academic film conferences offers another kind of stateless, portable milieu – as long as there is agreement on (or an assumption of) what particular films we (i.e., the audience at such events) know about and care about. Of course, in practice – at least judging from the academic guests who have spoken in Australia down the years – this assumed common culture tends to be comprised of a small academic canon of hit topics (film noir, melodrama, Afro-American cinema, etc.) plus what amounts to a mainstream film reviewer's (or fan's) sense of what's currently or recently popular, and hence eagerly consumed and memorised by all (*The Matrix* [1999], *The Simpsons*, *Crouching Tiger, Hidden Dragon* [2000], etc.).

I am interested in what happens – if it happens – when these demarcations and certainties break down: when one has to at last bust out of the comforting, suffocating circle of one's symbolic home; or when one confronts the fact that one's assumed canon of the familiar and the notable is indeed not shared by everyone everywhere in the world; or when one has to figure out what definition of home, of local culture, is in fact worth returning to and defending. Actually, it's a bit like those small town melodramas that many cinephiles love, perhaps unconsciously sensing some allegory of their own cultural predicament in them: to leave home is both frightening and necessary, both a melancholic loss of safety and security and tradition, and a bet on a potentially thrilling, wide-open future. . . .

As your own work (like your book on film noir, *More Than Night*[4]) shows so well, Jim, a sense of history, and of ideology, can help us be sensitive to and to navigate these shifts in the cultural landscape. I want to concentrate for a moment on just one of the many schisms in the map I have just sketched: the non-correspondence between the internationalist critic's agenda of what comprises new cinema, and the academic practitioner's working plan of what is worth teaching, analysing and researching.

I believe that academic film study tends (in general) towards a safe consolidation of what is known, a certain kind of consensus. The intellectual institutions tend to want to avoid states or phases of crisis and disequilibrium. There are periodic turnovers or tweakings of ruling paradigms (from structuralism to post-structuralism, from post-modernism to post-colonialism . . .) but not much revolution – at least, perhaps not since the whole semiotic push, which did powerfully challenge the previously reigning, humanist–literary mindset (a palace coup that some people – its victims – still grumble about!). I use the word crisis in a positive way, in the sense of an emergency – the difficult moment when something new is emerging, indistinctly at first. And I guess I'm wondering if film academia these days, as a system, as a way of thinking and proceeding, is really ever terribly interested in the new or the challenging in this sense.

I recently reread – but saw anew – a mind-boggling example of the conservatism of consensus and canonical thinking around film. It's a classic anthology of film criticism, Richard Roud's mammoth, two-volume *Cinema: A Critical Dictionary*, prepared all through the 70s and finally published in 1980. It's a mixed text, with noted critics as well as academics in it – at a time when, generally speaking, critics and academics were not so far apart as they are now. It's Roud's introduction which is particularly symptomatic. In it, he casually states a couple of rather remarkable things; at least, the passage of historic time makes them remarkable, destabilising their former commonsensicality. First, Roud asserts that 'the United States, France, Germany, Italy, Sweden, Russia and Japan' are the 'seven countries [that] have produced, shall we say, 95 per cent of the world's cinematic masterpieces'. Second, he claims that 'the United States, Britain [and] France' are the 'three countries' where the 'best and most influential writing is being produced today', because 'the study of film is necessarily restricted to the metropolises of the world, New York, London and Paris'.[5]

I'm not taking an easy shot at Roud here, because many of us could have written those words at that time, and a lot of what circulates now in the spaces of an emerging, global film culture did not circulate then. But Roud's text offers an amazing example of what happens when a period of confidence in film culture at large (including the academy) becomes overconfident and atrophied, and thus ripe for the waves of change. And that change begins the moment we start to collectively doubt these deeply embedded planks of our presumed cinematic knowledge: that we know from where the best or most important or most innovative or most challenging films are going to come; and that we have a critical language which will fully account for their action and significance, which can fruitfully evaluate them.

And here I think, with slightly mixed feelings, about someone, recently deceased, whose writing has been so important and inspiring to me: Raymond Durgnat. In the openness of his spirit and intellect, Durgnat was a true pioneer and a border crosser. In fact, I'll be unashamedly canonical: he is among the half-dozen greatest critics in cinema history. Yet when we look at his work, we see that he happened to embody a kind of old world of film tastes and interests. The cinema he bothered with was English language (mainly American and British) and European (and Eastern European). Asian cinema (apart from some Japanese erotica!) never really registered for him. And at the time of his death he had never heard of, and did not really care to find out about, Kiarostami and other vaunted masters who had emerged from previously overlooked regions of the film globe. Of course, like every individual with one life to live and particular interests, skills and passions, Ray Durgnat was selective, he made his choices. There is no cultural law that decrees we must all master every new figure who is deemed by someone, somewhere, to be important! But, by the same token, I also wonder if current situations, in global politics as in culture, oblige us to take stock and move on, to open ourselves to the world in ways that will be vital and generative.

But as to how this might play itself out in the universities, I would like to hear from you – who is much closer to the daily situations, dreams and politics of academic work than I – what some of the finer grained schisms and possibilities are within this particular piece of the cultural landscape. What do you think, for example, of the contested legacy of what is sometimes called (however unjustly or inaccurately) the Grand Film Theory of the 60s and 70s? What did the historiographic turn in cinema studies – which I date to the late 80s, when Grand Theory had somewhat exhausted itself and its appointed gurus – bring that has been of lasting value? And how – I know this is something you have pursued extensively in your own work – does one square cultural studies with aesthetics, and canons?

Yours eagerly,
Adrian

30 July 2002

Dear Adrian,
First I'd like to say a few words about Raymond Durgnat. Among writers on film who had a strong impact on me, he is somewhere near the top. I was pleased that you organised a fine tribute to him in Senses of Cinema on the occasion of his recent death.[6] One of his early books, *Films and Feelings*, was very important to my development, and I'm troubled by the fact that his achievement is so seldom recognised here in the States. His essays on *Psycho* (1960) and *This Island Earth* (1955), for example, ought to be collected in an academic anthology of the best writings ever about movies.[7]

   I had the pleasure of meeting Durgnat only once, in the mid to late 70s, when he came to Bloomington to give a lecture about Luis Buñuel. He seemed pleased when I told him I had read one of his poems in an anthology of new British verse, and we chatted briefly about the current state of film studies. Like me, he was interested in the many references to Jacques Lacan that were beginning to appear in *Screen*. He remarked, however, that he thought the new film theorists knew too little about Freud. This remark appeared to me symptomatic of a generational line dividing him and the post-structuralists. Durgnat was something of an auteurist (though he much preferred Huston to Hawks), and within that formation he represented the survival of a late Romantic and essentially Surrealist temperament that was on the verge of seeming out of date. Another way of describing his situation would be to say that he not only believed in Freud and Marx, but also in the power of artistic imagination. (His essay on *This Island Earth* is not only a sharp political analysis but also a celebration of what he calls 'The Wedding of Poetry and Pulp'.) For me, the closest examples of his particular kind of intelligence among movie writers today would be the remarkable independent scholar Paul Hammond and perhaps also the academic writer Sean Cubitt, both of whom are more erudite and in some ways more intellectually sophisticated than Durgnat. Certainly Durgnat had his limitations, as you point out, but he's still very much worth reading. He's also a good instance of a critic with considerable learning who was evaluative in a way that I admire. Consider his book on Hitchcock, which is deeply concerned with what Durgnat thinks is an over-valuation of a minor but intriguing artist, but which somehow makes Hitchcock all the more interesting. Here and elsewhere, Durgnat was able to deconstruct and seriously analyse films, even reveal their political/ideological unconscious without turning them into grist for a theoretical mill.

I agree with what you say about how social space or habitus influences what we write and what kind of judgments we make about film. It's undoubtedly true that our artistic taste and our politics are determined in some degree by the sociology of our professions. (Within academia certain divisions are exacerbated by departmentalisation and the pressure to develop professional networks and specialised, field-specific discourses.) I also agree that the three types of writers you mention – newspaper reviewers, festival critics and academics – often seem to inhabit different worlds. To some degree the separation is inevitable because so few newspapers provide a forum for intellectual reflection, and so few academic journals are actually oriented toward the public sphere. Then, too, the roles you describe are different. The festival critic is in a better position to bring us news, whereas the academic is in a better position to think about the past. By nature, academics are less prone to a thumbs up/thumbs down attitude; in fact they often teach students how to suspend judgment in order to better understand the systemic features of art. (Here I should perhaps note that two of the greatest works of literary scholarship and analysis I've ever read, Erich Auerbach's 1946 *Mimesis* and William Empson's 1935 *Some Versions of Pastoral*, have nothing to do with overt critical evaluation.[8]) But the journalistic critic and the academic scholar need one another, and they ought to work in dialectical relation. At any rate festival critics ought to have a strong knowledge of history and theory, and academics ought to be aware of important new artists. We need more writers like you and Jonathan Rosenbaum, who can bridge the gap between the two domains. Here in the States, we also need more journals like *Cineaste* and *Film Quarterly*, which at least try to bridge the gap, providing a good discussion of both aesthetics and politics.

In answer to your question about the legacy of what David Bordwell calls Grand Theory, I may not be the best judge and I don't know how to give a short answer. However, I'm convinced that neither art nor the theory of art goes out of date. If we toss away an older theory like an old dress or a used car, we lose an important part of a long conversation. Eisenstein and Bazin are still essential reading, as are the best writings of the 70s. That's why I described my own intellectual history as a palimpsest rather than a jump from one position to another. For me, the so-called Grand Theorists raise basic questions about representation, patriarchy and the interpellation of the human subject. To argue, as some do, that their theories aren't scientific or verifiable is beside the point. (The same thing can be said of Freud, who remains crucially important.) My own problem with the *Screen* theorists of the 70s is that they tended to make vast systemic generalisations, overlooking the messy details of history. They also concentrated almost entirely on sex and gender issues, leaving out questions of race and class, and they worried too much about certain kinds of eroticism and aesthetic pleasure. I especially disliked the grandiosity or superiority in their tone of voice. For example, I started getting really depressed in the late 70s when Stephen Heath, whose work I sometimes admired, asked the following rhetorical question: 'Is an interest in "the work of Max Ophuls" today anything more than the province of film studies and criticism?'[9] Maybe not, but one could have worse interests, and the scare quotes don't constitute an argument. When I read that question, I thought maybe I should give up academia and drive a truck.

The advantage of the cultural studies movement is that it redirected attention to the popular, which in some ways was what auteurism was about, except that auteurism never degenerated into populism. Populism is the sort of thing that made governor George Wallace stand in the door of the University of Alabama to keep black kids from attending school. But popular art can be as great as any elite art. For me personally, a TV show like *Ozzie and Harriet* has the same indefinable charm as certain Howard Hawks movies. And Ricky Nelson is as good on record as he is in *Rio Bravo* (1959). Certain episodes of Jackie Gleason's *The Honeymooners* seem to me as good as the short films of Buster Keaton or W. C. Fields. The problem here is that TV tends to be local or national compared to film. And the bigger problem with cultural studies is that it adopts a 'theoretical' stance toward the popular. Good criticism ought to be written from the heart rather than from a neutral perspective.

All things considered, I think that writing about movies is worthwhile, and that it needs to be informed by a spirit of discrimination and cinephilia. I'm generally pleased by what you and others call the turn to history in film studies, but it, too, needs to convey the sense of a good critic's pleasure and judgment. In fact I think the distinction between criticism, theory and history is to some extent artificial. How can one construct a theory without knowledge of history, and how can one write history without making critical judgments about the past? I greatly respect the tradition of what the Frankfurt School called Critical Theory, a term that nicely captures the need for critique in all writing about culture. I'm pleased by the renewed interest in figures like Siegfried Kracauer, and I applaud the work of contemporary academics like Tom Gunning and Miriam Hansen, who see film history in relation to the larger saga of modernity. It seems to me that the real enemy of academic film studies, and the thing it needs to avoid in the future, isn't theory or history or aesthetics (which, in the writings of figures like Kracauer and Walter Benjamin, have a close relation to politics) but positivism, which produces sterile formalism, self-perpetuating audience research and apolitical industrial history. If I keep harping on about aesthetics it's because my own aestheticism has always informed my politics, and I don't think film studies can do without it.

I'd like to hear more about what you call the crisis of the field, because I'm not sure I've experienced the complacency you describe. I'd be eager to know your perspective of what's happening.

Best regards,
Jim

26 August 2002

Dear Jim,

In relation to the university and the academy, my life has recently formed itself into a strange loop. I dropped out of university when I was eighteen. At the age of nineteen, I was invited back to teach at the place I had left, because I was fortunate enough to have encountered a nurturing and very talented critic/educator, Tom Ryan (now retired from academia and a weekly reviewer at the same newspaper I write for). Beginning in 1982, I taught for ten solid years at various campuses, on the lowest level of casual pay that these institutions were capable of fixing. All that time, I was writing reviews and essays on film, art, music, getting involved with small, intense magazines (one was called *Buff*, another *Stuff*!). After a decade of often exciting but not especially career-rewarding university work, I cut my ties with that world, and went hell for leather into freelance writing. One glaringly evident fact taught me the life lesson I needed: for ten years I had feverishly devised, lectured and administered courses, but written no books; two years after I quit my last teaching job, my first book appeared. But now, at the age of forty-three, I am in the process of writing a doctoral thesis; the Art and Design Department – not the Film and Media Department – of a local university offered me this opportunity (even though I have no previous degree) on the basis of my accumulated critical writing. My supervisor is Robert Nelson, the art critic on that same newspaper Tom and I work for – and a fine example of what Australia likes to call (with an ambivalent love/hate) its public intellectuals.

Maybe this will serve to give you the impression that, while I think of myself essentially as an outsider to the university system, I have always been close to it. More exactly, close to the university library! I'm one of those obsessive browsers at the journal shelves of academic libraries, and the Internet age hasn't yet knocked that out of me; when people sling around the caricature of cinephiles as creatures who haunt darkened rooms, that conjures to me the mysterious basements of huge libraries as much as the dimming lights of cinemas. Like you, I think of the world's history of critical writing as an archaeology or palimpsest, not an ever-changing hit parade geared to a rapid rate of obsolescence. I know that my library-lover wanderings produced in me, very early, a desire to personally synthesise two traditions I admired equally: the organic aesthetic critique of the loose *Movie/Monogram/Positif* school (Andrew Britton's work, for example, has always been a major reference point for me) and the militantly anti-organic approaches of the post-structuralists (Raymond Bellour, Peter Wollen, Paul Willemen). In fact, the synthesis of those two approaches, if I can manage to stage that encounter successfully in my imagination, is the topic of my current PhD!

But I also like to think of the annals of criticism, in Greil Marcus' term, as a secret history, full of unknown or scarcely consulted or misunderstood texts tucked away in obscure pockets, waiting to be discovered, eulogised, used, juxtaposed with some new film or going concern. ... We talk a lot these days about new, global networks and communities, as if all information (even intellectual information) is about to become transparent, tabulated, ready at the fingertips to be synthesised. But I think a lot of criticism functions as a message in a bottle: you throw it out, it bobs around on the waves, you have no idea where it will land, who will read it, or what they will make of it. Not everything in film culture (or any culture) can be curated and programmed in advance – as the history of government subsidy of the arts in many cities of the world shows!

In this sense, academic writing is certainly no different to any other writing, once you loosen it from the immediate confines of its institutional space. Like you, I feel no need to dismiss the 70s, as so many now do. Some essays by Thierry Kuntzel and Stephen Heath, for example, are more powerful, more inspiring today than they were twenty-five years ago. Sometimes – to take the cheeky advice of the unclassifiable, border-crossing Australian writer George Alexander – it's necessary to read hard theory as mad poetry in order to really feel and transmit its intensity and insight! And I guess that's why I have long been drawn to that area called (ugly term, I know) fictocriticism, where the line between imaginative creativity and intellectual conceptualising is not strictly drawn, where the essay really essays something hitherto unknown! Ray Durgnat was a major early figure of this kind in England, but I think I can safely boast that Australia has also pioneered in this realm: writers including Meaghan Morris, Lesley Stern, Edward Colless and Tara Brabazon, some known outside my country, some not yet.

American scholars including Robert Ray and Gregory Ulmer have set forth their own propositions about creative theory, but I find what they say a bit too programmatic and formula-bound, a bit disconnected from any actual social formation beyond the university journal/conference/anthology circuit. It seems peculiar to small nations like Australia that critical sensibilities and idiomatic styles get formed in the furious crossover between areas (art, literature, film) and the often treacherous paths that take freelancers from one precarious, part-time job to another (teaching, reviewing, consulting). Something else needs to be pointed out about this kind of cultural scene: whereas, on the one hand, being a public intellectual can be a thankless task offering the dubious, ephemeral pleasure of media celebrity where one becomes a TV talking head or a radio soundbite for thirty seconds at a time, it's also the case that many of Australia's fictocritics have had at least a passing dalliance with creative arts beyond the written word: performance, scriptwriting, music, etc. And that reminds me of Serge Daney's ideal model of the critic as a *passeur*, one who crosses different worlds and tries to build connecting bridges between them – which is effectively the flipside of the broken cultural geography image I brought up earlier. Personally, I look to the *passeurs* of the world, like Chris Fujiwara in Boston idiosyncratically rewriting film history for us piece by piece, or teacher-historian-producers like Peggy Chiao in Taiwan, or the new generation of film-activists in Paris like Stéphane de Mesnildot and David Matarasso who are all at once voracious cinephiles, judicious editor-publishers, and experimental film and video artists.

But I'm not saying one has to be beyond the academy to do groundbreaking or simply good work – certainly not to you, Jim! Although we've never met face to face, having been brought together for the purposes of this book, I've long taken your work on Hitchcock, Vincente Minnelli, screen acting and film noir as models of what you call critical theory. It's easy to knock (as we Australians say) the academic system when you're outside it, as I have been (for all practical purposes) for a long time now. When I think over my own often publicly expressed antipathy towards the university system and the kinds of knowledge it produces, I believe I was reacting to some of the same things that have rankled you from time to time: the territoriality, the pre-emptive intellectual strikes, the fickle fashions, the dutiful repetition of cookie-cutter analyses that produce the same, predictable results. But the future of academic cinema studies must be brighter than that if, as you say, the field can't be truthfully characterised as mired in complacency or simple, careerist opportunism. Over to you for the final minority report.

All best,
Adrian

1 September 2002

Dear Adrian,
I find it amusing that you need to explain to some people that the film theory of the 70s isn't useless. I'm becoming such an old geezer that I often feel the need to defend the 50s and 60s as well. What becomes more apparent to me as I get older is that theory and criticism don't develop in progressive fashion, as if we were moving ever closer to the Truth. At best, these activities establish certain values, provide historical knowledge, and determine the kinds of questions we ask. Looked at from a broader perspective, however, all writing about the movies is part of a larger discourse about modernity that dates back to the mid 19th century. It seems to me that this discourse sometimes contributes to progress (making us more aware of feminism and issues of race or social class, for example), but also that it keeps struggling with the same old problems under new forms.

From the 19th century onward, liberally educated people from a variety of backgrounds have had at least four ways of responding to the onward march of industrial capitalism and state-supported ideology: they can become bourgeois (like most college professors), they can become anarchists (which means dropping out and behaving badly, like Rimbaud, Tzara and the Sex Pistols), they can become aesthetes (like Baudelaire, Wilde, Joyce, Woolf and all the great modernists), or they can become revolutionary political activists (like Mother Jones, Lenin, Fanon and Malcolm X). One of the best dramatic representations of these alternatives is Tom Stoppard's very funny play, *Travesties*, which imagines a crazy encounter between Tzara, Joyce, Lenin and an ordinary bourgeois in Zurich during World War I. For my own part, I often feel as if my personal subjectivity were split among the four positions. At certain points in my history, some of my selves can form alliances, but at other points, which are the true moments of crisis, the bourgeois, the anarchist, and the aesthete tend to get pushed aside by the activist. Where modern society in general is concerned, one of the major crisis periods for artists and intellectuals was the 30s. Another was the late 60s, a period that left its mark on radical film theory in the 70s. As I write this response to you, American capitalism appears to be pushing the world ever closer to war, and the contradictions in the system are once again becoming apparent. Perhaps a new crisis will develop, in which case it will become increasingly difficult for any of us to maintain a balance between cinephilia and social action.

As I've said, I don't notice any special crisis of the moment in the small academic field known as film studies, which continues to produce good work despite over-professionalisation. I find Robert Ray and Greg Ulmer much more interesting than you seem to, partly because they are among the few academics who recognise that revolutions can occur in Surrealist fashion, at the level of the imagination. I could list many other academic writers who are important to me (especially those who write film history), but I would feel like one of those boring Academy Award recipients who thanks fifty people and inevitably forgets to mention somebody. Let me nevertheless add that film study in the academy is always challenged, and not only at the level of institutional politics or critical fashions. The whole of American pop culture – movies, music, TV broadcasting and mass market literature – is today in a sorry state, brought on by conglomerate capital, marketing hype and various types of horizontal and vertical integration. I live most of the year in a Midwestern college town where the McDonaldisation and juvenilisation of the movies is especially evident. In the past two years, I've seen only one big-budget Hollywood production in a cineplex (Spielberg/Kubrick's *AI: Artificial Intelligence* [2001]) that was interesting enough for me to want to write something about it. On the other hand, the digital era is creating new forms of production, distribution and exhibition that make it possible for people to have much greater access than ever before to alternative and foreign films. The best movies today aren't underground in Manny Farber's sense of unheralded commercial productions that manage to do subversive things around the edges; they're more like what you've called *passeur* art, in the sense that they blur generic boundaries and experiment with new technology. They're always created outside Hollywood, and they are in special need of latter-day critics with Farber's talent, who can make them better known. That's the chief reason why straightforward evaluation remains important to me, and why I think we need to engage in a certain amount of old-fashioned canon building (however decentred and contested it might be) for the contemporary scene.

In solidarity,
Jim

Notes

1. Jean-Pierre Gorin *et al.*, 'Manny Farber: Cinema's Painter-Critic', *Framework* no. 40, Summer 1999, p. 49.
2. Manny Farber, *Negative Space: Manny Farber on the Movies* (New York: Da Capo, 1998), p. 365.
3. Sylvia Lawson, 'Pieces of a Cultural Geography', *The Age Monthly Review*, February 1987, pp. 10–13.
4. James Naremore, *More Than Night: Film Noir in its Contexts* (Berkeley: University of California Press, 1998).
5. Richard Roud (ed.), *Cinema: A Critical Dictionary – The Major Film-makers* (New York: The Viking Press, 1980), vol. 1, pp. 18–20.
6. 'A Festschrift for Raymond Durgnat', *Senses of Cinema* no. 20, May–June 2002. http://www.sensesofcinema.com/contents/02/20/contents.html#durgnat.
7. Raymond Durgnat, *Films and Feelings* (London: Faber and Faber, 1967).
8. Erich Auerbach, *Mimesis: The Representation of Reality in Western Literature* (New Jersey: Princeton University Press, 1974); William Empson, *Some Versions of Pastoral* (New York: New Directions, 1992).
9. Stephen Heath, 'The Question Oshima', in Paul Willemen (ed.), *Ophuls* (London: British Film Institute, 1978).

9

On Four Prosaic Formulas Which Might Summarise Hou's Poetics

Fergus Daly (2001–2002)

The received wisdom on the cinema of Hou Hsiao-hsien rests on a number of general observations: these are intimate tales featuring characters entangled in the great movements of Taiwanese history; the characters barely feel involved in what happens to them; Hou's style consists of long still takes of relatively distant and repeated spaces; the sense of a scene emerges from factors such as temporal experience or the play of light rather than from the drama that unfolds before us. So often, a summary of the Hou aesthetic could just as easily be describing a range of modernist auteurs from Michelangelo Antonioni to Béla Tarr. It seems to me that there are four main principles guiding the construction and development of Hou's aesthetics:

1. Historical memory is impersonal.
2. My experiences don't belong to me.
3. The shot's centre of focus is forever drifting out of field.
4. We are clusters of signs and affects given form by light.

These formulas account for why Hou's characters are at a remove from the actuality of which they are part. The viewer senses that historical experience is never truly subjective or collective, and its recollection neither subjective nor intersubjective. An aura of strangeness envelops the spectator before the director's lengthy still takes. Events don't take place in space-time; space-time is the event taking place before our eyes. Its actualisation produces its own memory. The contemporary world has no place for psychological trips down memory lane; memory is impersonal, our recollections mere incarnations of its inscription in matter.

For Hou, History in film is that which Memory must constitute in order to lend the overwhelmed subject a point of orientation amid these impersonal Visions that include or implicate him/her. Flashbacks, even ellipses, are never convincing in a Hou film. A (Hi)story is rather the sum of 'shots, their movement and variation'[1] from the viewpoint of a subject who desperately seeks to halt the sweep of Time but cannot.

Hou's historical forays are never content to remain in the past but invariably contaminate a character's present circumstance; *Good Men, Good Women* (1995) is exemplary in this respect. Wang (Tony Leung) in *Flowers of Shanghai* (1998) and Kao (Jack Kao) in *Goodbye South, Goodbye* (1996) are rent by an internal difference, that 'sweet disjunction'[2] which explodes every unified thing in a Hou film. His frames are drifting blocks of signs and affects. Often his images seem like presentiments of future memories rather than representations of present happenings. Jean-François Rauger speaks of his 'embalmed' characters, 'surrounded by the silence of premonitory dreams'.[3] Alain Bergala's discussion of *Flowers of Shanghai* highlights the scene in which Wang is seen alone in the dead of night at the house of Rubis, confronted with a situation he cannot comprehend. Bergala reads this as a loss of psychological bearings because nobody is there to interpret for him the circumstance in which he finds himself; in other words to ground it in an inter-subjective experience.[4] It is an exemplary case of the impersonal Event in the process of actualising itself. As Burdeau says of *Goodbye South, Goodbye*, 'Hou passes from the manifest to the latent, the actualised to the virtual.'[5]

Reframing is minimal in Hou's work. The camera doesn't follow the characters because once they've slid beyond the frame's limit they are metamorphosed. Hou speaks of his frames as 'zones', declaring that 'certain shots appear empty, but that's an error'. The shot continues to contain affects, floating in its space. 'There is a parallel with Chinese prints in which you can believe there are empty spaces ... these aid in transporting the gaze. They encompass whatever is effectively represented. I conceive my shots in the same manner.'[6] Time and History are treated in like manner. In *The Puppetmaster* (1993), for example, an alternately 'visible/invisible, perceptible/imperceptible movement' expresses the 'progressive grasp of a memory in the process of formation, a troubled and lively memory',[7] actualising, then virtualising, the world's incessant becoming.

It seems to me that, in the final analysis, the socio-historical aspects of Hou's work are less important to him than it seems, and are not the essence of his originality. As Dudley Andrews said of Kenji Mizoguchi, social problems are 'emanations of a cosmic fiction',[8] and social degradation is often shown to be merely a barely perceptible fold in the complex tissue of reality. For Hou, as Kent Jones has noted, it is the 'ravishing arrangement of light and shapes' in 'half-defined spaces' suggesting an 'array of portals into new dimensions' that provide the ground of any possible morality or ethics. Hou succeeds in 'allowing what's visible within the frame to open out ... onto the world that extends beyond its parameters'.[9] His astonishingly original way of working with light serves to create just such a perforated or (in Gilles Deleuze and Felix Guattari's term) 'holey' space – frames that are like sifters through which every centre of expression or point of focus slips. This leads to his equally lacunary narratives, featuring characters with hiatuses where the West puts egos. Hou prefers contrasts, references, allusive sense. 'What interests me is not to follow an action, to "see it clearly", but to underline the gaps, the holes, the interrogations. I detach myself from an action, don't follow it in all its details but establish myself in the "general sense" of an event.'[10]

Translucency, rosy-hued interiors, the blue haze of twilight or the soft diffusion of oil-lamp light – Hou works these like a sonar (the flat in *Good Men, Good Women* has been likened to an aquarium, the sound in *Goodbye South, Goodbye* described as a magma).

Often there are contrasts, but never the high contrast expressionism of noir; a mode of chiaroscuro lends space porosity rather than depth of field. Hou seeks in this way to master the 'complete range between darkness and light'.[11] His characters can't relate to their most pressing problems, as per Burdeau's list: 'their memories (*Good Men, Good Women* and *The Puppetmaster*), the historical context in which they live (*A City of Sadness* [1989]), their projects (*The Boys of Fengkuei* [1983] and *Goodbye South, Goodbye*), their love affairs (*Dust in the Wind* [1987], *Flowers of Shanghai*)'.[12] Jones ties this to what he sees as Hou's fundamental problematic, that of how these characters 'have arrived at their own particular fate, how they have come to be in *this* particular place at *this* particular time under *this* particular set of circumstances'.[13] Perhaps this is a little too existentialist to account for Hou's singularity. If, as Jones so perceptively notes, 'every space is allowed to live as itself', then the question becomes the cosmogenetic one of how this reality is now actual, now virtual and why 'all that's visible is at the threshold where the shown tips over into the not-shown'.[14]

Hou opens up or rather vaporises the space-time of Western cinema. His perforated spaces distribute light in an incredibly inventive way, revealing subjects who are derived from this light: packets of signs and affects, phantasmatic figures or 'energetic facts' as Burdeau puts it.[15] In the words of Taoist philosopher Lie-Tzeu, cited by Stéphane Bouquet: 'You walk without knowing what pushes you, you stop without knowing what bars you, you eat without knowing how you digest. All that which you are is an effect of the irresistible cosmic emanation. Therefore, what belongs to you?'[16] Hou might answer: what belongs to you is whatever form light grants you for the briefest period. There is a Samuel Beckett side to Hou, a mood of resigned perseverance. When all is said and done, *it* 'goes on', being is *conatus*, it perseveres.

This is why repetition – of sites, scenes, gestures – plays such a major role in Hou's films. Through persistently repeated set-ups, Hou redefines and redescribes his space-time units. Repetition thereby undoes the linearity of narrative film-making, replacing development with passage and modulation. By way of repetition, every axis is unhinged. And the effect of all this on morality is that there is no fatum to which man is yoked. There is only Life and the Light and the Impersonal Images that it ceaselessly creates and unmakes.

> In my career, the history of Taiwan is behind me. Now I want to film the present. (Hou Hsiao-hsien, 1999)[17]

Critics have been in no doubt that Hou's intention in *Millennium Mambo* (2001) is to examine the disturbed and disoriented perception characteristic of the contemporary world – a perception to which it testifies in its 'superimposition of iridescent chromatic sheets, its great electronic planes, its undulatory variation of shots between the atonal and the explosive'.[18] But the film isn't only an audiovisual spectacle. Despite the dreamlike quality of the images, *Millennium Mambo* has nothing to do with dreaming. It's a film about memory – about memory as something that can occupy us or be occupied, that can haunt or be haunted. If the blocks of memory seem literally to be differently coloured, it's because these are memory-images involving moments and individual lives that were given life only through the light and the colours that once isolated them. These luminous states incorporate every conceivable texture, colour and intensity in a lesson in light-being that ranges from natural sunlight to the dubious luminosity of closed circuit TV imagery.

The choice of a techno club milieu is essential to Hou's project. As Didier Peron astutely notes: 'If, contra the supremacy of melody, techno works on the textures of sounds, rhythmic sequences, volumetric experiments on synthetic looping in an unlocalisable mental space, Hou performs an equivalent mutation in cinema.'[19] The film examines the world of techno clubs and characters whose lives are bound up in them in order to ask what it might still mean in the present to speak of separate interior and exterior spaces (or space-times), and to study the disappearing threshold between them.

Hou explores the competing spaces of our inner and outer worlds through rhythm. He ties sound and light together as twin prongs of a single force. The film suggests that, if Millennial time is truly 'out of joint', if the space-time we inhabit has lost its metric relations, and if individuals have lost all internal and external co-ordinates, then techno can be isolated as one of the forces that simultaneously performs a de- and re-territorialisation of bodies and brains. The character of Hao-hao (Chun-hao Tuan) functions like the prototype of this tendency, standing like a throbbing membrane at a turntable in the replica of the Blue Club he has set up in his bedroom.

What does memory mean in such a universe? To explore this question, Hou creates a distance from the now by looking back at the present from a time in the future; a voice-over comments on events in 2001, from a vantage point of ten years. Deleuze: 'In its very essence, memory is voice, which speaks, talks to itself, or whispers, and recounts what happened. Hence the voice-off which accompanies the flashback.'[20] But no viewer could ever mistake the sounds and images of *Millennium Mambo* for any narrator's flashback – nor for that matter could he mistake the voice-over for a narrator.

In the beginning was not the word but light – neon light. The film opens on an abstract configuration that's revealed to be a neon-lit subway-tunnel roof under which a young woman (Shu Qi) strides, the camera following closely behind her. Her arms flail in a rowing or flying motion; suddenly she looks back over her shoulder at the camera. This look seems to say: follow if you wish, but why me, what 'me'? She is immediately answered by a voice-over which begins: 'She broke up with Hao-hao, but he always tracked her down.' Does this explain her glances to camera? Perhaps she believes he has found her again. She seems happy, liberated that he hasn't. She skips and bounds down the subway steps and disappears from view. No longer locatable, like a floating shard of transparency.

This is Vicky, the film's subject. She will speak in the third person of her own recent past. Or are we too readily presuming that the voice and the body are one and the same character (even if we know the actress' voice)? This is a question the film will never resolve. At first glance what this opening promises is the image of a journey through an individual's memory. But *Millennium Mambo* is neither a fond reflection on days of being wild, nor a modernist, cerebral game. The world of the film is one of matter infused with sensation, matter brought to life as impersonal memory, impersonal affects now slipping between, now clinging to bodies and objects, materialising sensation. Nicole Brenez's words are apt: 'Emotions traverse situations, it little matters who displays them, provided that they're there.'[21] These affects tend to be contained in the images rather than being made available to the viewer through character identification – an essential aspect of Hou's famously indirect style of film-making. His experiment is in line with Baudelaire's project as glossed by Foucault: 'the high value of the present is indissociable from a desperate eagerness to imagine it, to imagine it otherwise than it is, and to transform it not by destroying it but by grasping it in what it is'.[22]

The choice of the club milieu and its music is again vital here. Techno is so tied to the present, its function is precisely to take over the dancer's body, turning it into an automaton who exists in a pure 'thereness'. Hou creates the perfect opportunity to crack open this thereness in order to reveal its components. The floating voice searches in the memory of the present, bores holes in it to reach 'what it is', a pure present image, one which offers an opening onto the future, providing a vision of life to come. The present as depicted has bifurcated into sound and visual images; the voice-over seems to pull the images one way as the incessant techno beat pulls them another.

Just as our eyes are pulled this way and that, so our ears hook on and off the incessant beat which functions like a flickering does for visual recall: both a summoning of recollections or a doorway into recall and a blockage to their taking or sitting in memory. Hou's films rest on the threshold of perceptibility. Here, the homogeneity of the beat is set against what are, for the most part, portrait shots and other non-eventful images, leaving the spectator's eye and ear occupying two distinct spaces. The music and voice-over which ought to provide the conventional mode of unification of the images are subject to dysfunction – the beat doesn't take you in, doesn't enter your nervous system as it does for example in a film like *Trainspotting* (1995). Instead it floats a little distant from the spectator, in fact it often has a menacing quality – like the aural dimension of a bad trip – before becoming, after a time, a 'deaf spot'. The techno beat serves the same function as the mobile phone in *Goodbye South, Goodbye*: 'This repetitive sound ends by constituting a motif of irritation, pulling the entire scene towards it and almost annulling the image: you can no longer see anything but this noise.'[23]

Shelly Kraicer estimates that 'dance music defines the beat of its shots, the drift of its camera, the endless loops within loops of its spiralling chronology'.[24] But the use of the beat is more ambiguous and complex. It is precisely in the visual images that Hou creates a true rhythm, in the sense in which Olivier Messiaen defined rhythm as that which doesn't have a regular beat. Hou's visuals are unhinged, lacking co-ordinates, without measure. It's the head-to-head between audio and visual rhythms that produces the *Millennium Mambo*'s unique effects.

The film's structure is intriguing. There are six isolatable blocks of audiovisual images, like plasmic bubbles of space-time, each one separated by a mobile threshold and accompanied by a voice-over. How is each block occupied? What are its internal limits? What are the thresholds between blocks, and what violates them? Screenwriter Chu Tien-lu describes the method of constructing *The Puppetmaster*: 'Like putting together passing clouds.'[25] It is impossible to measure the limits of these blocks or clouds; they overlap with and delocalise each other. There is no definitive, consistent and articulable logic guiding the trajectory of these shifting thresholds and the modulations between blocks, beyond the barely perceptible 'passage from one luminous state to another'.[26] The film finds an exemplary formal equivalent for its thematisation of a world without isolatable co-ordinates or reference points.

Kraicer suggests that Hou has substantially altered his aesthetic choices in the way he 'directs the viewer's eye' in *Millennium Mambo*, as opposed to his usual 'exploring the space he lays out for us'.[27] But there is no need to see this as a regression from the ultra-modernism of his two previous films. This time he does get closer to bodies, often filming in medium close-up and shallow focus, but in so doing he pushes further his experiments with what Bergala terms the 'aquarium shot' – the concentration of bodies and props within an enclosed space or décor.[28] The spectator hits upon Vicky's body like a 'missing person', a creature who appeals to director and viewer: 'Please locate me! Give me some co-ordinates!' If the previous films succeeded in displacing the centre of focus, largely through the use of group movements, then *Millennium Mambo* desperately seeks to stay with the body lest the entire image implodes or slides off the screen. The camera dwells on Vicky's body, but it's not at all like Godard did with Myriem Roussel in *Hail Mary* (1984), to show the body's impenetrability; Hou displays its porosity, declares it to be excessively penetrable, prone to decomposition.

Is this the true reason for Hou's seeming return to single character film-making? His poetic experiments have progressed from explorations of Historical Memory, to the porous space of the everyday, to filming lives drifting out of focus and out of field. Now he can examine the porosity of the contemporary individual, internally rent, or rather turned inside out; bodies subject to automation by controlling forces 'as if under a spell' (as Vicky says), prosthetic bodies rejecting identity and intentionality through drugs and alcohol, without choice or resistance but subject to being tracked down, located. Take for example the magnificent scenes where Vicky returns from clubbing and Hao-hao probes her body with his nose, as if going over her body with a detector. What is he searching for? Signs of sex? Of humanity? Is he searching for cracks, holes through which he can reach what's inside? And, inversely, Vicky is like the limit of Hao-hao's autistic perception; he must perform a humanity test on her each time to ground, however temporarily, his own impaired senses. *Millennium Mambo*'s great novelty *vis-à-vis* Hou's previous films is the manner in which it casts his negotiation of limits and thresholds onto the very surface of bodies.

Perhaps by flattening space – as if he believed he had exhausted all the possibilities of chiaroscuro and depth in his films about history and memory – and through replacing the holey space of his earlier films with a kind of demented fauvist colour that slides on the screen's surface, Hou succeeds in making the surface itself porous. In this way the body becomes sharded ... by light, by colour, by all kinds of shimmering and stroboscopic effects, the intensification of vivid colours becoming 'pure incandescence or blazing of a terrible light which burned the world and its creatures'.[29]

In terms of the thematic of visual degeneration, in a world where being equals light, the character of Jack (Jack Kao) is essential. 'He's not here,' Vicky insists; she's not only referring to his unlocatability in Japan but to a fundamental ontological unlocatability. Jack exists only technologically – a virtual voice and a virtual image. In one extraordinary sequence, he returns to his apartment; we watch him entering on a closed circuit TV screen but without any gain in substantiality in the move out of the video image. Vicky lies there asleep and Jack, like a vampire, proceeds to haunt the space. Neither she nor we can find spatial co-ordinates for this subjectively insubstantial, unlocatable creature. He disappears soon after, nothing but a voice message left on a mobile phone.

In the film's final image-block – last for the spectator but in essence only one moment in a circuit – 'she' (the memory-probe) succeeds in penetrating the magma and 'finds an image'. That it involves snow has a certain inevitability about it because snow is precisely the substance that settles; here it's something that 'sits' in Memory, even if the image is one of metamorphosis or melting, one through which sense is bestowed on her relationship with Hao-hao, on the vampiric transmutation of Hao-hao, disappearing with the sunrise 'just like the snowman'.

Malaise, torpor, inertia, melancholia, autism, fatalism, ennui, lassitude, vacuity – these are the words critics have employed to describe the dominant attitude to life of Hou's recent characters. But their very disparity testifies to the director's resistance to creating any straightforward affective hook for the spectator – which may well be his greatest modernist achievement. He has no interest in judging the contemporary individual; rather, he maps out the co-ordinates of the contemporary individual's life.

Notes

1. Emmanuel Burdeau, 'Goodbye South, Goodbye', in Jean-Michel Frodon (ed.), Hou Hsiao-hsien (Paris: Cahiers du cinéma, 1999), p. 160.
2. Emmanuel Burdeau, 'Les aléas de l'indirect', in Jean-Michel Frodon (ed.), Hou Hsiao-hsien (Paris: Cahiers du cinéma, 1999), p. 33.
3. Jean-François Rauger, 'Naissance d'une nation', Cahiers du cinéma no. 469, June 1993, p. 18.
4. Alain Bergala, 'Les Fleurs de Shanghai', in Jean-Michel Frodon (ed.), Hou Hsiao-hsien (Paris: Cahiers du cinéma, 1999), p. 175.
5. Burdeau, 'Goodbye South, Goodbye', p. 170.
6. Thierry Jousse, 'Entretien avec Hou Hsiao-hsien', Cahiers du cinéma no. 474, December 1993, p. 45.
7. Jacques Morice, 'La Mémoire impressionée', Cahiers du cinéma no. 474, December 1993, p. 40.
8. Cited by David Williams in John Wakeman (ed.), World Film Directors Vol. I (New York: H. W. Wilson, 1987), p. 802.
9. Kent Jones, 'Cinema with a Roof over its Head', Film Comment, September–October 1999, p. 47.
10. Antoine de Baecque, Colette Mazabrard and Frédéric Strauss, 'Le temps suspendu. Entretien avec Hou Hsiao-hsien', Cahiers du cinéma no. 438, December 1990, p. 28.
11. Burdeau, 'Goodbye South, Goodbye', p. 169.
12. Burdeau, 'Les aléas de l'indirect', p. 33.
13. Jones, 'Cinema with a Roof over its Head', p. 47.
14. Burdeau, 'Goodbye South, Goodbye', p. 169.
15. Burdeau, 'Les aléas de l'indirect', p. 33.

16. Stéphane Bouquet, 'Un peu de danse ne fait pas de mal, ou deux ou trois choses sur la place de spectateur', *Cahiers du cinéma* no. 516, September 1997, p. 42.

17. Emmanuel Burdeau, 'Rencontre avec Hou Hsiao-hsien', in Jean-Michel Frodon (ed.), *Hou Hsiao-hsien* (Paris: Cahiers du cinéma, 1999), p. 104.

18. Didier Peron, 'Terminus Techno', *Libération*, 31 October 2001.

19. Ibid.

20. Gilles Deleuze, 'Literature and Life', *Essays Critical and Clinical* (London: Verso, 1998), p. 3.

21. Nicole Brenez, 'The Actor in (the) Place of the Edit', *Senses of Cinema* no. 21, August 2002. http://www.sensesofcinema.com/contents/02/21/sd_actor_edit.html.

22. Baudelaire cited in Michel Foucault, 'What is Enlightenment?', in Paul Rabinow (ed.), *The Foucault Reader* (London: Penguin, 1984), p. 41.

23. Mathias Lavin, 'Plans écliptiques (*Goodbye South, Goodbye*)', *Cinergon* no. 11, 2001, p. 98.

24. Shelly Kraicer, 'East Asian Films at the 26th Toronto Film Festival', *Senses of Cinema* no. 17, November–December 2001. http://www.sensesofcinema.com/contents/01/17/toronto_east_asia.html.

25. Cited in Gabe Klinger, 'Decoding Hou: Analysing Structural Coincidences in *The Puppetmaster*', *Senses of Cinema* no. 8, July–August 2000. http://www.sensesofcinema.com/contents/00/8/puppetmaster.html.

26. Bergala, '*Les Fleurs de Shanghai*', p. 177.

27. Gilles Deleuze, *Cinema 1: The Movement-Image* (London: Athlone Press, 1986), p. 53.

28. Stéphane Bouquet, 'Un art qui transporte', *Cahiers du cinéma* no. 512, April 1997, p. 25.

29. Kraicer, 'East Asian Films at the 26th Toronto Film Festival'.

10

Movies Go Multinational

Nataša Durovičová and Jonathan Rosenbaum (2001–2002)

JONATHAN ROSENBAUM: As someone who grew up in Bratislava (the former Czechoslovakia) and Uppsala in Sweden, and has a speaking and reading knowledge of six languages (Slovak, German, Russian, Swedish, French and Italian), plus a reading knowledge of at least five others (Czech, Polish, Serbo-Croatian, Norwegian and Danish), I'm sure you've had plenty of occasions to think about national differences. In fact, the area of research you've specialised in over the past decade – the early multinational talkies made in separate language versions in both Hollywood and Europe – focuses in part on this very issue. How would you account for the fact that today, when globalised markets and the Internet appear to make countries more and more aware of one another – or at least more aware of one another's cultural products, like movies – the population of the United States should appear to be more isolationist now than it was even during the Cold War? Is this merely a side-effect of marketing practices, or does it point toward some ideological trend that's independent of them? Or do you disagree with the assumptions behind my question?

NATAŠA DUROVIČOVÁ: It's not at all that I disagree with your premise, but my time scale may be different enough from yours that I see the picture just a bit differently. And 9/11/01 then really gauges that difference because it puts a period, an end, to an era. What I actually wonder, then, is whether it wouldn't be more accurate to say that the US was not nearly as isolationist during the Cold War as it has been for the last decade between 1989 and the September 2001 attacks.

For, whatever else one may say about the Cold War, surely its constitutive trait was that 'the Other' that is, for all practical purposes, the Soviet bloc was somehow always part of the general field of vision, whether for politicians or for normal Americans. Mostly this was of course in the negative, as in 'Cuba', then 'Vietnam' and then later 'nuclear deterrence'. But some of the overarching global concepts/ideas we today make most everyday use of – ecology, human rights – have come centre stage because of the US' forty-year effort to try to beat this Other in a world sum game (ecology as a way of showing we care about the world more than the Chernobyl management does, human rights to show we care about citizens and the public sphere – not just markets – more than the Moscow guys do, etc.) The bulk of the foreign languages and cultures students have learned for the last forty years at US universities was taught in the so-called 'area studies' programmes – the South Asian, the Middle Eastern, the Latin American, the Russian programmes, established quickly after World War II to generate expertise in cultures and languages outside of the mainstream middlebrow Ivy League French. It is thanks to the rapid atrophy of these programmes in the last decade that the US intelligence service is now relegated to subcontracting its interpreter services from the Mormon Church (which still pitilessly subjects its thousands of missionaries to minor Mongolian dialects or Wolof alongside the more mainstream languages like Arabic and Polish).

For film, this inescapable and all-pervasive internationalism was the case at least from the mid 50s until the early 70s. If you look at the American Film Institute catalogue of fiction films for the 1960–70 period, you'll see that the very *definition* of 'American' fell apart totally during that decade. Just about every other of the maybe 2,000 films listed there has some kind of 'foreign' participation – actors, locations, producers, themes, etc. It's not that Ingmar Bergman would have been a household name in the US in 1965, but inescapably, in the movies at least, the outside world was a good and constant source of excitement, or newness, or attractiveness. This went for James Bond, Julie Christie, Euro soft porn and spaghetti Westerns as much as for Rambo, *Apocalypse Now* (1979), *Queimada!* (*Burn!*, 1968) or Bernardo Bertolucci, not to mention Jean-Luc Godard. An actress like Meryl Streep could rise to stardom (OK, sort of stardom) on the strength of her ability to act with an accent. It really is striking how the US cinema began reconsolidating its world power in the mid 70s with Lucas' double-pronged strategy: on one hand with the a-local, proto-global, totally synthetic *Star Wars* (1977), on the other with *American Graffiti* (1973), with its hyper-precise time-space co-ordinates of Bakersfield, California, circa 1960. Whatever world there was between the moon and the West Coast gradually ceased to matter.

Without question the isolationism you point to is the reason for the deeply felt and all-pervasive surprise about even the possibility that America could provoke a hostility intense enough to lead to the September attack. And that surprise is a direct consequence of the post-1989 situation, of a shift from a bipolar to a mono-polar world system. Monopolists tend to not (have to) listen: the widely noted near-elimination of foreign correspondents at all the major networks and at many of the major newspapers over the last decade is a case in point. The more the world became accessible, the less it began to matter to access it, other than on our own terms. But I wonder whether the concurrent proliferation of technologies that make all the other world-spaces, as well as our immediate past, more accessible didn't have the direct, immediately obverse effect on the desire to actually check it out. There can be no doubt that it is easier for you or me, sitting next to a computer and at walking distance from a university library, to now have better access to a Malay or Italian film than we did before the video/web nexus became so common. But at that same time both the pressure to find one, and the eagerness, the curiosity about what one might look like, seem to have gradually atrophied – certainly in proportion to what is possible. Bollywood now has its own suburban video outlets, as parallel and as invisible to the American cultural mainstream as the huge supply of unsubtitled Asian videos long available behind the cashier's desk in your local 'oriental' grocery.

We've all had that experience of being too lazy and too busy to work our way through that (unsubtitled) Vietnamese family drama, and niche marketing has come to our rescue, as it were, offering us a very functional and very pernicious tool to avoid having to deal with this torrent of unsorted new stuff. For the widespread expectation now is that unless some sort of advertising copy alerts me to it, and interprets it for me, the experience I'm about to pay for is probably too iffy to be worth the effort: when in doubt, go with a brand name.

There is for instance the long-standing strategy, at least since the mid 20s, of slotting into the 'art' drawer anything foreign that moves on screen. The unchallenged consensus of our social tradition – formulated in a media driven exclusively by advertising – is that a cultural product's first obligation is to *guarantee* pleasure; that is, to entertain; that is, to avoid risk. The term 'art' and ergo anything foreign – a strategy carefully and deliberately cultivated in both the American film trade press and by Hollywood to stand as an antonym to the idea of 'fun' – was tantamount to a label with a toxic warning.

The 90s had some other real similarities with the 20s. In both moments the tsunami of American exports of all sorts followed in the wake of a reshuffled post-war order and filled various voids – consumerist, social. But at both moments this Americanisation of the media was achieved not necessarily by the local markets craving US goods – as the market ideologues wanted and still want us to believe – but also by direct political pressures by the US diplomatic machinery. In the 20s, this took place against the backdrop of war debts and reparations; in the 90s against the background of the GATT debates and free trade agreements. But in both cases a campaign to allow the free 'flow' of US films into the rest of the world was driven by Washington at least as much as by Hollywood.

And in both periods this huge wave of exports was predicated on and packaged in a mix of advertising and a generic 'media English', an English enriched not only by the key terms for the new technologies but also by a mix of brand names – 'McDonaldisation' being the prime example, 'CNN' being another. I wonder then whether this lingua franca, this elastic and commercial – and therefore not too rule-driven – 'omni-English' is not a kind of perceptual screen preventing Americans increasingly from imagining a world different from their own. While on one hand providing an essential tool for efficient universal communication, much like Latin for botanists – take the pilot and flight control tower English – and for the enormous masses permanently or temporarily mobile to be able to function even minimally, this resolutely a-cultured, not-rooted 'world English' obscures all that is precisely lost in translation – nuance, tradition, mastery, personal style.

In most other societies a second language is a part of a daily routine and an unquestioned necessity. And the web now only amplifies what other forms of mechanically reproduced mass culture have been disseminating at least since the jazz era, followed by the arrival of the sound film. In the gap between the primary/strong and secondary/weak language is then born a certain consciousness of what it is like to live on the other side of a language barrier. In the worst possible case this can then translate into pathological nationalism, leading in turn to wars. But the official US, by increasingly operating in this invisible and isolating bubble of monolingualism, not only blocks out awareness of 'the Other' on its own terms, but moreover reduces anyone who wants to speak to it into a condition of the always-imperfect. It used to be that foreign heads of state or high ranking officials would use their native language to retain their own dignity (not to mention gain time for thinking) by using translators for official occasions. Increasingly, however, everyone now – including the French – feels obliged to speak in a more or less precise English, and sounding sometimes more, sometimes less like the foreign Teacher's Aid you used to have in your math class. Reverse the picture and imagine Dick Cheney addressing the politburo in Beijing in mediocre Chinese. Or George W. seeking NATO's support in accented German. In the current world ranking order the rules of the game are written in English. Yet, much like those laminated exit row instruction handouts on planes telling you that if you can't read this please notify the flight attendant, this monolingual fallacy is by and large invisible to its main victims – the monolingual English speakers. It's not so much a matter of being able to tell whether Osama bin Laden addresses us in Arabic, Urdu or Pashtun on those tapes we aren't supposed to watch and listen to too much of. It's a matter of remembering to ask the question – something easily forgotten in a universe where no subtitled film, that is, no non-English soundtrack, has ever penetrated the fortified mall cinemas until last year's surprise hit *Crouching Tiger, Hidden Dragon* (2000).

I imagined something like this to be an explanatory framework around Lars von Trier's recent *Dancer in the Dark* (2001). As if trying to sneak past the US distributors' art film patrol and out of the festival niche ghettos, it made several efforts at an idiom acceptable to a broader audience here in order to show Americans what their country might look like from the other side. Unlike most foreign film-makers who try for their 'American' film by working within the US environment, von Trier addresses himself to the US on its own linguistic terms from another environment. His Pacific Northwest, eerily well 'acted' by a Danish location, is populated by generic characters familiar from US films, performed, as is the custom, by bigger-than-life stars (Deneuve, Björk), and supposedly paying homage to the most ur-American of genres, the musical. Von Trier deploys this 'Hollywood vernacular' not only to attract a large(r) audience, however, but also to deliver to them a moral tract on the topic, 'the cruelty of the death penalty' – the death penalty being one of the issues, in the last decade, around which anti-Americanism has crystallised the most in large parts of Europe. So the film is not just a bravado (anti-Dogme) case of trying to do a tragic opera in the style of a musical. It's also, I think, an attempt to send a letter to America in its own language, to say something like 'this is how you look to us from where we stand', composed in an entertainment idiom that would be somewhat familiar and therefore possibly acceptable to US audiences. The accent was too heavy, in the last analysis, and the 'message' doomed to remain outside the malls' walls. I am not trying to argue indiscriminately in favour of the film; I'm just saying that what it had to say and how it was saying it can give us an insider's insight into a particular outsider's view of the US. That if one wanted to put up with its 'broken Hollywood English', as it were, one could hear a kind of early warning, even one possible proleptic answer to that key post-9/11/01 question, 'Why do they hate us so?'

JR: One thing I find fascinating about your comparison between the 20s and the 90s – with the flood of American exports in each case filling 'various voids' in the aftermath 'of a reshuffled post-war order' – is how perfectly this also describes the Marshall Plan in the mid 40s, facilitating the rediscovery of American cinema in French criticism during the 50s that ushered in *la politique des auteurs*. This in turn inspired the American auteur theory, valorising Hollywood directors like Hitchcock and Hawks, Sirk, Ray and Fuller during the 60s, and thereby upgrading the American cinema as soon as it could be perceived as a stylish export item – truthfully, that's the way I learned how to love most of these directors, and I was far from being the only one. In other words, by the 60s, when a certain internationalism in American culture was nearing its peak – still the Golden Age of movies for most of my contemporaries, in part because it seemed to develop neck and neck with a broader discovery of the planet – it paradoxically became possible again for Americans to take American movies seriously as art, for the first time since the 20s.

Sadly, this eventually degenerated into something like an exclusive taste, heralded by the partiality of critics like Pauline Kael for movies like *Bonnie and Clyde* (1967) and *The Godfather* (1972) and *The Godfather Part II* (1974) that absorbed European influences the same way that America tends to absorb its immigrants – such as François Truffaut in the first case and Luchino Visconti in the second – to the point where they effectively became invisible, or at least unnecessary. Mission accomplished, one might say: the American cinema could go back to pretending it was the only game in town, a cultural monopoly that has remained in place ever since.

Yet there's another side to this that needs to be explored – the disappearance of nationality itself that accompanies globalisation, a disappearance affecting the US along with everywhere else. As I suggest in my book *Movie Wars*[1], 'McDonaldisation' isn't the same thing as 'Americanisation' – not if the McDonald's outlets in Tokyo sell corn soup – and I've also argued elsewhere that the moment Coke machines are installed in Tehran, American customs will stop fingerprinting every Iranian who enters the US. Because the paradoxical thing about the apparent increase in tribalism around the world is the fact that countries are now being defined so exclusively as markets that, existentially speaking, one might argue that they're becoming just markets. Insofar as most countries are starting to share the same global culture in the same toneless 'world English', you might even say that we have more things in common than we ever did in the past. Yet the conviction of the marketers is that we're profoundly different from one another, mainly because we presumably require profoundly different ad campaigns. Frankly, I'm more than a little sceptical about this. The terrible fact is that we're somehow letting the people who dream up the marketing campaigns tell us who we are – which also usually means who we aren't supposed to be as well.

ND: You may be right that we are more similar than we are different. But to me an essential point must be added: your and my 'personhood' is tantamount to the possibility of deciding in what ways I see myself to be like you, and in what ways I understand myself to be different from you, as well as from the rest of the world. Language, environment, political discourses, food, parenting – let's say these may be some of the emotional domains in which we look for solidarity between ourselves and others. Memory, sex, smell, space, art may be domains in which, in the best romantic sense, I'd prefer to emphasise difference rather than similarity. And film may scramble for you where you thought your 'differences' and your 'similarities' were. So, the sound of Maggie Cheung's high heels on the steps of her Hong Kong walk-up rental may make you feel like you resonate with this person's inwardness, while the 'universal family' idea on which Mira Nair clearly got her financing for *Monsoon Wedding* (2001) gives a new – scarier yet – meaning to the idea of 'tribal'.

That's what a film, in always being of a particular, concrete moment, can do: it offers a latent sensitive surface, as it were, onto which we cathect, more or less, an occasion for resonating to a greater or lesser degree with depending on what is shown. Just what Adrian was saying. In the movie theatre's mix of solitude and togetherness one feels safe to go either way (which is my contribution to the ongoing TV/DVD debate). Choosing and watching a film alone, I'm inclined to go for a safer bet. In a movie theatre, even a film that makes you feel too different, unresponsive to the ideas and textures you are immersed in – also known as a film you hate – still catches you in the net of the audience's togetherness; ultimately, you have to give it the time of day.

As with the previous question, I'm in your general ballpark, but want to adjust the optic for looking at its grid. And so will break down your long comment/question into two parts. First, a few more words about the extremely productive Cold War decade of US/West European film relations, and its legacy. Second, on America's 'indigenous' relationship to nationalism, in counterdistinction to its caricatured version, 'Americanism'.

What made the 50s and 60s so interesting from the point of view of film was that, thanks to the momentarily TV-atrophied Hollywood, it wasn't chiefly about film. The number one behemoth world cultural industry curled up into a cocoon; as a result not only did the various national film industries step up into the opened world space (Japan, even India with Ray, the 'thawed' Soviets, and the various European industries which each generated their own New Waves). The various arts also came into a better mix: film butted up more tightly against music (between jazz and rock), against painting (abstract expressionism and proto-minimalism), against literature (cross-bred with philosophy), even dance (which fertilised a lot of latent body art, and fed the experimental cinema) – all under the common heading of pop art. For pop art removed the stigma of commercialism, dissolving terminally what was left of the pre-war high/low distinction with its political legacy and agenda, and thinning the formal and genre membranes. The arsenal of what a decade later would collectively be identified as post-modernism was beginning to be built up: parody, pastiche, citation, total self-reflexivity. Maybe this had something to do with the American TV industry's closer historical affiliation with, and dependence on, New York.

Conceptually refined and distilled in the just-emerging liberal-arts film schools such as University of California Los Angeles (in contrast to professional film schools like University of Southern California, which had been going strong since the late 20s), this pop sensibility came to animate many (though not all) American authors of the 70s. Contra the 'I'm John Ford, I make Westerns' macho insouciance that the *Cahiers* critics' cinephilia so fundamentally depended on, Lucas now legitimised the predictability of his narratives with the help of his college-acquired Levi-Strauss, as served up by Joseph Campbell; 'folk' met 'market' at just the right time and angle. In Vietnam's long and Reaganesque aftermath, in an intellectual climate that celebrated the virulently anti-modernist, anti-political, anti-analytic and pro-pop stance in the vivid, self-confident and contemptuously opinionated voice of a Kael, Hollywood gradually returned to conventionally American products, having regained its full self-confident contempt for 'alternative' ways of thinking about film.

That contempt, bred out of a vague film-school familiarity, came out in the ridiculous scenes of the late 90s as Spielberg and company – all raised on a watered-down post-*Cahiers* auteurism – repeatedly chastised the European film-makers as milquetoasts for wanting to retain some measure of protectionism around the state-supported European Union film industries. 'The genius of the system' . . . but what to do when Bazin has been hijacked by Jack Valenti?

For the next decade or so, even while in the mid 80s the parallel system of video distribution became commonplace and part of the American film landscape as a whole, the presence of other cinemas – and I am still here speaking mostly about the Euro axis – mutated from a presence of film objects to a presence of film-makers. Since there was no significant possibility of importing a non-American film into the US for a theatrical release, Percy Adlon, Michelangelo Antonioni, Bertolucci, Costa Gavras, Milos Forman, Ivan Passer, Slava Tsukerman, Jerzy Skolimowski, Louis Malle, Nikita Michalkov, Wenders, Sergio Leone, Verhoeven (and then in the 90s Jean-Jacques Annaud, Emir Kusturica, Lasse Hallstrom, Roland Emmerich, Wolfgang Petersen, Ang Lee, John Woo) opted to come, as it were, in person to deliver what they had to say.

Perhaps this phenomenon, too, is cyclical. In a way there is a similarity between this gradual 80s' shutdown after a period of relative openness, and the general phasing out of imported films into the US by the mid 30s, after they had provided a temporary but crucial presence on the American film scene in the 20s and even in the early 30s, right after the arrival of sound. At both moments the American film industry consolidated (that is, as some scholars would now say, 'innovated' enough to regain a momentum lost in its industrially-scaled routine), but the imports' afterglow, the circulatory surplus value and cachet which they imparted to their makers and their domestic industries, bought some among them enough leverage to negotiate a 'personal' Hollywood deal.

This in itself is not an uninteresting phenomenon – in fact, I'd hypothetically propose that there is a whole category here of films about America 'seen otherwise' and 'seen elsewhere', often drawing attention to events/domains/landscapes/areas that remain invisible to the domestic eye. Think about how strange the American worlds of *What's Eating Gilbert Grape?* (1993), not to mention *Paris, Texas* (1984) or *Rosalie Goes Shopping* (1989) are. But this phenomenon is, in a dialectical movement, a pendulum-swing – and in fact precisely antithetical to, i.e. away from, the claim on our attention of the near-physical evidence of other worlds out there inherent in 'imported' films. Forget Baudrillard and simulacra: what seems to me to be important is the anthropological documentation, and so a kind of 'physical redemption of reality', that films are the best conduit for: precise images, dis-

tinct light, actual voices, slightly different temporality, unpredictable perspectives, viscer-
ally different textures, sounds, etc., all evidence of an elsewhere in the world.
Phenomenological rootedness. Well before we debate whether a narrative is just another
local application of a classical Hollywood narrative or a break with its stylistic norms, it's
about seeing that people blow their noses somewhat differently in Swedish films, or about
the fact that Taiwanese apartment buildings' elevators are the same, or what rain gutters
look like in Tehran, or what fast talk looks like in comparison to slow talk in a Swiss film.
And these visceral little proofs of the differential potential of the world are, as I keep
stressing, what is so painfully absent – not so much from actual American video rental
catalogues as from the general national world-view that ought to have been influenced by
them. I think that Americans have really been short-changed here by the Orwellian lie
about the market providing for them just what they want.

Yes, yes, I know, this all has a lot of holes in it as theories of representation go: Tom
Hanks is not a real American but only acts like one, and a trashcan looks different in a
Wajda and a Kieślowski film. But I'm really convinced of this as a gut level cultural gripe.

By the same token, I actually share your nervousness about the mindless anti-
Americanism out there, and God knows there is a lot of it, generated as an unintended
side-effect of the asymmetrical circulation as well as scale of images. In the smallish town
in France where I just spent six months, the US is present largely through the offering of
the local video store, and the picture that emerges is some kind of living hell, populated
only by violent men and their cars. Obviously, the selection has been assembled not by
Valenti or the State Department but by the ur-French guy who owns the store, and who's
responsible for tipping the line up more towards comedies that are French, with a sprin-
kling of Woody Allen and Robert Altman. But compounded by a sound bite of the 'axis
of evil' kind, and the principally crime-driven made-for-TV movies that fill the late-evening
slot on most European commercial channels, the US today strikes fear in the heart of a
huge proportion – probably the majority – of the average EU citizens. *Oprah* is the closest thing to a documentation of ongoing issues in the US that the world out there sees.

In the case of films, exporting by necessity a 'coarse-grained' image of the US abroad
has worried American officials since the 20s. And in fact was consistently modified by the
Hays Office, on the insistence of the State Department. Ruth Vasey's book *The World
According to Hollywood* [2] gives some pretty interesting examples of *de facto* national interest
censorship in the pre-war years designed to curtail the most 'socially corrosive' representation of American mores – though it was then the consumerism/sex nexus that was
considered most problematic. And the Office of War Information (OWI) – the propa-
ganda arm of the State and Defense departments during and right after the war – tried,
much in the same vein, to provide a 'national-interest screen' for the urgent pressure
exerted by the Motion Picture Producers and Distributors of America (MPPDA) to export
its backlog as soon as the fighting was over. The whole loop of noir – its fetishisation in
France taking place precisely because it wasn't offering the predictably optimistic view of
the US – wouldn't have happened if the OWI had really succeeded in having its way
before being dismantled.

The one good thing that may have come out of the whole 9/11 disaster – in which I include the squandering of the moral capital the US had instantly acquired for the price of those killed – is this idea of the US as a 'homeland', that is, a home. Because 'home' is a shifter, a relational term like 'I' or 'you' or 'there', and thus it inevitably calls forth geopolitical co-ordinates. So if we have a 'home' here that means not only that we don't have it 'there', say in the Middle East. It also means, I'd think, that a lot of people might gradually make themselves more responsible for an US that is a 'home' rather than a hyperpower, with an attendant shift in optics. Maybe the success of Michael Moore at this month's Cannes festival [May 2002], with *Bowling for Columbine*, has something to do with this.

Notes

1. Jonathan Rosenbaum, *Movie Wars* (New York: A Capella, 2000)
2. Ruth Vasey, *The World According to Hollywood* (Exeter: University of Exeter Press, 1997).

11

Circumatlantic Media Migrations

Catherine Benamou and Lucia Saks (2002)

1. Old and new suitcases

Ann Arbor, Bastille Day 2002

Dear Lucia,

It is good to hear from you as you make your move from Durban to Johannesburg, and are preparing to make the leap across the Atlantic. As the descendant of European Jews, born and bred in South Africa and educated in part in the US, you share with me a sense of periodic displacement that affects our sense of ethnic and national identity at the same time that the boundaries shaping those identities are shifting. (In my case, this has to do with being part French-Algerian Jew and part Anglo-German American – which is why I hold two passports.) The distances you're covering now, which I had never contemplated in my own transatlantic travels, are prompting comparisons between the modern and allegedly multicultural nations in which we live. It seems that differences can only be reckoned with if one is willing to acknowledge similarities: the US and South Africa were both founded on alternate waves of immigration, neo-colonialism, genocide as a 'necessity' of settlement, apartheid (both legal and social), aggressive exploitation of the hinterland for its mineral wealth, and civil protest. One country is now making use of blatantly oligarchic strategies to remain at the centre of empire (as it continues to be more affected than it is willing to admit by the plight of countries in which it has meddled, a malady endemic to post-war neo-colonialism); the other is still in the throes of a democratic experiment, trying to keep from being swept back into the periphery, and treading an imaginary tightrope between its affiliation with the G8 [the eight main industrial democracies] and the so-called Third World, neither of which it can afford to abandon.

How this all plays out in terms of screen culture is still slightly opaque to me as an inter-Americanist. At least on the surface it seems that although South Africa remains much closer to its ethnic traditions, both US and South African cinema have long tackled race and immigration as indelible features of their national realities, if not

always as political issues for the audience to grapple with. This is in sharp contrast to their European and Asian mainstream counterparts (with the possible exceptions of the multilingual, multiregional Spain, Belgium and India), which continue to be amazingly oblivious (if not outright averse) to these subjects. This is not to say that European and Asian audiences are not fascinated with South African and US films when they address these issues, but rather that, on their home fronts, immigration and race still represent a source of interference in the screen fabrication of national integrity and the unified national subject. Japanese film-maker Masato Harada has mentioned how impossible it was for him to have a film (*Kamikaze Taxi*, 1995) about the Nikkeijin – the returning Japanese migrants from South America – produced by any major Japanese studio, even though the Nikkeijin currently make up a significant portion of the workforce and have long managed to introduce strains of Latin American cultural expression, including soccer and samba, into the Japanese public sphere. When films about race and immigration emerge in the European context, such as Isaac Julien's black British cinema, they often take the form of diasporic or ethnic expression, which is certainly not a bad thing, but the circuits for such films are recognisably smaller than they are for the mainstream.

The parallels between the US and South Africa – I hope I'm not exaggerating – not only point to the remnants of the 'Third World' that are still in our midst, with all of the questions that poses for screen representation, but also point to the extent to which the late twentieth-century schism between the 'First' and 'Third' worlds might no longer hold, either descriptively or strategically. At the same time, I don't think we've reached the point of interconnected, 'globalised' metropoles, each with its own periphery, as some analysts of post-1989 globalisation have argued. Your mention of the movers in your house and their rapt engagement with the ongoing soccer World Cup, mixed with their consumption of tea and lunch in between carrying boxes, led me to think about just what has changed in the transnational transmission of media, and what is meant by its 'globalisation effect' on our social and cultural lives; is it qualitatively different than what was the case twenty years ago? What has happened aside from an expansion of media use, a branching out of production and distribution modes, and an increased technical proficiency around the globe to build markets? (Granted, these improvements theoretically benefit practices other than those of corporate produced and sponsored media.)

Naturally, there's a greater sense of connectedness brought about by our sensory experience of an event that we know to be experienced simultaneously by others who are spatially distant from us, as though one could close the very gap between looking and being. When the channels of connectedness are activated repeatedly or consistently enough, this can produce what John Tomlinson has called disembedding – the uprooting and dispersal of cultural expression and social experience from one geohistorical context to another, leading to any number of transnational links and cultural mixes.

Yet this is often accompanied by an anxiety of participation, since our capacity for full consumption is diminished by intermittent watching, the smallness of the

electronic screen, and the implied (and thus immeasurable) scale of mediated events. We easily find ourselves caught in the global loop, hegemonic or alternative, but how close can we ever get to the epicentre of the action? How do we define our relationship to our interlocutors – by the time we get 'there', is it still 'us' speaking? And if we ever do reach the centres of production and diffusion, to what extent can we become agents in relation to the global whole? (In the Latin American periphery, there are now direct flights to Disney World. Yet most aspiring denizens of the US dream mecca realise, upon full immersion, that they are no more enfranchised and privileged than they were before.)

This condition affects non-corporate producers, film-makers and spectators alike. Yet the semblance of access and agency is exactly what is being proffered as the side-benefit and hook of the global media message: the world 'at your fingertips', or, speaking of soccer, the world 'in a cup'. Juxtaposed with the promise of the totality is the inevitable cognitive dissonance produced for most viewers when the globalised image fails to jibe with what we can witness and touch in our everyday lives. Even when we've 'been there', and 'done' or 'had that', our fragmentary access makes us continue to miss and desire real experience in an eerie way, yet this experience can no longer be had without some form of mediation (Aldous Huxley's 'feelies', perhaps?). To return to the World Cup: here we have the ultimate expression of global synchrony and communication combined with a dubious, ritualistic revival of nationalism – are the real and symbolic stakes of the game the same for Croatia, Ecuador, Turkey or even Brazil as compared to Germany or France? Does the national continue to coincide with these geopolitical boundaries? And, as you mention, off screen, there are the not-so-post-colonial rituals and expectations of the everyday.

What seems to be lacking in most current analyses is precisely the messier *middle ground* between corporatised global culture and local manifestations of consumption and resistance. In our range of options, we're still caught in the rhetorical grip of Mothra vs Godzilla (or Biollante, if you prefer), as we plough through a barrage of electronic logo-bearing billboards even as we try to email each other. Plausibly, we can attribute the shrinking and eclipsing of this middle ground not to the dissipation of nationalism and its media expressions – on the contrary, Western European avoidance of immigration and race is nothing but a knee-jerk expression of nationalism – but rather to the occlusion by byzantine conglomerates and subsidiaries of transnational film culture. This culture takes multiple forms: 'art cinema' and explicitly radical film movements, which have often wielded the banner of the national, yet have been highly dependent upon international forums of exhibition and distribution (Cannes, Viña del Mar, Venice, Berlin, etc.); and the semi-clandestine flow of B films to neighbourhood theatres and empty TV slots around the globe. Whether or not this middle realm still exists (and as a Benjaminian at heart, I prefer to think of it as being 'suppressed' rather than simply vanishing, and of being more central to our current understanding of globalisation than might first appear), it is important to retrieve it as a useful vantage point from which to evaluate how the new 'global age' – or rather this new phase of globalisation, since the cinema has always been global – has changed the

cultural elasticity of film, and, just as importantly, the terms of interaction between transnational media and its audiences.

Moves are not only about taking leave and embracing the new, but also about luring us back into bits of our past, which we hold up against the present. Perhaps, as I move intellectually between the 'Good Neighbour' 40s and the NAFTA [North American Free Trade Agreement] 90s in my observation of media flows between the Americas, I can retrieve a bit of this hazy middle realm by returning to the immediate prehistory of cinema's latest global phase – a past that, like a collective media unconscious, is still being mined for its popular appeal (like 70s' blaxploitation in *Jackie Brown* [1997] or the diverse references in *Austin Powers in Goldmember* [2002] and *Undercover Brother* [2002]) by the savvy producer or media entrepreneur.

Yet something more is needed here than the demystification of commodified global media, accomplished by focusing on the seductive hold of the increasingly hidden and extensive apparatus over the individual psyche, redefining 'community' and what it means to 'participate' in it, or recognising the nation state as a rhetorical construct that can still pack a punch with brutal state force, aided and abetted by global capital (Guatemala, Indonesia, Israel, Russia, the US). Nor is the dangerous impulse for generalisation remedied by resorting to the idiosyncratic local appropriations of the global, which have momentarily succeeded in translating logo-laden hegemonic messages into culturally meaningful acts that psychically, if not materially, mitigate the effects of 'cultural domination'. Haven't multinational, multiculturally 'smart' advertisers already learned how to counterfeit a centre-periphery power inversion by promoting the logo as the ultimate global currency, rather than the sign of cultural domination? Aren't we already being told that we are all logo-centric, yet in different ways? I'm thinking here of the World Cup TV ads, in which we see people of different nationalities swapping their shirts, all paid for in different currencies by MasterCard; and the Japanese sports announcer who is finally able to belt out a full-fledged, Latin-style 'Goooooo-al!' coached by a Mexican sports announcer, but only after taking a swig of ubiquitous and unambiguous Coca-Cola.

Imperfect mastery and cultural conversion: over twenty years ago, on a film expedition through the Andes, I wandered into a neighbourhood movie theatre in Lima, Peru. Not surprisingly, it was very difficult then to view Peruvian films in commercial theatres; instead, one saw well-worn prints of post-war Hollywood films and Bollywood musical epics (with no apparent logic as to the time of theatrical release). The film being shown that afternoon was *Shaft's Big Score!* (1972), playing to a reasonably sized, mixed-class audience, mostly single and male. What, I wondered, could be of relevance in this celebration of black urban masculinity and defence of integrity in a warped, hostile, 'white' American world for the displaced and lonely Peruvian *serrano* (highlands) viewer? A few days later, upon venturing into the central highlands, not yet ravaged by the campaigns of the Shining Path, I began to find the answer. Here, in every town and marketplace, the breathless whining of the Bee Gees could be heard, wafting into one's distracted consciousness among the more

vernacular sounds of *huayños* (electrified indigenous ballads) and spoken Quechua.
Traces of *Saturday Night Fever* (1977) were everywhere, and young *cholo* men were
styling their hair, wearing the pants and walking the walk of Jhon (sic) Travolta. In
performing these acts of consumption, the young men were expressing their desire to
remake their own social personae not in the image of powerful Manhattan tycoons (an
absent presence in the film), or the archetypically nefarious and bumbling *gringo* of the
highlands imaginary (so aptly epitomised by Jorge Sanjines in *Blood of the Condor*
[1969]), but in the image of the hard-working, socially mobile and thoroughly
urbanised working-class youth from the boroughs that Travolta and his dance partner
represented. The masculinity of both Travolta and Shaft was sustained and projected
by their picaresque styles, in which they could each 'get over' by displaying their
innate physical talents, cunning and courage, without asking permission from anyone.
Thus the dramas of Shaft and Travolta were avidly absorbed by these money-poor yet
globally-savvy local male audiences, not according to the nuances of the dialogue or
the historical references of the plots, but on a deeper, more visceral level of struggle
and identification.

The actors who played the lead roles in these films (Richard Roundtree and, yes,
even John Travolta) were hardly stars then by mainstream standards, yet their
characters loomed heroic because they, too, like the highlands *cholo* or urban *mestizo*
man (who had been rendered vulnerable by incomplete social assimilation and
unstable employment in a zigzagging post-military economy), were able to recognise,
cultivate and even assert their own ethnic difference, while inventing a modern
identity and striving for a better future. Moreover, this was something one could
achieve individually without waiting for radical change or being bogged down by
national and political trends. What clearly distinguished Travolta's and Roundtree's
screen performances from the more ubiquitous recordings of the Bee Gees was that
the latter remained confined to the sphere of the global, beyond reach in style and
language except through some kind of awkward mimesis; whereas these films still
proffered the possibility of cross-cultural identification and, eventually,
transculturation.

What's striking about Peruvian reception of US media in the 70s is that these
audiences were able to create their own consumption rituals, through which new
mythologies could be woven around the ritualised myth of the medium itself. If world
televised soccer is about preserving the myth of ritual (and now players are even
faking injuries for theatrical effect), indifferent to the cultural identity of the spectator,
the cinema, on the other hand, seems to permit the building of ritual around powerful
social myths and efforts at demystification. It is perhaps by observing these rituals that
the current substance of the 'middle realm' can come back into view.

Second, while it's possible that the performers and the producers of Top Forty
songs and box office hits might have known their work would flow outside the
perimeter of the Anglophone world, neither the performances nor the plots, nor even
the packaging of the product, was conceived along transnational lines. Instead, these
works were simply dumped by the industry on 'Third World' circuits to recover

whatever surplus value they could glean. This lack of premeditation is glaringly apparent in the lack of any marketing effort to lure local audiences to the theatre or record store, save for a poster or two. While the dumping without fanfare might have contributed to incomplete comprehension – and therefore 'imperfect' consumption – of the texts in their original formulations, this ethnocentric neglect of multicultural modes of usage also created a margin for the spectator's agency that was fully taken advantage of by Peruvians, and doubtless many others.

Moreover, the haphazard exhibition schedules created by indiscriminate dumping can pave the way for a different alchemy to take place between cultural positionings and screen genres: Chilean-born director Raul Ruiz, who this year was sitting on the official jury at Cannes as a 'French' film-maker, owes his own narrative innovations to the plethora of American B movies he saw in Chile as a teenager. At the same time, his 'Frenchification' has less to do with a change in cultural identity than with the availability in France of state and private funding for the 35mm films he makes. Thus, it is increasingly difficult to place certain directors, like Ruiz and Harada, within the trajectory of a given national cinema, even though they remain resolutely preoccupied with the respective trajectories, politically and culturally, of their nations of origin. We should also allow for the possibility that such directors will be able to transform the national cinema, provoking a U-turn or boomerang of cultural vectors, by virtue of their international status. For example, Ruiz has just returned again to Chile to make an experimental TV series through the Chilean Ministry of Culture.

What has happened then is that films circulating globally – including indigenous videos from the Brazilian hinterland – are now produced with global audiences in mind. This has produced a new 'rules of the game' for the relations obtaining between film-maker and producing organisation, as well as tangible pressures at the level of the film text (this has also occurred in transnational TV, apart from US products). Whereas there was no clear-cut global standard of representation during the era of indiscriminate media dumping, beyond a self-imposed and internalised concept of Hollywood production values and grammar (while leaving narrative content, casting, plot structure and thematic orientations within the realm of local definition), there is now an undeclared international standard that is being strategically adhered to by Mexican, Peruvian, Bolivian, Brazilian and even European directors who depend on companies such as Miramax for production and distribution. This dependence is a necessity rather than an option for all directors who cannot count on adequate access to their domestic markets, and would like to make more than one film. It would seem, then, that the chances for mimesis, and its correlate, masquerade, to take place within an imperial cultural network are stronger than ever, even as dissonant voices and screen alchemists persist in their efforts.

I've focused very little on specific films here: perhaps we can address the new global cinema in more concrete and contemporary terms later. Mira Nair's *Monsoon Wedding* (2001) was just released in art cinemas in Rio de Janeiro, and I am curious to know about its reception in Durban, and what this might tell us about new transnational trends.

Very much looking forward to hearing from you, from whatever point along your journey this letter finds you. . . .

Transnationally yours,
Catherine

Johannesburg, 27 July 2002

Dear Catherine,
Your letter is filled with so many fascinating and pertinent observations – not only about transnational cinema (which I take to also include video, television and computer technologies) and the kind of media migrations that it engenders, but also to my personal situation since I am in transit between nations, lives, families and jobs as I begin the move from Durban to Ann Arbor. As you rightly say, this is an enormous leap across not only the Atlantic but also the Indian Ocean, and it is one I have made before when I emigrated to California from South Africa just after the Soweto uprising – never dreaming that I would return almost twenty years later to the brave new democracy of South Africa with Nelson Mandela, a mythical figure hidden away in Robben Island for over two decades, as the new president.

As you so cogently put it, since that time South Africa has been walking a tightrope between its desire and need to placate and attract the developed world and its capital, and its equal need to present itself as the leader of the African continent. Hence NEPAD, President Thabo Mbeki's plan for a new economic and political blueprint for Africa's relationship with G8 countries, and his idea of an African Renaissance – a very Eurocentric event – in the original birthplace of mankind, which leans heavily on the discourses of negritude, pan-Africanism and the colonial critique of Frantz Fanon. In keeping with the contemporary moment, Mbeki's concept of an African Renaissance is, at face, an inclusive gesture. But there are also exclusive gestures that occur during moments of immense change and movement. Membership in society can become more closed and discriminatory by using the powers of local governance – homeowner associations, gated communities, private clubs and schools, by-laws, and fines – to keep those deemed undesirable out.

Both of these gestures are present in contemporary South Africa, which has become the melting pot for sub-Saharan Africa. A quick tour of the pavement economy in the Hillbrow section near the centre of Johannesburg will bring you into contact with Ethiopians and Congolese street vendors selling watches, bags, vegetables, beads and make-up. A restaurant that used to be Greek has become Angolan, and so on. On the other hand, a tour of the old white suburbs that now house the new urban black elite reveals gated communities with razor wire on top of ten-foot walls and electronic gates. In the townships and the inner city there is a growing dislike of all that is perceived as foreign and strange. Rising crime and unemployment rates have led to a xenophobic backlash against black foreigners or strangers who are perceived as stealing jobs from South African blacks, using up scarce public resources, and committing crimes.

Internally there has been a complete restructuring of laws, institutions, economic regulations, and electoral and social policies as part of the process of transforming South Africa into a progressive democracy. But of course such an idea, utopian as it is, requires representation and narrative construction to produce the new forms of community and identity that go along with such mutations. Perhaps the only word to explain the explosion of new coalitions that has occurred at all levels in South Africa is the Italian word *provare*, which means to try on. And that's exactly what is happening as people try on and take off different identities and guises and behaviours. Of course, this has also engendered the expected backlash of conservative essentialism, justified by the idea of ethnic tradition and custom.

But the media has exploited this explosion of new social 'types' – particularly the advertising agencies. One campaign springs to mind: using huge outdoor billboards that hang over the main freeway into Johannesburg, an agency has played with the idea of race as fashion, something to be put on and taken off. The client, a black talk-radio station, is clearly trying to appeal to a crossover audience to attract the new urban Joburg sophisticate, irrespective of race. The advertisements boast a variety of black South Africans, all beautiful, young, hip and urban (including an Albino woman and a flamboyant gay man) with different coloured hair – blonde, red, blue – and blue and green contact lenses. 'What makes you Black?' is the question posed above these images, and answered by the logo and tag of the radio station. Blackness is a state of listening to the right music and talk, which of course allows everyone to be black, including the white kids who are also struggling to be African. A case of logo-centricity, as you so cleverly put it, or a way of acknowledging the fungibility of race and ethnicity – the *provare* factor? Given South Africa's terrible history of quantifying race, of writing it on the body, the campaign can be seen as celebrating the change that has taken place.

South African popular culture has been deeply influenced by American popular culture. The long-term cultural connections between Africa and America have gotten lost in cinema theory by the creation of typologies such as mainstream/Hollywood cinema, oppositional/alternative cinema, or even national cinemas. Important and useful as they have been in the history of film scholarship, these typologies have also tended to become dogmatic and frozen, obscuring the global connections which cinema history, as part of broader history *per se*, must seek to acknowledge and understand even as it also registers the differences at work. Indeed, the connection with American popular culture, especially American black culture, is so central to the story of South African black culture that the rise of black urban spaces like Sophiatown or District Six has been predicated on the transposition, imitation, translation and remaking of American culture there. In the 30s, the films of Fred Astaire influenced African dance performance. In the 50s, jazz bands like the Manhattan Brothers, the Woody Woodpeckers, and the Harlem Swingsters were integral to the creation of Sophiatown's urban black culture, while *Drum* magazine featured a Philip Marlowe character and a style of presentation almost indistinguishable from *Life* and *Look*. The pan-Africanist discourses of the Black Consciousness Movement (Steve Biko, most famously) have been predicated on the writings of W. E. B. Du Bois about Africa as the site of a racialistic unity defined by lines of cultural descent, a legacy to the present that equates black consciousness with nationalist consciousness.

A right to a cinema of one's own: there is no better site from which to retrieve what you call the 'suppressed middle ground' than to look at the discourse swirling around South Africa's desire to have its own media, capable of 'reflecting the nation's own culture in its cinema and television'. The quote comes from the Department of Art, Science, Culture and Technology, and it's redolent with the politics of cultural ownership in South Africa today, which has become the site of intense battles that retrace historical fault-lines of race, culture, gender and class. Both the media and the film industry have been accused of suffering an 'unbearable whiteness of being'.

Transformation has not been fast enough; the industry favours those who already have training, resources and access, which inevitably means the whites. It is hostile to the tradition of oral culture, unfriendly to would-be black film-makers, and suffers from what Haile Gerima has called a lack of image equity. There is no longer any single image of the people, which in post-modern, post-Marxist, neo-liberal times can be relied upon in framing the question of national cinema in relation to cultural rights (and representation). A diverse group of South Africans with diverse cultural backgrounds, distinct languages and astonishingly different historical trajectories (emotionally charged places on the sullen map of the past) cannot be assimilated into any single picture of how the media might best express their right to representation, and their larger cultural rights generally. Even if one is clear on what a cultural right is, one still remains unclear about its content. Hence the reigning image in South African cinematic and media theorisation of a rainbow nation, which projects a group characterised by unity through diversity in virtue of a common project, a common landscape, a common history and a common requirement: to bind themselves into a new whole while remaining diverse. What is wanted is a harmonious refraction of colour bands, each into the others, to produce a beautiful thing, while each retains its own colour properties. This is the aesthetics of multiracialism, a harmony of types, each formerly at war with the other, now glowing in the light of the other. How some kind of Technicolor can achieve this rainbow effect while also catering to quite distinct audiences is the central theoretical problem in South African media pronouncements. As Benedict Anderson noted in his classic book *Imagined Communities*, a sense of national belonging is the most universally legitimate sense and provides the framework for all kinds of political activity, and yet its terms of representation tend to be homogenising: taking disparate texts and bringing them together as one, under the false auspices of a shared imagined community.[1]

In some ways transnational media fare offers an escape route out of this conundrum. It can be a corrective to overpowering national repression at worst and lack of invention at best. Under apartheid, the cultural imagination became obsessed with apartheid as the only subject for representation. Ironically, this generated an immediate if specialised global audience for anti-apartheid films and literature. Now the question is what to represent, who, and how? South African films have to develop a global market if they are to survive since the domestic market is too small to recoup production costs and cultivate audiences at home. This is not easy, as evidenced by the problems encountered by Anant Singh, a Durban-based and South Africa's only international film producer. He produced *Mr Bones* (2001), an *Ace Ventura* clone set in the Lost City, an incredibly expensive simulacrum of an 'African' city set in rolling hills with world-class golf courses near Johannesburg. This was the only film made in sub-Saharan Africa (not just South Africa) that was for sale at the Los Angeles Film Mart this year. It starred a popular local comic, Leon Schuster, as a white *sangoma* (witch doctor), thus inverting stereotypes about African primitivism, but the main point here is that it hoped to find a market globally by combining local talent with two African-American up-and-coming actors, David Ramsey and Faizon Love, and adopting Hollywood production values. Apparently it worked: the film was picked up by German and by some South American buyers, and it is expected to open in the US later this year.

Singh, who has produced everything from anti-apartheid movies (*Sarafina!* [1992] being the best known) to the remake of *Cry the Beloved Country* (1995) with James Earl Jones and Richard Harris, owns the film rights to Mandela's famous autobiography *Long Walk to Freedom*. For the past six years, he has been trying to find an actor to play Mandela, but cannot find anyone that would be acceptable to both local and global audiences. The South African audience would be offended if anyone but a South African played the most famous son of all, while the global audience (however one wishes to define it) requires, according to Singh, a star like Denzel Washington in the role. Clearly the terms of interaction between transnational media and its audiences are, depending on the text, complicated and less elastic than is often assumed.

There is a further point about films coming out of Africa. They have, as you rightly say, been part of a self-conscious international film circuit, limited to European art houses and film festivals. They have had little exhibition within the continent. In this sense, they are truly transnational products, or products for export only. (In this respect, one wonders how *Monsoon Wedding* was received and exhibited in India.) The South African Broadcasting Company (SVS), as part of its Reithian public broadcasting mandate to uplift and educate the public, recently bought and showed many of the classic African films that had never been seen before. The problem was that they showed them on their digital satellite channel, and the majority of people who saw them were white: digital TV is expensive and mostly has a white viewership. So once again African films travelled the art circuit, except this time on the small screen and through virtual space.

Things are changing, however, when it comes to the way African films and particularly African film directors position themselves, and the change is one that should have an effect on the way African (and South African) film is perceived in the pantheon of world cinema. The first wave of African cinema from the 60s and 70s was first and foremost a political idea. It emerged out of the early days of African independence as part and parcel of the thought that Africans could not only carve out independent states for themselves, but also alternative spaces for making films outside of the Hollywood model. It was a social cinema; a cinema of liberation and purpose dedicated to re-educating a new generation growing up in a new age. Today many of the leading film-makers in Africa are rejecting the concept of 'African cinema' and the label of 'African film director'. They do not want their work to be placed in a box marked 'African films', separated off from the rest of the world's film output. They reject being co-opted under the name of state nationalism, or being seen as important only in terms of their contribution to the nation or the continent at large. Gaston Kabore has commented that just because he comes from Africa, his films should not have to represent the whole continent. The fact that he makes films in Africa merely reflects his own individuality and history.

The second wave of African film-makers is very concerned with marketing its product. There is a turn towards pragmatism, an emphasis on reaching a wider audience, both within the continent and abroad, on finding solutions to the ongoing problems of distribution, inconsistent state funding and state censorship, and the fact that African cinema is an industry falsely separated from its consumers. If reaching a wider audience means making films in English, appropriating the narrative codes of mainstream cinema, or moving away from anti-colonial movies to more layered and diverse subjects such as contemporary life in urban Africa (Idrissa Ouedraogo's *Kini and Adams* [1997]), women's inequality (Tsitsi Dangarembge's *Everyone's Child* [1996]), and the immigrant experience in Europe (Jean-Marie Teno's *Clando* [1996] and Jean-Pierre Bekolo's *Aristotle's Plot* [1997]), then so be it. Audiences are seen not as potential revolutionaries who need to be educated and culturally transformed, but consumers, participants in the worldwide entertainment and leisure industry. Even the more didactically inclined Francophone film-makers are talking of making films in English which they could then re-route through South Africa, the Hong Kong of Africa, so as to reach the larger global audience.

In its previous incarnation, South Africa thought of itself as a Western outpost at the bottom of Africa, an accident of geography that should find reflection in its cultural forms. It therefore sought validation from the countries that 'mattered' – the Western world – with which it continued to maintain, despite economic sanctions and moral rejection, an imaginary bond.

Well, let me leave it there for now, not in Cape Town but in Johannesburg at the tip of Africa waiting for my own export to the USA. I look forward to our next conversation and the moving mutations to my thoughts and ideas that it will bring.

My best to you,
Lucia

2. *In situ*

Ann Arbor, 25 August 2002

CATHERINE BENAMOU: In your letter, I was struck by the challenges South Africa is facing, rehabilitating a national cinema through a globally oriented model in this post-Socialist, post-apartheid era. What does this portend, exactly, for the local spectator?

LUCIA SAKS: We have to make a distinction between Francophone African and Anglophone African cinema. The first has a rich culture and historical background – and there are all sorts of reasons for that. . . .

CB: Yes, the formerly 'responsible' post-colonial state, which has now divested itself of its responsibility towards Francophone African film-makers.

LS: Exactly, and the idea of France seeing its ex-colonies as outposts of potential French culture, and encouraging film-making and exhibition. But this wasn't the case in Anglophone post-colonial or colonial contexts. That was a British system, a system of economics, not a system of culture to the same extent. Some people commented ironically that that was good because it left people alone. It therefore didn't produce any intense, nuanced analysis of the post-colonial situation. Now the post-apartheid era is even more complicated, because it's not exactly post-colonial. It's hard to explain why particular styles are adopted by certain countries, and why other styles are not. Why didn't South Africa adopt the practices of Cinema Nôvo, a more intellectual approach – a kind of avant-garde, didactic, polemical approach that you might find in Mozambique?

CB: As the Brazilian director Glauber Rocha summed it up, 'An idea in the head, a camera in the hand.'

LS: First you have to look at the fact that it was Anglophone colonialism, and then a protracted period of apartheid. This is not a complete answer, but it's a significant factor.

CB: So this oppositional cinema couldn't imagine the nation beyond apartheid?

LS: No, it couldn't. It also became very much concerned with the realist aesthetic, almost in the sense that it was considered . . .

CB: . . . a cinema of demystification?

LS: Right. Because apartheid was so severe and so obviously wrong. Therefore a cinema that argued for formalistic interventions of that nature at the textual level was considered to be almost a luxury, so witnessing and recording became more important, and this limited the idea of cinematic invention.

CB: There have been great debates in Latin America about what is the correct way to proceed, and there were splits at certain points in time. Realists and those who felt that you had to use a documentary approach thought that any kind of formalistic approach was acting as a smokescreen and was preventing a direct address to social crises, so there *are* some analogies there. What's interesting is that, today, a curious return has been made to some of those realist strategies, but it's being mixed with a very self-conscious and iconoclastic approach to form, in the more successful cases, because of a kind of cynicism that has come about as a result of neo-liberal, post-dictatorship policies in Latin America. I like to call it the cinema of disenchantment. You're seeing it in Mexico, in Brazil (and to a lesser extent in Argentina and Venezuela, which also have very active audiovisual industries): it's a kind of 'in your face', very gritty, Zola-type realism, combined with some post-modernist quotation and very different ideas about narrative continuity. In other words, an emphasis on narrative continuity means complicity: it means you've fully bought into the ingestion of the Hollywood model, which is inappropriate to these historical contexts. So yes, let's have state-of-the-art production values, 35mm, large crews, and distribution from New Line and Miramax, but let's insist on episodic structures, or at least imperfectly sutured narrative where the continuities and contiguities are used to foreground the contradictions: 'seamy' films that show the seamier side of life. I'm thinking specifically of two Mexican films, Alejandro González Iñarritu's *Amores Perros* (2000) and Alfonso Cuarón's road movie *Y tu mamá también* (2001). In Brazil, Sergio Bianchi's *Chronically Unfeasible* (2001), about the demoralised state of civic life in post-dictatorship Brazil, refuses to let the spectator off the hook. It shows all Brazilian classes in day-to-day interactions, but it is the self-designated politically correct spectator as well as the more conventional bourgeois subjects who become Bianchi's targets. These films focus on the micro level at the conflicts which take place in the everyday, and so they're using a commercial veneer, well-known genres such as the *telenovela* and the road movie, to look at the same filmic objects that the radical New Latin American Cinema (such as Solanas and Getino's *Hour of the Furnaces* [1968]) would have looked at, only in a much more rough-hewn way. This aggressive post-modern cinema – the Argentine *Nine Queens* (2001) is also a good example – takes a very polished approach to very unpleasant situations, and I find it's an entirely new cinema, which really hasn't been appreciated because people are trying to evaluate it from the point of view of international box office and actors' performances. Let's say that Antonio Banderas might appear in one of these films, or very well-known Mexican actors, such as *telenovela* heart-throb Jorge Salinas, or the veteran Brazilian actress Fernanda Montenegro, who was in Walter Salles' *Central Station* (1999). Their appearances get commented on, but the intervention that's being made at the level of form is usually skirted around, because there is this fear of interfering with the films as transnational commodities.

LS: I'm starting to realise just how far behind South African cinema is at the moment. There have been pronouncements, rhetoric, bills passed, calls for South African cinema to drag itself out of the apartheid ghetto into the post-apartheid, but very little has happened. Where to go? In fact, Nadine Gordimer has written an essay called 'Living in the

Interregnum'[2] which asks, 'What do we write about now?' That's one of the problems: nobody really wants to talk about apartheid anymore.

Many young people are ashamed that their parents went through apartheid, and feel they sold out, or they gave in for many years. Many of them were only eight or nine when Nelson Mandela was released in 1994. In fact, classic apartheid, as it was known, ended in the early 70s. After that there were states of emergency, and general chaos, and then the end of apartheid, the negotiated end. So it's very difficult to know what subject to address. People don't go to South African films; there's a lot of discussion as to why the few that are produced are not well attended. But there are local TV soap operas, which tend to follow the *telenovela* format and are popular. One of the most popular is *Generations*, which is now in its fourth or fifth year. It's about an ad agency, and everybody's beautiful, they're white *and* black, they also have affairs, and it's all very yuppy. I mean this is not exactly representative of social conditions for most black South Africans, but it's extremely popular, and the producers defend it as having 'aspirational value'.

I think it's Armand Mattelart who said that three-quarters of all the people in the developing world are absolutely marginal to the market forces of that world; but they are completely sutured into the symbolic content, and then they participate in it, through the symbolic, and it's such a rich, powerful participation. This has been dismissed by cultural studies critics as, 'Oh, you have no real power', but who's to tell that person that he or she has no power? If it's perceived that texts really have power, then we have to believe in this kind of spectatorship. I think it's also important to realise – and this is happening in South Africa – that these global-oriented texts are not just produced by multinational corporations that are then beaming them into or selling them to South Africa; they are produced locally.

CB: So the nation has reached a certain level of representational competence in the eyes of the viewers.

LS: Yes, and also in terms of the nation's interactions with the global.

CB: And that permits a sense of national identity to take shape: if the state and these companies are successful in negotiating air space for a soap opera that has the production values that a Brazilian soap opera might have, then that's a sign of success that permits identification at the national level.

This returns us to the whole question of South Africa having to face the fact not only that it's post-apartheid, and needs to move beyond white supremacy, but that it's multi-ethnic. There are often tensions between the idea of nation building and that of multi-ethnicity. Just to give you an example from the US: I remember a film by Bolivian film-maker Marcos Loayza called *Cuestión de Fé* (*A Question of Faith* [1995]), a kind of a post-modern road movie that reverses the country-to-city paradigm and leaves La Paz to look at what's happening in the Bolivian countryside: the decadence due to the drug trade, moral hypocrisy around the question of religion and, at the same time, a celebration of the multiplicity of Bolivian identity, which is composed of people who are indigenous and don't speak any Spanish; people who are Spanish-dominant; and *mestizo* people who live between those worlds. We showed this film only one evening here in Ann Arbor, but in order to justify such a screening, I had to demonstrate the existence of a local audience, and to get that audience, I had to do audience outreach. At the screening there were actually Bolivians from Chicago—urbanite areas who 'went to the provinces' to see a Bolivian film, plus whoever was Bolivian or Andean in Southeastern Michigan. These viewers were able to reaffirm and restate their sense of national identity, even though they might have already been US citizens. They were there to rekindle a nostalgic relationship to this country they had left behind.

Flora Gomes' new musical, *Nha Fala* (2002), which is about to be screened at the Venice Film Festival, addresses the effects of the migration of Portuguese and Creole-speaking Guinea-Bissauians to Paris, yet also has to answer to the expectations and interests of producers in Portugal, Luxembourg and France. . . . During an early discussion about the screenplay in Paris, I suggested to a diverse group of production people that since the film was already foregrounding gender by making its main character a young Guinea-Bissauian woman, it might be a good idea to problematise the French identity of the lover she meets in Paris by making him North African and/or Jewish. The producers were appalled! France really has no multicultural cinema.

LS: Even when the cinema tries to reflect multicultural issues, it is difficult to assign validity to the very *concept* of national cinema today, not only because of global cultural flows, but also because the local texts themselves deal with people who are so diasporic and migrant, living in exile, or who go and return. For example, in *Monsoon Wedding*, the young man has come back from the US to find a bride, and obviously he's going to take her back to the US with him. So even in its characterisation, the movie is concerned with people who are in states of movement, and I think that this is partly why it appeals so much to the diaspora. It isn't the old Heimat film; it's about these people who are in between, in transition or in exile.

CB: A new generation that is breaking with tradition, yet negotiating a return to it anyway.

LS: You've even got the same thing in England, with *Bhaji on the Beach* (1993). . . . In Durban, it's quite interesting, because we have such a large Indian diaspora that came in 1840. It's the largest in the world, comprising a million and a half. *Monsoon Wedding* was tremendously successful in Durban, and not only with the Indian audience. It had a crossover appeal. It was lauded for being a film that could appeal to everybody. Even though it came through the art film circuit, it opened like a mainstream film on twenty screens on the same weekend as *K-Pax* (2002), and it took in even more money.

CB: One of the problems with the Hollywood/Third World antinomy is that it really distracts us from these other places that have always been centres for the diffusion of film culture. The Philippines has long exported Philippine cinema in the form of videos to the US, because we have a large Filipino community here. So it already was transnational in its distribution concept, yet nationally oriented in terms of content since it relied on the Filipino diaspora for its commercialisation.

LS: So it was already global cinema, it had a global market waiting for it.

CB: Until recently along the border in Northern Mexico, they were producing B movies for American export, not only for the audience in Mexico. They knew these films would be picked up by TV stations in the US, and they went as far as Russia, where for some reason audiences were relating to B movies about migration and about smuggling across the US/Mexican border. These producers were able to keep offices in Texas and in Mexico so they could generate US dollars to finance low-budget pictures. So it was extremely marginal to the film industry in Mexico City and to the kind of cinema the state wanted to send to Cannes, but probably more extensive in its reach, because it could be distributed on videotape to Mexican grocery stores in Chicago, for example. Bollywood is another great example: when I was in the Andes years ago seeing *Jaws 2* (1978) and *Saturday Night Fever*, one of the most popular draws for Saturday afternoon in the highlands was a Bollywood film. So India has always had a broad export market for its films, and that's how in a multilingual and multireligious nation such as India, an industry has been able to sustain itself.

LS: In closing, we should mention that people often use the word transnational very much as a substitute for multicultural, but I don't think the two are the same at all. . . .

CB: No, they're not; nor are they the same as international cinema. I would define transnational cinema as a cinema which will circulate outside of a certain geopolitical territory, and which self-consciously reflects that circulation.

LS: Which moves us away from preconceived categories into the concrete.

Notes

1. Benedict Anderson, *Imagined Communities: Reflections on the Origin and Spread of Nationalism* (London: Verso, 1983).
2. Nadine Gordimer, 'Living in the Interregnum', in Stephen Clingman (ed.), *The Essential Gesture: Writing, Politics and Places* (New York: Knopf, 1988), pp. 261–84.

12

Movie Mutations 2: Second Round

Quintín, Mark Peranson, Nicole Brenez, Adrian Martin and Jonathan Rosenbaum (2001–2002)

Buenos Aires, 18 December 2001

Dear Mark,
A few days ago I wrote about *Amélie* (*Le fabuleux destin d'Amélie Poulain*, 2001) for your magazine, *Cinema Scope*. According to you, it's the only negative review of the film that's appeared in the Toronto press. This fact alone may justify a new series of letters as a follow-up to those published in *Trafic* in 1997: it's good for critics not to feel alone. However, the original set of letters, grouped together under the title *Movie Mutations*, is much more than a gathering of like-minded individuals, and when I read them for the first time – I've been rereading them since then – I was certain that they were a landmark in the history of film criticism. To begin with, they represent a decisive step beyond the 'death of cinema' discourse that was so important to cinephilia throughout the mid 90s. At the same time, the reconfiguration of film culture that the letters propose and the path that they take towards the future of cinema are at the other side of the spectrum from the new trend of 'world cinema' designed along the same lines as 'world music', of which *Amélie* is a perfect example.

By contrast, the internationalism of *Movie Mutations* shows that cinema still establishes a kind of communication between films and viewers outside the pressures of hype – a communication that has its own history, which the letters help bring to the surface. They also reveal an aesthetic emotion shared by a generation that exists beyond borders – an important element in what generated the original cinephilia back in the 50s, setting the basis for a renewed debate where passion remains intact in spite of everything. I think that when Jonathan proposed to people younger than himself that they clarify the origins and co-ordinates of a way of appreciating movies that he doesn't entirely share but feels essential for a film culture of the twenty-first century (I know, the expression sounds pompous, but it's just), he's doing something more than indulging his curiosity; he's testing his own beliefs with the hope of challenging and modifying them. Personally, I need something like that myself. Badly.

Especially, for one thing, because I live in Argentina. Apart from the country's terrible economic crisis, which I can't avoid mentioning, a peripheral position in the world doesn't help the circulation of films or texts that represent alternatives to the great film and publishing conglomerates (though, paradoxically, it may be good for local films). The Internet may help a lot, but the intellectual networks and interpersonal links are very hard to build. (It seems significant that the *Movie Mutations* letters were available online only during a brief period, and on a website that was very difficult to find.) But even more difficult is the circulation of people across vast geographical reaches. So, when I first read the letters, I couldn't help but feel that I was colliding with an object from outer space, even if what I read responded to a profound need on my part. At this point, I had read some of Jonathan's work and a little bit by Kent, but Nicole, Alex and Adrian were completely unknown to me, even as names. And in fact it was the texts of those three that stood out as the most emblematic because of their radical novelty: they came from the antipodes of my own story.

To be clear about this, I would need more space than I have here, and more time to make it clear even to myself. But let me mention a couple of things. I was born in 1951, which makes me closer in age to Jonathan than to the others, but I started out as a critic when I was close to forty, which makes me by far the least experienced of everyone here. Also, before I started to write, I wasn't even a cinephile, and I'm probably not one now. The two facts that may justify my participation in this chain of letters are a fortuitous circumstance and a personal disposition. And the second of these is twofold. I like to talk about films even more than I like to watch movies, so I always like to have people to talk with. And, in choosing my company, I find critics more stimulating than directors, precisely for the reasons that make directors glamorous and critics not. Critics are not a priori interesting in themselves, so many of them can avoid speaking about themselves. I know that this may sound strange to Nicole, who finds Abel Ferrara, without having yet met him, an admirable person (personally, I would be scared of meeting him). Or to Jonathan, who feels genuinely excited when he meets Jim Jarmusch or any of his other favourite film-makers. Or to Kent, who works with Martin Scorsese, another terrifying character to me.

That's one of the reasons why I don't qualify for cinephilia: because its heroes never arouse the least bit of personal curiosity on my part. But the critics do – especially the *Movie Mutations* ones, of whom I've become some sort of dedicated fan. I finally met them thanks to the opportunity afforded to me by becoming, a year ago, the director of the Buenos Aires Festival of Independent Film. Since then, I've become friends with Jonathan and Adrian, and managed to persuade both of them that it was important to come to my city last April. (Nicole came too, but for a shorter time.) And I spoke briefly to the others, with whom I was less lucky in the invitations. In any case, my quest of discovering the mutants proved to be worthwhile. I owe to Flavia de la Fuente, my wife and companion in cinematic adventures, the remark that these people have something special: a certain way of being in the world, a special joy proper to people emboldened by a mission of great nobility. Cinephilia, like any religion, has its saints, and the mutants may well be among them.

But let's abandon this confessional mode. Please allow me to try to justify this new series of letters – a project that emerged from a dinner during the Vancouver International Film Festival in October, which you and I attended, as well as Jonathan and Adrian. My idea was to ask what changes had taken place since the original set of letters, how the map of cinema should now be redrawn and what its shape will be in the future. The interventions would hopefully point to the birth of a new cinematic canon and organise conceptually a dispersion considered by many as an impoverishment compared to a supposed golden age, and by many others as a random explosion. But over the last few months, we have the proof that the mutations haven't stopped. For instance, Kent published a long piece in praise of *Moulin Rouge* (2001), a film that in Cannes provoked nothing but contempt. On the other hand, Nicole has written energetically to support the revolutionary significance of a film that horrifies supporters of good taste, *Baise-moi* (2000). I was with Adrian on a jury where his favourite film was the Korean *Teenage Hooker Became Killing Machine in Daehakno* (2001) – a bizarre object that still baffles me, although I'm sure that he has a strong justification. I heard Alex announce that the best film in Rotterdam 2000 (out of over 400 films) was *Face* (2000), a Japanese movie that nobody cared about and that I'm still lamenting we couldn't bring to our festival.

Such isolated data singled out by the mutants amount to much more than a list of critical preferences. *Movie Mutations* points towards a precise albeit fragmented region of cinema for which traditional criticism doesn't have an answer. To make it visible was, I suppose, Jonathan's original intention. And also to establish that members of this generation should be in charge of charting the borders of this new territory. At the Vancouver dinner, Jonathan suggested also that someone even younger should participate in this second series of letters to illuminate new changes in perspective. So you, as a writer and magazine editor in your 20s, came across as the perfect baby correspondent. As a somewhat more seasoned editor, I confess that I'm pleased with your presence for a darker reason related to my own magazine. *El Amante* has also recently mutated – around the time the original *Movie Mutations* letters appeared – through young collaborators who are now willing to die for *Moulin Rouge*, celebrate Asian genre films and share Kent's vision about the links between cinema and pop music production. I imagine them as the true recipients of the dialogue around pop culture, an issue completely alien to my concerns. The Argentinian isolation is, in spite of everything, a fertile soil for mutations.

There's another reason to praise the *Movie Mutations* group for its clairvoyance, but I need to introduce a character who has been missing so far. I'm speaking of Raymond Bellour, whose intervention closed and commented upon all the others. I have difficulty identifying Bellour as a member of the group. He's a scholar in the proper sense (more so than Nicole, the more scholarly in orientation of the others). His letter challenged the cinephilic cult of Cassavetes, a common idol of the mutants, and he wrote against the core beliefs of the group, against its common ground, although his high intellectual level allowed him to qualify his discourse and become a genuine participant. But reading his piece after September 11, I was literally shocked. I remember that on this infamous date you and I were both in Toronto, attending a film festival where everything gets shown and everything is oriented towards American business. In those days, being Argentinian was tough and being Canadian was tougher. Our common identity consisted of being customers of CNN waiting for speeches from George W. Bush. The internationalism of our movie discussions seemed to be denied by the most blatant expression of the global world, by a fact that swallowed all facts and admitted no reflection. Bellour had written:

> The studio period, between the end of the conquest of the West and the beginning of the Vietnam War, has to be the only moment when the US was a civilised country, when it could still affirm itself, despite all of its ideological weight, as one country among others, before becoming insufferably the law of all others.

After the horror of September 11, one of the few conclusions that may be safely drawn is that the US has explicitly stated the will of becoming the law of all nations.

So, if the official interpretation of September 11 admits no reply, what's the use of *Movie Mutations*? And, worse, is the love for a cinema of the body (and with no reference at all to the public sphere) epitomised by Cassavetes a way of forgetting about civilisation and leaving it in the hands of the rulers of the world, as Bellour's text implies? Were we looking all the time in the wrong direction while the world was mutating on its own terms? I admit that this question is beyond my ability to answer and I pass it on to you as a poisoned gift.

I also leave you the task of asking more questions and redefining from the North of the North the new place for cinephilia and film criticism in these difficult times.

Quintín

Toronto, 8 January 2002

Dear Quintín and Nicole,

As much as I'm honoured by the invitation to participate in this exchange, I enter this project with a great deal of anxiety as the anointed baby. But actions speak just as loud as words. Running a magazine, an activity fraught with the peril of budgets, deadlines and self-doubt, seems a lot like producing an independent film – and you never really know how the audience will react. When most traditional critics in your immediate environment seem not to care, well, to a contrarian, that's a challenge. Just as much as the events of September 11 or the current situation in Argentina, this vantage point may account for the tone of Quintín's introduction, more anxious than pessimistic: it's a letter written more by a disgruntled editor – and, more recently, a festival director – than a critic.

We both work on magazines that cross national lines and introduce the works of international critics to a (hopefully) wider audience: in my case, this stems from a lack of interesting, accessible voices in Canada who are willing to challenge the party line.

Along with helping in this regard, I began *Cinema Scope* two years ago to seek out fellow Canadian mutants and give them a voice in a critical environment characterised by Alex's deadly sins: cultural pessimism, affirmation of the market and irony. (To this, I'll add the smug belief in the infallibility of one's own opinion.) Or, to use a terminology our 60s' counterparts might appreciate, I wanted to see if there is a consciousness that can be raised, a spirit to be animated, in a place where any intellectual thought in public, popular culture is anathema.

Tastes and attitudes are shaped by what's in front of you at the right time: the seeds of my cinephilia were planted early, but took a while to spring to life. Like Jonathan, my grandfather owned a movie theatre, a rep cinema in Toronto, though he sold it when I was six years old. I first started obsessing over films that I encountered not in the theatres or on video, but on television – in particular, Hitchcock. I didn't become a true cinephile until 1994–5, when I was at graduate school in New York, studying political science; to discover film, I had to leave home. As befitting any religion, I had an epiphany: seeing a projection (one feels the need to qualify this) of Godard's *La Chinoise* (1967), still a startling film of ideas – and immediately thereafter reading Pauline Kael's review, as her books were the easiest to find at the time. A whack of canonical viewing soon followed, mostly on video, but always accompanied by reading about film. My cinephilia was formed in reaction to the academic world, in a general state of alienation. I've never taken a film class in my life – which is both a minus (I'm still playing catch-up) and a plus (though I've rejected academia, I never had the opportunity to reject film theory, and remain pluralistic).

In 1997, when I tripped over the original *Movie Mutations* letters, I had just begun to write about film, and quickly felt isolated in a place where intellectual cinephilia is synonymous with cultural elitism. (One of my guiding principles is that the so-called populist critics, who underestimate the population, are the true elitists: they stand above them, presuming to know what 'the masses' will like, urging them to naïvely identify with the characters.) Just as important, in 1999 I was invited to the Rotterdam Film Festival as a critic's trainee. Travel and cinephilia are now linked for me: there's an excitement born from seeing films in another place – a subject I haven't seen adequately explored – but, more importantly, it exposes what critics and programmers from other countries deem crucial. Not enough critics realise the need to actually seek out non-traditional work. That year I saw 'minor cinema' like Abolfazl Jalili's *A True Story* (1996), Alexander Sokurov's *Confession* (1998), Hong Sang-soo's *The Power of Kangwon Province* (1998) and the films of Daniele Ciprì and Franco Maresco, none of which had played in Toronto at the time. A few have since, at Cinematheque Ontario, not the festival – minor film doesn't play well in major North American markets. Many such film-makers remain unknown outside of a small cadre of international festivalgoers. This inspires me, and it inspires me to urge others to watch as much as possible. This also explains why many of *Cinema Scope*'s issues are organised around festival coverage, and always include substantial features on films without domestic distribution. At the same time, my work for the Vancouver International Film Festival is another manifestation of the same impulse, and an even more concrete endeavour;

the hands-on experience of programming should be mandatory for all critics, as it helps one to understand the many factors that are involved in what films are even available for local viewers to see, and how programmers' tastes are one (often the least crucial) factor.

I need to explain something about us younger kids. Just as important as music and far more important than home video for my non-essentialist generation has been television. We discovered movies, for the most part, on television, and endless hours of after-school television trained us from an early age to look a certain way; it found its parallel in 80s' teen movies of the John Hughes variety, which possess few discernible formal qualities. They have mutated our taste, bridging the low and high (and help me see what's valuable in the Farrellys). We have an unconscious itch for kitsch, and a film like *Moulin Rouge* – a daring gamble made by an erstwhile hack, which skirts over the body like a needle used to skip over a record – may satisfy it. Television is also characterised by a mode of narration that sees the body as a vehicle for the story. It's natural that cinephiles of the television/video generation tend to look at films as wholes as opposed to comprised of parts. In other words, some younger cinephiles may like the same film-makers as the cinephiles of the 60s' generation, like Cassavetes and Eustache, *but for different reasons* – one of which for me is an entry point to an historical energy outside of my personal (and generational) experience. Rather than hail Cassavetes as a film-maker for whom the body is the last site of authenticity, most Cassavetes fans I know see films through a moralistic filter. For this reason, *A Woman under the Influence* (1974) is preferred – the behaviour of Mabel Longhetti (Gena Rowlands) is easy to understand, sympathise with, and explain away as crazy, unlike that of Cosmo Vittelli (Ben Gazzara). More admired today is an attitude, a stance towards the characters, even a political message. It might be easy to conceptualise as a (North) American, rather than European, sensibility. One of my goals is to integrate this attitude with a formalism captured in the original *Movie Mutations* letters.

At any rate, the real question for me isn't why some younger cinephiles like *Moulin Rouge* – the general reaction at Cannes was not as unified as Quintín would have us believe – it's why don't they like Manoel de Oliveira, whose most recent films convince me that art will always be possible at the cinema, and it may be because de Oliveira, a stuffy Old World film-maker, has nothing at all in common with television. Nor does de Oliveira mean much to children of the Internet, a social, interactive medium, and a tool that has done more to benefit the international exchange of ideas than television. (How did magazines come together before email?) Even so, my anxiety relates to the increasing role of the Internet, both in terms of how it might influence criticism – in a rush to judgment, for example, that simply exacerbates a tendency already present in traditional criticism – and film itself (in the yearning for a community of isolated individuals). I agree that film is hurting, but the cause is not the Internet or digital video, but, as Quintín via Bellour puts it, 'the law of all nations'. This is multinational capitalism, or American neo-liberal commerce, which holds some of the blame for Quintín's country's economic collapse.

In Canada, a country with a constant anxiety regarding its cultural colonisation, the same opinion pieces pop up every December: why don't more Canadians see Canadian films? I can't help but think this is misguided: doesn't this box office failure in some roundabout way prove our artists aren't succumbing to this universal law? Canadian films are often seen in the same light as foreign art films here and perhaps their core audiences are met through festivals and smaller regional outlets of distribution. And if valuable 'popular' films are those that are most hated, the Hollywood auteurs worth supporting are those who criticise Hollywood (so few could care about the rest of the world) and don't care about being loved – such as Paul Verhoeven, Jean-Pierre Jeunet's opposite. The belief that this law of commerce is immutable relates to Quintín's review of *Amélie*, and he answers his own question: though the film might give evidence of the end of History, the oppositions to it show there will always be revolutionaries. I also see critics of different nationalities inducing their own nuanced laws as to how they relate to their own national cinemas, a sense of community that's localised – something, too, that might be traced back to Cassavetes. As opposed to expressing what it's like to be Canadian in an abstract sense, I would argue the necessity for films that speak to what it means to live in Canada now. (Or Australia, Argentina or, even, America.) This accounts for why the Canadian films I like may be different than the ones Adrian likes, or why none of the foreign critics in Buenos Aires last year gave a hoot about *El Descanso* (2001).

But there must be some common ground, even in this new order. The original set of letters presented the thesis and the antithesis: what's lacking is the synthesis. My theory is a tool-box ready to be lugged out if the occasion provides it, and my tools come from the original *Mutations*: Kent's notions of driving and being driven; Jonathan's extra-philosophical concern for politics; Alex's film-makers who 'speak in concrete words and voices, from a concrete place, about concrete places and characters'; Adrian's open cinema; Nicole's concern for representing power; and Raymond's civilised intelligence. I'll add, to cite the title of Mike Leigh's satirical short which I saw this year in Vancouver, a sense of history: a film should tackle life in a space outside of the influence of global capital flows (a recent example is Quintín's countryman's *La Libertad* [2001]), chart their development, or take a stance in opposition to it. In other words, to make the invisible visible which, almost inevitably, brings me back to Godard (and to Bresson and Rossellini).

A great example of a cinema that integrates these qualities, a cinema that can be read a number of ways, is Jia Zhangke's *Platform* (2000) – the long version that (one assumes) can no longer be seen for, despite all voices to the contrary, market reasons. If it happens to hold up to the holistic test, namely, that the film is invested with a style – simply put, that which (to paraphrase Dreyer) allows us to see the material through the director's eyes – all the better. Claire Denis' *Beau travail* (1999) might also qualify: narrowly seeing this as a film of the body elides much of its accomplishments. I would bet the ranch that George Lam's 'Genghis Khan' holds an equal place in Jia's heart as, say, Nico's 'These Days' does to Wes Anderson or the music of the Tindersticks does to Denis – even if I prefer the soundtrack of *Trouble*

Every Day (2001) to the film – and Wang Hongwei's performance in *Platform* is just as open as anything by Ben Gazzara. Maybe because I discovered these films at the same time as older cinephiles, maybe because it too speaks of the anxiety of influence (of Hou Hsiao-hsien), yet also speaks a kind of foreign language as it relates to Chinese cinema, *Platform* strikes a plangent chord that's altogether real: rather than seeing this new mutant film, which possesses an historical energy of its own, as belonging to either a cinema of the body or of the mind, befitting Quintín's religious analogy, I'd like to see it as a cinema of the soul.

Affectionately yours,
Mark

Paris, 15 February 2002

Dear Quintín from Argentina, dear Mark in Canada, dear Adrian from Australia, dear all of you for whom the real homeland seems to be the multi-territoriality of cinephilia,

Two thousand words, two thousand words to describe to you what's happening in France today: if I write 'mission: impossible', that explains where I'm coming from. But two thousand aren't enough, so I'll start with the two extra words you've granted me, no doubt to honour the date when we're exchanging these new texts, five years after the first *Movie Mutations* letters and also after a change in millennium; all right, here in Paris, in two words, it's the Turntable Age.

What does that mean? For me, concretely, it means that each week I'm discovering new films, new authors, new practices, new projection sites. And more generally, in terms of the *Zeitgeist*, it means that everyone here is experiencing the sensation of bathing in a lavish, effervescent, intense atmosphere. To sum up the mood: today, in France, the cinema has become reconciled with the avant-garde. To give you only one indication of this: last week, who do you think went to FEMIS[1] to teach the students how to achieve an image? It was David coming to the aid of Goliath: the members of one of the key active experimental workshops in Paris today, Etna. To what can one attribute this reconciliation and what are the principal characteristics, so that one can appreciate the full extent of it? First, one can assign it a date: it dates from the release of *Sombre* (1998), the masterpiece by Philippe Grandrieux, who has reinvigorated in a masterful fashion the great avant-garde tradition that vanished with Jean Epstein. Next, one can cite the convergence of three factors: the multiplication of creative instruments; the diversifications of practices and of artistic models; and a radical political awakening that will only make the history of this period more difficult to recount.

A few striking facts: first, the appearance of major authors and works, whether their venues happen to be art houses, galleries or various underground locations . . .

you're familiar with some of them, maybe not all, and inevitably I'm going to forget some others: Grandrieux, Gaspar Noé, Virginie Despentes and Coralie Trinh-Ti, Jean-François Richet, Patricia Mazuy, Dominique Gonzalez-Foerster, the Étant Donnés group, Sothean Nhieim, Régis Cotentin, Johanna Vaude, Jena-Philippe Farber, Stéfani de Loppinot, Nicolas Rey, Hugo Verlinde, Othello Vilgard, David Matarasso, Xavier Baert, Yves-Marie Mahé, Philippe Jacq ... while the preceding generations continue to create and sometimes produce their most beautiful masterpieces, such as Claire Denis with *Beau travail*, for example. René Vautier, Maurice Lemaître, Marcel Hanoun, Lionel Soukaz, Philippe Garrel, Ange Leccia, Raymonde Carasco, F. J. Ossang, Maria Klonaris and Katerina Thomadaki, Rose Lowder, Cécile Fontaine and certainly others never stop producing, inventing, proposing, so that the first cross-pollination is taking place, initially between generations and then only between their aesthetic tools. Aesthetically, in fact, this mixture of tools represents the artists' major field of reflection and intervention: films become palimpsests where the intersecting of analogue and digital, Super 8, 16mm, 35mm, video and computer becomes allied, confused, and confronted in every possible way, yielding sometimes beautifully confounding textural and rhythmic results, as in *Sombre*, Leccia/Gonzalez-Foerster's *Ile de beauté* (1996), the second half of Godard's *Éloge de l'amour* (2001), Augustin Gimel's *Il n'y a rien de plus inutile qu'un organe* ('There's nothing more useless than an organ', 1999) or Anne-Sophie Brabant/Pierre Gerboux's *My Room the Grand Canal* (2001) – fully demonstrating here one of the principal forces of cinema: its technical complexity, its nature as apparatus, allowing it to graft itself onto a completely different technology or indeed any ritual, living spectacle, theatre, performance, music hall, concert or celebration. How is this renewal expressed in terms of the repoliticising of cinema? What are the demands and objectives of this new generation? What formal, ethical and, indeed, existential testing-grounds are opening up today?

One of the stories that touched me this year is that of Peter Tscherkassky: visiting Paris, he was recognised and greeted by a Latin Quarter bookseller, something that had never happened to him in Vienna. Here the cinema is lived like a national cause. Under the aegis of a great analyst, Alain Bergala, cinema is on its way to becoming a pedagogical discipline. An incredibly tight network of festivals, events and sites of reception covers the territory: one finds festivals devoted to every genre, format, length, subject and theme, from national cinemas to the tiniest localities, and the tininess often guarantees the quality of the programming. Film magazines proliferate, both general and specialised, institutional and fan driven, and the least conformist ones aren't necessarily the ones you would guess; today for instance, beyond the scholarly magazines such as *Trafic*, *Exploding*, *Cinergon*, *Repérages* or *Balthazar*, the avant-garde is finding itself defended by *Bref*, a magazine of the CNC[2] devoted to short films, *Le Technicien du film*, a magazine for professional technicians, and *La Gazette des scénaristes*, an organ of the screenwriters guild. A national cause also in the sense that people easily and collectively become enflamed for or against a film, for and against an issue. The recent attempt to make an issue of a film-maker complaining about being mistreated by the critics has raised an outcry; in France there's a certain pride in criticism, a tradition to which Godard justly paid homage at the beginning of *2 x 50 Years of French Cinema* (1995). (That said, one has to point out that the first conference on the work of Philippe Garrel was organised by an Irishman, Fergus Daly, in Dublin, while the largest international conference on Godard occurred in London, organised by Michael Temple, James Williams and Michael Witt.)

For me, the polemics clarified the lay of the land by showing clearly that three kinds of critics exist: the collaborators, who sell the film by copying out the press book, journalists that a studio can therefore invent in every particular, as happened recently in the US; the partisans, who discriminate between the industrial products – sometimes with genius, as Daney did, for example; and the snipers, who depart from industrial logic and delve into the research of other kinds of film-making, gestures, behaviours. But without the latter, who are the least numerous because this activity has nothing lucrative about it, one couldn't write the history of cinema, and Quintín is certainly right to take them under his wing.

Since the first batch of *Movie Mutations* letters, two events have occurred in my life. The first was the conception and realisation of a retrospective devoted to the history of avant-garde cinema in France, which I entitled *Jeune, dure et pure* ('Young, Strong and Pure'). Over the course of long and laborious months of preparation, two principles progressively, almost surreptitiously, came to light and became imprinted on me. First principle: the history of cinema completely remains to be written. Second principle: the more important a film is, the less it is seen. Excessive? Well, then, see the films of René Vautier or of Patrice Kirchhofer, see Djouhra Abouda and Alain Bonnamy's *Ali in Wonderland* (1976), see the films of Tobias Engel or of Bruno Muel. . . . These films mean nothing to you, or not very much? They are essential; it's starting from them that a true history of cinema must be written, and not starting from the notoriety of works that reflect only the quantitative criteria imposed by the industry. To say that such films are marginal automatically disqualifies those who qualify them in this way: the history of cinema must deliver itself from the history of commerce or of sociology with which it is too often confused today.

With a few notable exceptions (Jean Mitry, Noël Burch . . .), the history of cinema up until now has been principally drafted from the point of view of the industry. This doesn't mean in any way denying the industrial cinema, which certainly possesses its own martyrs and sacrificial victims, from Émile Reynaud to André Sauvage, from Eli Lotar to Monte Hellman. On the contrary, one of the characteristics of the experimental generation without dogmas is its way of knowing perfectly how to situate itself in relation to production, how to look at and analyse any film – whereas the name of Robert Bresson made the previous generation laugh. In exemplary fashion, one of the specificities of current film-makers consists of working with found footage in an analytical and no longer merely polemical fashion, crossing the lineage of Ken Jacobs' *Tom Tom the Piper's Son* (1971) with that of Kirk Tougas' *Politics of Perception* (1973): the sublime CinemaScope trilogy of Peter Tscherkassky, or – to only mention examples from the past few years – *Exposed* by his student Siegfried Fruhauf, or Vilgard's *High* based on Ferrara's *The Addiction* (1995), MTK's *Mody Bleach* based on

Moby Dick (1956), Baert's *Revelation* based on *In the Mood for Love* (2000), or Vaude's *Samourai* based on (among others) *The Blade* (1995), representing poetic initiatives as much as high-density theory.

Today, the violence of the cultural industry, what Adorno very aptly called 'masochistic mass culture', flourishes with such cynicism that one can almost posit a law of inverse proportions between the social surface of a film's visibility and its real importance – to the extent that it becomes necessary to subvert a whole production apparatus, as Verhoeven managed to do superbly with his satirical superproduction *Starship Troopers* (1997). In this undertaking, the true critics (Jonathan, Adrian, Mark, in France Raphaël Bassan on film and Raymond on video), the true programmers (Kent Jones in New York, Jean-François Rauger in Paris), the true directors of festivals (Quintín in Buenos Aires, Simon Field in Rotterdam, Bernard Benoliel in Belfort, Jacques Ledoux formerly in Belgium) or cinematheques (Alex today in Vienna, Dominique Païni yesterday in Paris) or sites (*Senses of Cinema*) – in short, the snipers (I give your names as emblems; there are undoubtedly many others and our job is to find them) – situate the landmarks and construct the parallel circuits. Without these actions, all non-standardised creation would become not impossible but inaccessible.

Sometimes, faced with the unjust lot reserved for whatever film is unseen and whose print proves to be in danger, I tell myself that, for the 'true' in Godard's 'true history of the cinema', it would be fitting to substitute the more violent *truthful*, in the sense that to all appearances certain dominant images are there only to cover up and screen others, making them invisible and inaudible. Can one imagine the history of literature without *The Songs of Maldoror*? And in fact the history of cinema is full of crucial objects that are as fragile as Lautréamont's manuscript. We have already lost some of them, like Jean Grémillon's *The Life of Italian Immigrant Workers in France* (1926), Philippe Garrel's *Actua I* (1968) or almost all of the films of the Cinéma du Peuple co-operative made over the course of the teens. Can one say that losing the Grémillon, censoring Vautier's *Afrique 50* (1951) and placing its author in prison, not showing *Ali in Wonderland* or *Black Liberation* (1964) – four crucial pamphlets on racism – participates in the same logic as that which consists of refusing to consider the links between the Same and the Other, therefore of plunging three-quarters of the world into this scornful and imperial obscurity leading to, among other catastrophes, the outrages of September 11 and the economic crisis of Argentina? Before being able to respond, I'd like to know the opinion of Kent, who has written a profoundly sensitive text on the televisual treatment of the New York attacks.[3]

To write the history of contemporary cinema seems more urgent and difficult because, thanks to the increase and greater accessibility of technological tools, thanks to the diversity of artistic models, because of the spreading need for images, production is exploding. First phenomenon: like a painter or a writer, a director can find a studio in his own room and create a magnificent oeuvre all alone and in complete freedom; in France that's the situation for the video artist Jean-Philippe Farber or the film-maker David Matarasso, for instance. Second phenomenon: the proliferation of networks and alternative sites, as much for production as for distribution, allows many individuals to refuse to enter not only industrial conditions but also the art market, perceived as corrupt, cut off from and destructive of reality. The term 'artist' applies today equally to popular singers and visual masters, no longer representing a fatally discredited object of derision. One can only rejoice at this turn of events.

Added to this, the second event in my life makes me very confident. Thanks to the first series of *Movie Mutations* letters, I met a historian who has become indispensable to me, Brad Stevens. Brad is a young English critic. He writes film history; he discovers authors, works, ideas; he has written books on Ferrara and Hellman. Each time that he writes to me, he helps me discover new links between images. Recently, for example, he informed me that Michael Winner's film *The Mechanic* (1972), the material used in that critical masterpiece, the film *The Politics of Perception*, had its script supervised by Hellman and should have been directed by him, which explains to a large extent its crepuscular genius. (Let me also pass on here the wise words of Francis Moury, specialist in underground cinema and co-editor of a *History of French Erotic and Pornographic Cinema* currently in production: 'An amusing fact: some people know the entire oeuvre of Fritz Lang, but have never seen a Michael Winner film. A sad fact: others know the entire oeuvre of Michael Winner but have never seen a Fritz Lang film.'⁴) Now, Brad works all alone in his little London suburb, attached to no university or research group or institution whatsoever – and that's probably why he can move mountains.

From day to day, it reassures me to think of Brad and a few other sublime, tutelary figures such as Vautier, leaving completely on his own to make, at the age of twenty-two, *Afrique 50* in opposition to the entire colonial empire, against governments, economic imperialism, even his own political party; or Edouard de Laurot, making *Black Liberation* for the Black Panthers, equally alone, and in opposition to the American police state; or Muel, flying off to Chile at the announcement of Pinochet's *coup d'état*, mandated by no one, purely on the human impulse of a film-maker; or Stan Brakhage, feverishly reinventing the cinema as he watches a moth dying in the night; or Hanoun, exhausted from fighting a legal case which ruined him financially, assembling in a few weeks an anthological book, *Cinéma Cinéaste*, the contemporary equivalent of Robert Bresson's *Notes on the Cinematograph*, but by an ultra-leftist Bresson.⁵ . . .

Today, to speak personally, I find myself confronted by a paradox. On the one hand, I have not given up either my collectivist childhood or my Bataillian and Foucauldian adolescence – that is, a fundamental hatred for values founded on the individual, to the extent that the single note of positivity allowed by Adorno, the very Stendhalian, simple promise of happiness, is meaningless to me. On the other hand, I have never actually encountered instances of humanity nobler or worthier than Vautier or Muel, whose historic intelligence and actions rest, at base, entirely on personal conviction and individual initiative. But cinema, I find, has rarely been as intelligent as it is today, like it was in the grand eras of Michael Powell's *Peeping Tom* (1960) or Fassbinder and Pasolini. Godard, Grandrieux, Garrel, Ferrara, Kinji Fukasaku, Carpenter, Yervant Gianikian and Angela Ricci Lucchi, Straub and Huillet, Pedro

Costa – all of them help me less to reflect than to *not forget* all the processes of confiscation that attack humanity. They are developing an ethical discourse the equivalent of which I cannot detect in any other discipline, and their latest films fill me with a desire to reread Hobbes, Saint-Just and Gracchus Babœuf – which is certainly the greatest compliment I can imagine.

I send you many electronic kisses,
Nicole

Melbourne, 24 February 2002

Dear friends,

> Things were different now. You could no longer feel safe just because you were lucky enough to live in the West. Just because you were lucky enough not to be a refugee, or not to be living in Afghanistan or the Middle East. It didn't matter who you thought the baddies were, the World Order had changed. Now, apparently, there were good people and bad people, enemies and allies, friends and foes.

These are not the words of a politician, journalist or critical commentator. It's the opening voice-over narration from a fictional character in the new series of a popular Australian TV show, *The Secret Life of Us* – the ultimate lifestyle programme for that niche market creation, Generation X. It is a completely apolitical show – extremists of either left or right are regularly mocked; love is all they need. Every episode is based on a jazzy metaphor: life is like the stock market, the dating game is like a shooting range. So the reason all its characters are fleetingly involved in something terribly topical – watching the news coverage of September 11 – is to set up the latest *Zeitgeist* tag: 'There's a New World Order in our lives.' How quickly earth-changing, historic events are mulched into lifestyle accessories – like the new *Interview* cover I just glimpsed at the corner newsagent: 'Top Directors Photograph New York'.

Quintín posed a hard question: has September 11 rendered the ideas canvassed in the 1997 *Movie Mutations* letters obsolete, irrelevant, even ridiculous? In the immediate aftermath of those events, we heard and read a lot about how any art or pop culture were useless, pathetic, hopelessly insensitive responses to such a crisis. In one area, at least, I felt like agreeing: it was depressing to read so many opportunistic commentaries diagnosing whether September 11 had fulfilled either Baudrillard's, Virilio's or Zizek's prophecies about the 'precession of simulacra' in our media-saturated age – as if it were all a theoretical exam question rather than a political and human catastrophe.

But I resist being held hostage to this 'the world has changed forever' rhetoric of the past six months. I used to scoff at those dour Marxists who would intervene in every cultural debate with the solemn proclamation that everything must be historicised. But nowadays I tend to the same precaution.

When September 11 struck the Western world, I did not feel the desire to unplug my VCR or give up my film reviewing job. Quite the contrary, I experienced the hunger of a primal cinephilia in a way that had not overcome me in years. And I mean this in a nakedly instrumental, almost medicinal way: I felt compelled to watch disaster movies set in New York, like *Tycus* (1998), whose cover depicting that city's collapsing towers was discreetly covered over at my local video shop; films about the fragile borders of the New World Order, like Wim Wenders' *The End of Violence* (1997); meditations on war like Terrence Malick's *The Thin Red Line* (1998); comedies of anarchic, antisocial demolition like Frank Tashlin's *The Disorderly Orderly* (1964) or Tex Avery's most apocalyptic cartoons; Jean-Luc Godard's spookily prophetic video *Origin of the 21st Century* (2000), which is for me like the image-track to Leonard Cohen's CD *The Future* (1992); gory horror movies; and Luis Buñuel's blackest comedies (Buñuel, whose final, unfilmed project was a scenario about a terrorist attack on the Louvre and the insane, surreal, international war it catalyses). Throughout all this, I remembered some mysterious, inflamed words of Nicole's from a 2001 panel in Buenos Aires: 'Images care for us.'

Was I just seeking catharsis, discharge, through the screen? Escapism has nothing – or not much – to do with it. Frankly, I have never been able to separate the body content of cinephilia – its raw emotions and phantasmatic undercurrents, its physical reverberations and childlike thrills – from the brain food. I raid films for the concepts, metaphors and diagrams they can give me in periods of crisis or confusion, as well as for release of various kinds; for wisdom as well as sensation.

How can art – or indeed, criticism – ever be rendered obsolete by history, even for a second? Art speaks to levels of our being-in-the-world that are not timeless (as per the meaningless cliché pedalled by Jungian-Campbellian mythomaniacs) but rather out of time, untimely. John Berger put it best in a TV documentary: art cannot solve anything or change anything, he said – but it can save something. A memory, a feeling, a testament, a way of coping.

You have to understand that, in Australia, the attacks of September 11 coincided with both a national election and what is known as the refugee crisis: boatloads of people fleeing troubled lands, refused admission into our country by the government and held indefinitely in detention centres – precisely because the scare-panic could be opportunistically raised in the public sphere by the conservative (Liberal) party in power that any stranger to our shores might be a deadly, subversive, anti-Western terrorist. In other words (as political commentator Robert Manne put it), the vote crystallised around fears generated by the emotive issue of border control – and the central illusion (powerfully undermined on September 11) that Western nations are fortresses, safe places protected from many kinds of intrusions and influences (physical, cultural, political ...). And now I remember Nicholas Ray's description of the concluding (or was it the opening?) image of his unfilmed 50s' project, *Passport*: a man finds a child tearing up his stolen passport and watching the pieces scattering with the tides as he wonders aloud, 'Where does the tide become national?'

This brings me to *Movie Mutations* yesterday and today. All of us who have been involved in it have tried to welcome the waves of internationalism to our shores, our borders. We have tried, in our ways, to break down prejudices and tear down prisons of many kinds. How successful have we been? I confess that the promises of the Internet age, and of a world cinema, have left me a little disappointed and frustrated. Take the flows of language, for example. Journals like *Senses of Cinema* and *Cinema Scope* celebrate Iranian and Korean cinema; pieces by Jonathan and myself have been translated in (respectively) Farsi and Korean film journals or websites. But how many Iranian and Korean critics have we translated into English – and do we even know who they are? World film culture still seems primarily a one-way street leading to the West (despite some remarkable early signs of a truly radical, multilinguistic system of exchange, like the book series *Traces*, devoted to cultural theory and translation, made available simultaneously in Chinese, Japanese, Korean and English editions; and Paul Willemen's pedagogical project towards founding a curriculum of comparative film studies).

My comment can seem less definitive if we historicise the situation. In my lifetime I have witnessed a slow, massive, difficult conversion from an almost exclusively Euro-Anglo axis in Western film cultures (fixating especially on American and French cinemas) to a supposed New World Order that embraces previously marginalised or occluded nations. But let us not fool ourselves as to how far this conversion has actually taken place: on the macro level, Asian films are almost impossible to release in many Western markets (*Crouching Tiger, Hidden Dragon* [2000] notwithstanding) and, when they do break through, they can encounter the most extraordinary, crypto-racist resistances from viewers and gatekeeping reviewers alike. And, on the micro level, our personal histories (of family, travel, contacts, reading, education, etc.) have positioned many of us firmly under the influence, and in the proximity, of the old Euro-Anglo axis – we are still more likely to pay respectful attention to the film theory emanating from Paris or New York than from Tokyo or Cairo. Realising this is the first – but only the first – step toward moving beyond it.

We live in a time when utopianism has attached itself to a dream of 'one world'. But for myself now, I have to say that some of the wisest, most moving and provocative films of recent times have been those that insist – even to the point of coldness, fatalism and misanthropic despair – on irreducible, fundamental differences between cultures, nations, levels and types of experience. In Michael Haneke's best film, *Code Unknown* (2000), every problem or crisis spins around missing translations: from the argument with a homeless, immigrant refugee on the street to the ability to gain access to a Paris apartment, the code is unknown or lost. More enigmatically, Tsai Ming-liang's *What Time Is It There?* (2001) is all about uncommunicating vessels: Paris and Taipei, a man and a woman, the living and the dead, unsynchronised time zones, incompatible languages, unreciprocal desires. There is a moment – it comes around in cycles – when we need such cruel reminders of the realities that disturb any premature fantasies of oneness.

This very colloquium around *Movie Mutations* risks creating its own fantasy of oneness. I confess that too many invocations of the holy crest line of Kiarostami–Hou–Denis–de Oliveira, etc. make me want to watch my stretched videotape of the gloriously silly comedy *Superstar* (1999) for the fiftieth time, or champion a middlebrow hit like *Amélie*, so damned by Quintín and Mark. For which of us is to deny someone, somewhere on the planet right now, getting that rush, that necessary trigger to cinephilia, from Jean-Pierre Jeunet rather than Jia Zhangke? (Of course, it would be better if both were equally available to be seen.) I am not interested in erecting a new system of taste – which can only be another limiting, exclusive prison, as taste systems always are.

A sense of history can also defuse the self-identifying dreams of generations. It amuses me when Mark describes himself as a member of the TV generation, because that's exactly what *my* generation (kids in the 60s) thought it was. I don't believe that the meaningful differences in film culture are bound to generations, or even the rise of new technologies (or viewing fads like DVD) *per se*; there are priorities that cut deeper. So it amuses me even more that I can't even *imagine* Jonathan or Nicole ever watching a broadcast episode of reality programmes like *Survivor* or *Loft Story* on their much-used TV sets. But the best experimental film I ever saw was on commercial TV one night in Athens, Greece, and it was certainly reality TV: the live coverage of the demonstrations over Clinton's visit there, which divided the screen into two halves – one half a placid panning shot back and forth across static, waiting dignitaries in a plush ballroom (Michael Snow), the other half a wild, hand-held lunge into the rioting on the streets (*Rosetta* [1999]). If only I had taped it for pirate distribution ... but then, I think that film culture, even in this age of the infinite supermarket, still needs its invisible, tantalising legends. The secret life of cinephilia ...

One piece of ground which has been lost in the Internet years is the open, ultra-serious, ever-curious, investigative and termitic approach to cinema's popular (and sub-popular) genres. I believe the highly selective tendency to draft into the new canon the likes of *Starship Troopers*, *Moulin Rouge* or *The Royal Tenenbaums* (2001) is a poor substitute for actually traversing popular culture without the crutch of auteurism. As for most other genre or trash films, they have been left to the normative clutches of fanzines and Internet sites that are often openly philistine.

I have to confront a contradiction within myself here. On the one hand, I am temperamentally opposed to any kind of elitism. On the other hand, I remain attached to the 80s' subcultural creed – that all interesting, innovative movements in culture are small in number, fiercely partisan in character, and capillary in their social action. A passage in Stanley Cavell's *Pursuits of Happiness* says it well:

> It is possible that [...] nothing valuable and comprehensible to each of us is valuable and comprehensible to all. And it is possible that every idea of value, like every object of value, must still arise as the possession of a cult, and that one must accordingly hope that some are more benign and useful than others.[6]

So what would be the politics of a benign and useful film cult, in its attempts to reconcile and negotiate (as Nicole reminds us) Same (or Self) and Other? A mid 60s' quote from Octavio Paz speaks eloquently to our present moment: 'We fight to preserve our souls; we speak so that the other may recognise our soul and so that we may recognise ourselves in his soul, which is different from ours.'[7] I have been sceptical about oneness here, but, like everyone, I long for it. I well remember the intellectual terrorism of the years of academic identity politics, when any attempt to approach, encompass or embrace the Other – even if only within the imaginary of film – was greeted by the difference-police with a censorious inquiry: 'Who are you to speak?' The years between the two volleys of *Movie Mutations* letters have certainly seen the flowering of one aspect of a democratic ideal: the more who speak, the better. The challenge now is to improve our skills of listening.

Your comrade,
Adrian

Chicago, 1 March 2002

Dear Fellow Mutants,
This letter, concluding (at least provisionally) an experiment launched five years ago, has to serve double duty. First of all it has to bring closure to a series of letters started just over two months ago by Quintín, destined for publication in Spanish six weeks from now at the Buenos Aires Festival of International Film, along with the original set of letters. Second, it's supposed to terminate a much larger book in English that the two sets of letters are intended to frame, destined for publication by the British Film Institute next year. Furthermore, what started out in English (the first three letters) and German (the fourth) was initially published in French, whereas the second round started with Quintín's Spanish and will initially be published in that language – even though the last four letters are in English or French, and Quintín's letter had to acquire an English version for these authors. The centrality of translation to this enterprise has even become part of its meaning, because each shift of languages has subtly altered as well as expanded the playing field.

    A lot more has happened in five years. Kent and Alex have stepped into major programming positions – Kent at the Walter Reade Theater in New York, and Alex just two months ago at the Vienna Film Museum. Nicole has effectively woken a sleeping giant by becoming a major pioneer in discovering, organising, showcasing and celebrating the French avant-garde through the agency of the Paris Cinémathèque – a giant comprising a highly interactive audience as well as a group of film-makers. And Adrian, writing more than ever, is currently working on no less than five books – one of them the English-language *Movie Mutations* book he's co-editing with me. The launching of new international film magazines in English – offering alternatives to the directions taken by *Sight and Sound* (when it became more American) and *Film*

Comment (when it became more institutionally oriented) – has already been described in Mark's letter, so let me simply add that these welcome arrivals have partially done for criticism and its audience what Nicole has been doing for French experimental work. We've also been affected by the growth of the Internet, which has certainly made the world smaller and our overlapping interconnections much more intense. (Not all of us even had email back in 1997.)

Most of the eight authors from six countries in the two sets of letters have become friends, and one of the most significant alliances has been between Adrian and Nicole – giving portions of her work an English-speaking audience, mainly through his translations in *Senses of Cinema*. There were also translations of the first six letters into Dutch, German, Italian, English and now Spanish – accompanied, in most cases, by more letters from other writers – as well as the effort of Quintín last year to bring all the original mutants to Buenos Aires.[8]

What started out as a taped dialogue with Adrian in a suburb of Melbourne on 20 October 1996 eventually took shape about a year and a half later as a series of letters written (and, in four cases, translated) for *Trafic*. Some time later this became reconfigured as a book of international exchanges about some of the directions in which world cinema and cinephilia was heading – initially to be co-edited by Kent, the only other American in the group. Then, roughly a year after a contract was signed with the British Film Institute – once it became clear that Kent's new duties as a programmer and his continuing work as a writer (as well as co-screenwriter on Scorsese's *Il Mio Viaggio in Italia* [2002]) made his involvement in the project more difficult – Adrian agreed, with Kent's blessing, to step in as his replacement, a decision actually made in Buenos Aires about ten months ago.

Moving from the role of instigator to that of team player in this ever-expanding venture has been an interesting but at times confusing experience for me. It's embarrassing to admit this, but I've had ambitions from the outset of this project that are strangely allied to those underlying my first book, *Moving Places* – a desire to combine writing with activism (that is, to change the world by writing about it and to achieve some empowerment by doing so), and at the same time to embark on a certain kind of adventure leading into unknown territory, creating its own cumulative logic as it proceeds. Admittedly the impulse behind the earlier book was extremely personal, though even there I originally had the notion of including previously published material written by others to prove that the book wasn't only about me. (The specifics of this are given in my preface to the second edition.) While the unknown territory in that book was the past (mainly my own, but also that of my family's movie theatre chain), the *terra incognita* of *Movie Mutations* has been the future of cinephilia as seen from across the planet, and increasingly in social terms. The notion of our collective project as an artistic as well as political endeavour was astutely picked up on by Nicole in the first round when she suggested that I had 'gently directed' the original set of mutants 'like Rivette characters, but in reality'. Another way of putting this might be to say that my semi-conscious model was André Bazin rather than Dr Mabuse. But I certainly don't mean to suggest that the project was ever simply or exclusively mine. For starters, *Trafic* – another international magazine that played a substantial role in this intervention – had to be persuaded to allow the project to begin. But it does seem worth pointing out that I was deliberately interested in straddling a contradiction by launching an enterprise that would be both part of my own work and something generated and realised by (and belonging to) many others far beyond my control. All of which, I'm happy to say, has happened. Even this second set of letters is mainly the product of Quintín's initiative rather than my own. This allows me some freedom in commenting on the recent letters as a relatively disinterested observer, one-time ringmaster turned kibbutzer – and, to continue this intertextual self-indulgence, I tried to end my recent book *Movie Wars* in the same fashion.[9]

Furthermore, from the outset there's been a danger in this second series of simple internationalism mutating into even more simple anti-Americanism – a danger to which I as an American may be even more susceptible than the rest of us. Though I'm grateful for Quintín's recapitulation of Raymond's insight about what's civilised and not so civilised about the US, it's also important to bear in mind that America – like Argentina, Australia, Canada and France – is many things. Australia, for instance, has both its refugee crisis and SBS, a state-sponsored multicultural TV channel that any other country could be proud of. To historicise the present moment (and I agree with Adrian that we must), these letters have been written during the launching of the Euro and the delivery of George W. Bush's 'axis of evil' speech – two versions of what it means to live in the Western Hemisphere at this particular moment, though surely not the only things happening (and many of the others still too low for our radar to detect). Maybe I associate the two because I was in Rotterdam and Paris, happily spending Dutch and French Euros, when Bush's war chants first reached me. But if I honestly believed that his idiotic formulation could simply be equated with 'America' – any more than the people of Iran and Iraq (long at war with one another, both of them armed by 'us') and North Korea (with scant relation to the other two) could be equated with some 'evil axis' – then I'd truly have to believe that September 11 has made our utopian fancies obsolete. More precisely, I think that watershed event has produced antithetical and contradictory responses – including a painful forcing of America into the dangerous zone occupied by the rest of the world, accompanied by a regressive and aggressive denial of that shared experience. For me, this is epitomised by the insistence of various dingbats that the September 11 attacks were 'attacks on America' – rather than, say, human beings who happened to be in the World Trade Center – thereby allowing assumptions about dead terrorists to define the identity of their victims and thereby eliding all the non-Americans killed. In other words, a discovery that nationality is both more *and* less important than it's usually cracked up to be.

Maybe I'm still being naïve, but I persist in mainly seeing nationality today as the reach and limits of certain markets – all too readily confused with either weaponry or cultural issues of race, religion, language, ethnicity. Eric Hobsbawm has recently noted that, unlike our more civilised nineteenth-century ancestors, we no longer even know the difference between war and peace, so defining ourselves according to arbitrary national borders seems like the worst kind of self-deception and self-diminishment. That's what's so encouraging about the Euro, and so discouraging about the 'evil axis'. Of course, if you read Robert Darnton, you'll see the idea of the Euro traced back to the eighteenth-century Enlightenment,[10] and it's even easier to see 'axis of evil' growing out of the spectacularly unenlightened Cold War of the mid 20th century.

Trying to figure out how such contradictory notions can co-exist is the problem we're all concerned with. They even come up when we purchase videos and VCRs, DVDs and DVD players. It's pretty easy to buy a tristandard VCR in Europe, but to get one in Chicago I had to order it from New York – a media equipment outlet that Jim Jarmusch sent me the catalogue for. It's much easier to find DVD players in the US that can accommodate all the territories. Of course, this drives the Jack Valentis of the world nuts, because the rights to certain films are supposed to be territorialised along with their access – which is presumably why I had to buy my DVD of *Johnny Guitar* (1954) in Paris. On the other hand, such niche-market purchasing is peanuts alongside the pirating of brand new Hollywood films on video, dupey and unsubtitled, in countries like Iran, which I'm told accounts for *most* of the film viewing there. But in this case it's clearly the desire of viewers more than any market imperialism that's responsible, so we're once again faced with contradictory cross-currents.

That doesn't mean we shouldn't go on contesting American arrogance and presumption. But sometimes what we're lamenting isn't so much what Americans say and do as it is what certain leaders (elected or self-elected) say and do on their behalf – including, I must say, the scandalous indifference towards Argentina's economic crisis. The fantasies of consensus and the self-fulfilling prophecies of polls in test-marketing movies, whereby the audience is profiled in advance as a pack of idiots, apply to the test-marketing of politicians and policies as well, and too many people are eager to jump to conclusions about the minds of Americans – something that I've been arguing for some time, especially in *Movie Wars*, we know precious little about. Even if some of our alternative profiles of the audience and public prove to be overly optimistic, don't these assumptions still give us more to work with than the monotonously well-worn grooves of cynicism, which invariably favour and ratify the forces in power?

Admittedly, knowledge about the rest of the world is genuinely threadbare in my country – as it is in all huge and relatively isolationist countries – and I can't even absent myself from this limitation. It's also true, as Adrian points out, that the flows of language – like those of so many other cultural products, ranging from movies to Coca-Cola – are mainly one-sided, for reasons that are clearly multifaceted. But when he asks how many Iranian and Korean critics we've translated and whether 'we even know who they are', I can begin to answer him, because I've just co-written a book about Kiarostami with one Iranian critic – a chapter of which *Senses of Cinema* published late last year, around the same time it appeared in Farsi in the Iranian *Film Monthly*. I helped my co-author with her English (one kind of translation) and she did most of the translation of our dialogue into Farsi, meanwhile teaching me, among other things, how to write my own name in that language, when we had to write and fax a letter to Kiarostami. This isn't much, but it's a start, and Mehrnaz is far from being the only Iranian film critic whose positions I've engaged with. (At the Fajr Film Festival last year, a few local critics cornered me to debate the ending of *Taste of Cherry*, for instance.) Anyway, my point is that ignorance isn't the same thing as attitude or position, and we have to start whenever and however we can, recognising and correcting our errors as we proceed.

Oddly enough, one of the ways Adrian illustrates his scepticism is with a film I just reviewed this week for the *Chicago Reader, What Time Is It There?* – for me a triumph of communication and even a certain kind of togetherness. Let's not forget that this is a Taiwanese–French co-production, and that Tsai does reveal a certain connectedness, congruence, unity, and even hope – not so much on the screen but inside each viewer's consciousness, where it really counts. There's even what I'd call a happy ending!

As for Adrian's worries about elitism, I regard this less as a danger than as a fragrant possibility that's hovered since our correspondence began, and one I'm more inclined to embrace than repudiate – even though I realise that elitism is a relative matter, and cinema itself might be construed as an elitist concern in some parts of the world. (Still, Mark is absolutely right when he writes that 'the so-called populist critics, who underestimate the population, are the true elitists'.) Long live such cliques – which are what fertilised post-revolutionary Russian cinema, Italian neo-realism, the French *nouvelle vague*, North American structural film-making, New German Cinema, and the more recent New Waves of Iran and Taiwan! Far from serving as any obstacle to community, they form the very basis of it. Such is the implicit theory and practice of Quintín when he brings together the mutants to enhance and mingle with the film community of Buenos Aires. This is because such communities nowadays are ultimately no longer framed by individual cities, or even by clusters of cities – or countries, for that matter – but by the reach of the Internet, making for a new kind of collective power. If it weren't for this Internet, I might not have met Quintín and Flavia, because my first trip to Buenos Aires in the fall of 2000, when I first saw them, was as a guest of the local branch of FIPRESCI, the international film critics organisation – a group of young critics who had discovered me on the web. And it was through the same Internet, via the nexus of *Senses of Cinema*, that the Dublin-based Garrel event took shape last June – an event that Nicole, team player *par excellence*, generously helped to organise but then found herself too busy to attend.

One could argue that communities of cinephilia are sometimes configured a little like boys clubs. A few years back, noticing the video swapping between Kent and me, our mutual friend Bérénice Reynaud noted that it was a little bit like boys trading baseball cards. But with Nicole, Mehrnaz Saeed-Vafa, Nataša Durovičová, Catherine Benamou, Lucia Saks, Flavia de la Fuente, Chika Kinoshita, Helen Bandis, Lynne Kirby, Dana Linssen, Belinda van de Graaf and Bérénice herself, among others, all having become part of our 'clique', at different times and in different ways, it no longer seems accurate to call this group gender-based. I'd rather accept the epithet of

childish or infantile – thinking now of the particular spin on this recently offered by
Peter Wollen:

> To Serge Daney, looking back, cinephilia seemed a 'sickness', a malady which became a duty,
> almost a religious duty, a form of clandestine self-immolation in the darkness, a voluntary
> exclusion from social life. At the same time, a sickness that brought immense pleasure,
> moments which, much later, you recognised had changed your life. I see it differently, not as
> a sickness, but as the symptom of a desire to remain within the child's view of the world,
> always fascinated by a mysterious parental drama, always seeking to master one's anxiety by
> compulsive repetition. Much more than just another leisure activity.[11]

So maybe what we all need to be considering is not simply how to reconcile the Euro
with the 'axis of evil', but also how to reconcile de Oliveira's notions of civilisation, so
beautifully evoked and described by Raymond, with Wollen's notion of cinephilia –
that is, how to remain a child and a grown-up at the same time, individually as well as
collectively. It's the business of art to attempt this in some fashion, and perhaps what
pleases me the most about the eleven letters in these two exchanges is the way they've
seriously (and frivolously) adopted both aspirations as they've circled and recircled the
planet. We may not have reached the perfect balance of mellow and callow yet, but
there's no doubt that we're all looking – and finding certain other things that we
barely knew existed in the process. Doing this together obviously makes it much more
enjoyable, as well as more instructive.

My love to you all,
Jonathan

Notes

1. Foundation Européanne de l'Image et du Son (the European Foundation for Sound and
   Image), formerly the IDHEC, the main film school in France.
2. Centre National de Cinématographie.
3. Kent Jones, 'Premiere Prise', *Trafic* no. 40, Winter 2001, pp. 16–18.
4. In response to a questionnaire on cinephilia proposed by Françoise de Paepe, which can be
   read and responded to on the Internet site www.cinerivage.com.
5. Marcel Hanoun, *Cinéma Cinéaste. Notes sur l'image écrite* (Crisnée: Yellow Now, 2001).
6. Stanley Cavell, *Pursuits of Happiness: The Hollywood Comedy of Remarriage* (Cambridge:
   Harvard University Press, 1981), p. 273.
7. Octavio Paz, *Alternating Current* (London: Wildwood House, 1974), p. 202.
8. In French, *Trafic* no. 24, Winter 1997; in Dutch, *Skrien* nos 221–5, March–August 1998; in
   German, *Meteor* nos 12–13, 1998; in Italian, *Close Up* no. 4, August–September 1998; in
   Spanish, *Movie Mutations. Cartas de cine* (Buenos Aires: Ediciones Nuevos Tiempos, 2002);
   in English, *Film Quarterly*, vol. 52 no. 1, Fall 1998. *Skrien* and *Close Up* supplemented the
   text with commentaries by their own writers. Lamentably but characteristically, the English
   version was edited down to about half its original length due to space limitations, though the

full English text was available for a time on a website provided by the University of
California Press – a website alluded to in Quintín's letter.

9. Jonathan Rosenbaum, *Movie Wars: How Hollywood and the Media Conspire to Limit What Films We Can See* (Chicago: A Cappella, 2000).

10. Robert Darnton, *The New York Review of Books*, 28 February 2002.

11. Peter Wollen, 'An Alphabet of Cinema', *New Left Review* no. 12, November–December 2001, p. 119.

Index